Our Black Mothers

Brave, Bold and Beautiful!

Joslyn Gaines Vanderpool & Anita McGee Royston

Five Sisters Publishing

Five Sisters Publishing
PO Box 217
Gretna VA 24557
www.5sisterspublishing.com

First Edition: September 2015
Published in North America by AR Publishing. For information, please contact Five Sisters Publishing c/o Anita McGee Royston, PO Box 217, Gretna, VA 24557.

Library of Congress Cataloguing-In-Publication Data
Library of Congress Control Number: 2015918540
Joslyn Gaines Vanderpool and Anita McGee Royston
Our Black Mothers Brave, Bold and Beautiful! Joslyn Gaines Vanderpool and Anita McGee Royston and /– 1st ed
p. cm.

ISBN – 978-0-981-7784-8-8
1. SOCIAL SCIENCE / Ethnic Studies / African American Studies. 2. BIOGRAPHY & AUTOBIOGRAPHY / African American & Black see Cultural Heritage. 3. FAMILY & RELATIONSHIPS / Parenting / Motherhood. 4. ART / American / African American. 5. HISTORY / United States / 20th Century. 6. SOCIAL SCIENCE / Women's Studies

10 9 8 7 6 5 4 3 2 1

Comments about *Our Black Mothers Brave, Bold and Beautiful!* and requests for additional copies, book club rates and author speaking appearances may be addressed to Joslyn Gaines Vanderpool and Anita McGee Royston and or Five Sisters Publishing c/o Anita Royston, PO Box 217, Gretna VA, 24557, or you can send your comments and requests via e-mail to www.5sisterpublishing.com

Also available as an eBook from Internet retailers and from Five Sisters Publishing

Book Design and layout by Fabiola Figueroa

Printed in the United States of America

Dr. Nora Jefferson McGee

Our Black Mothers: Brave, Bold and Beautiful!

 The Brave, Bold and Beautiful series was created to inspire, empower, enlighten and recount the personal histories of the forgotten, unknown and unacknowledged that live or have lived bravely, boldly and beautifully. As storytellers and keepers of the gate, our role is to unleash our truths and preserve our stories for posterity.

Ruth Jones Gaines   *Nora Jefferson McGee*

Dedication

To our remarkable mothers:

Ruth Jones Gaines and Nora Jefferson McGee, for providing

powerful legacies of love, strength and unfailing faith in us.

Special Acknowledgements and Thanks

We would like to express sincere gratitude to all of the authors who contributed true stories of inspiration to this important piece of history. Through this anthology, mothers and matriarchs of African descent will live on forever and be remembered for their roles in raising, teaching and nurturing generations of children. Sacrificing everything, they have strived to ensure their offspring have had sturdy enough wings to soar in the face of any challenge.

We would also like to thank our beautiful families, as well as all the individuals who offered assistance, a word of encouragement and a warm embrace through this process.

To our incredible layout artist, Fabiola Figueroa, we appreciate your creative eye and amazing talents. We would also like to acknowledge the ladies of the Gretna Public Library: Adrian, Debbie, Jeanette, Debra, and Barbra—thank you for your patient assistance. To Mr. Logan for suggesting and assisting with Ms. Sadie, and to Felecia McGee, we are eternally grateful to you for filling in when there was a need.

Thank you to my next door neighbor, Dr. Sue Wood and friend Barry Koplen, for believing that all children are created equal and deserve a free public education. You did not merely believe—you acted.

And last, but not least, we want to thank our incredible mothers, Mrs. Nora Jefferson McGee and Mrs. Ruth Jones Gaines for believing in us, sharing their faith in us, and providing an abundance of love to supply us for a lifetime. Their efforts (along with our fathers), have been crucial in making a powerful impact in helping us to become the women we are today.

This truly has been a labor of love, and a testament to never giving up and working through setbacks and trials to complete this book of history and inspiration for all to enjoy.

Introduction

Our Black Mothers Brave, Bold and Beautiful! came about to acknowledge matriarchs of African descent. Honoring and bringing attention to legions of black mothers before and beyond the days of slavery to present day is imperative, because many have given their all, and all that they own, to raise up their children to greatness. The stories within the pages of this anthology are about mothers from all walks of life, various generations, and diverse socioeconomic backgrounds, who all share one common denominator—a legacy that must be revealed!

The words that tell the stories will inspire, like Anita's mother, Nora's, pearls of wisdom: *"What do you believe?"* which is a phrase she asked her children when they were confronted by thoughts that countered their beliefs, and *"Never make anyone feel uncomfortable in your home,"* which Anita and her siblings readily practice. According to Anita, when seeking information that she and her siblings didn't know, *"my mother told us to look it up!"* Anita still subscribes to her mother's sayings.

Joslyn still lives by her mother, Ruth's, straight-from-the-heart advice, which includes the following: *"If you are just trying to hang on,"* she boldly stated, *"then take hold!"* and if you aspire to do something, then, *"Go for it!"* And the most powerful of all, *"Never let anyone make you think that you are less than who you truly are."*

Other words within this anthology will ignite, enlighten and empower! Our hope is that you will be so inclined and deeply-inspired to spread the word, that the legacies of *Our Black Mothers, Brave, Bold and Beautiful!* must be heard and read in homes, churches, classrooms, boardrooms, colleges, local communities and around the globe for generations to come!

Contents

Section One: *Mother Wit: In Her Own Words*

Black Mamas
Joslyn Gaines Vanderpool   1

My Black
Mahalia Barrow   2

Prayer for My Son
Joslyn Gaines Vanderpool   4

A Mother's Prayer
Camille Younger   5

**Tenacious! A Mother's Story of Trials,
Tragedy and Triumph**
Aisha Rene Hall   7

Gretna's Gold
Sadie Haley & Anita Royston   14

Living By God's Plan
Nora Lee Jefferson McGee   23

**A Mother of Sons, the Farmer's Wife and
One Smart Ass Grandma**
Sunda Taylor Meyers   32

Bygone Days, Lifelong Memories
Doris Lovelace   37

Something Special about Sydney
Joslyn Gaines Vanderpool   42

Section Two: *Mama Said...Mama Did!*

PJ, Mama and the Case for a New Pair of Shoes
Percy Taylor   59

Five Feet of Courage
Ruth Mitchell   64

True Grace
Kimberly Biggs   66

Remarkable Woman with an Uncommon Name
Peter Vanderpool   71

Matrilineal Reminiscing
Dr. V.S. Chochezi   75

Beautiful Line
Staajabu   81

A Faithful & Fearless Mother
Ruby H. Robinson   83

My Enraptured Melody
Francene G. Weatherspoon   90

My Mother, My Rose
Sandy Holman   97

Sister Moma
Anita McGee Royston   *101*

Section Three: *Pioneering Women*

Born Free
Melissa Cadet   *113*

Homemaker Extraordinaire: A Genuine Pioneer
Fannie Callands   *119*

Of Sweet Tea and Quilts
Dera Williams   *122*

Breaking the Classroom Color Line
Johnnie M. Fullerwinder   *128*

My Multi-Faceted, Multi-Dimensional Mama!
April Clark   *132*

**Trailblazer: From Military to Motherhood –
A Life of Service**
Jeri Marshall   *137*

5th Generation Girl
Tammy"Goody" Ballard   *144*

PFC to PhD
Frank Withrow & Joslyn Gaines Vanderpool   *147*

My Mum: The Major General
Pauline Zawadi   *152*

Testimony to the Spirit of Black Woman
Joslyn Gaines Vanderpool   155

A Sacred Inheritance
Claire P. Taylor   157

The Original Multi-Tasking Mother
Linda Monroe   160

A Feast for Life
Macia Fuller   163

And Still I Watch and Pray
Gloria W. Campbell   171

Section Four: *Heart and Sole Provider*

I'm Here
Sha Vonn Smith   183

The Blind, Beautiful Faith of a Child
Tammy "Goody" Ballard   185

She's the Reason Why
Clarence Griffin   189

A Woman for All Seasons
Terry Williams   191

My Mother, My Masterpiece
Clarence Griffin   197

Keeping the Faith
Ovetta P. Jefferson   199

The Adventures of Sylvia:
The Free, the Brave, the Spirited!
Irene Brown   *203*

Mother of the Year
Peter S. Vanderpool   *208*

Section Five: *Earth Angels*

Grace the Amazing
Stajaabu   *215*

Mothers Have to Take Care of Their Children
Anita Vanessa Dawn White   *217*

Unqualified Nurse
Sam Kalimba   *219*

Mama
Terry Moore   *224*

Memories of My Strong,
Determined, Loving Mother
De'Lone Waddell King   *225*

Bringer of Light
Erica D. Smith   *230*

She Is
Arianne Adams   *235*

The Guardian Angel
Angelique Peters   *237*

She
Noah Hayes   239

My Bold, Black and Beautiful Mothers!
Mike Cleveland   240

Grandma Mable and Me: A Love Story
Francene G. Weatherspoon   246

Incredible Spirit, Incredible Mother
Terry Moore   251

The Book of Ruth
Joslyn Gaines Vanderpool   253

Section Six: *Mama to the Rescue*

The Personification of a Mother's Love
Jacqueline Webb   265

Virtuous Momma
Vanessa Coleman   269

Black Fictive Kinship
Tammy Goody Ballard   271

The Unschooled Scholar
Rodney Snell   275

My Mother, My Advocate
J. G. Vanderpool, F. Weatherspoon and Ruth Gaines   282

Queen....Saint...Mama the Great!
Tony Gunter Jr.
288

Lady Day
Naa Harper
293

The Limitless Bounds of a Mother's Love
Jerome McGee
298

Ebony Queen
Frank Withrow
301

Section Seven: *Transformation*

Fortitude over Fear: A Survivor's Tale
Marsha Washington
303

**Beauty is Not a Size—Beauty
is Fearfully and Wonderfully Made!**
Denise Allen
307

It's All Mother's Fault
Theresa Gonsalves
309

Rue: The Story of My Beautiful Butterfly
Cindy Smith
310

Strong Towers
Camille Stone Younger
314

Eighty and Fourteen
Steven A. Royston
316

In Memoriam

For Those Who Healed Hate

A Farewell to Mommy
Charlotte Cooper

Remembering Ms. Bettie

Epilogue

About the Authors

About the Creators

Resources

Section One

Mother Wit: In Her Own Words

Black Mamas

by
Joslyn Gaines Vanderpool

Dedicated to All Mamas

Black Mamas are love
Black Mamas are fierce
Black Mamas linger
around
to save us from ourselves
Black Mamas seem to
know what we need to
hear
Black Mamas so brave,
they extinguish our fears
Black Mamas are
impassioned
Black Mamas are strong
Black Mamas souls…
the essence of a song…
Black Mamas are
omnipotent
Black Mamas are never
wrong?
Black Mamas patience, like
some days …long
Black Mamas are promises
that lift us through pain,
Black Mamas are there,
when others have left
Black Mamas are a Blues portraiture
juxtaposed on walls…
Black Mamas are murals
embedded in us all…

Ruth J. Gaines, circa 1950

My Black *by* Mahalia Barrow
In Homage to Black Mothers

My black is not hiding
It is not shame and degradation and abuse
It is not generations of self-cursing and verbal mutilation
No
My black is beautiful
My black is eye-catching, like a rich jewel in an Ethiop's ear
My black is a heart-beat
pumping blood to the beat of a djembe
drum in West Africa
My black is chocolate and peanut butter
and raisins and figs and honey
Each with its own unique flavor
And sweet in its own way
My black is stories like quilts
colorful warmth passed down from
generation to generation
With each birth, a new thread is woven in

My black is a lion's pride
An eternal strength – regal and vibrant
Undeniable both in power and in grace
My black is braids, dreadlocks, afro puffs
and weaves

Author

And Saturday night relaxers in preparation for Sunday morning
service
My black is triumph over adversity
Because we shall overcome
Until there is nothing left to conquer
My black is the dream of a King
And the proclamation of a president
My black is the strong, calloused hands of a hard worker
gentle enough to wipe away a baby 's tears

My black is respectful nods to graying men
Acknowledging the veterans in our common struggle
My black is brothers and sisters wherever I go
And enough aunties and uncles to fill a mega church
My black is lullaby laugh and literary muse
My black is a Caribbean accent
And good, slow-aging genes
My black is a sermon
Preaching the trials of prophets
As a message for the troubles of modern times
My black is endless words of wisdom
Shared around a table filled with the evidence of a satisfying meal
My black is his story and her story and their story
Merging to become my story
My black is my family
My black is my people
And my black....is beautiful

*Author's great-grandmother
and grandmother*

Prayer for My Son
by
Joslyn Gaines Vanderpool

Dedicated to All Mothers Whose Sons Have Moved Away Like Time

The heavens didn't cast their radiance
on my son today...

No moon, no rain, no sun

Instinctively I kneel to pray
as he moves away like time

I observe gangbangers eyeing my son,
see troopers encroaching from nowhere to
corner him, and I wonder...
would God watch over my son?

I've witnessed my son struggle
in this world of guns, of drugs, of pain
I wanted to protect him from his strife
but he moves away like time

After I pray he pulls me up from my knees
assures me, "Ma, I'll be fine."
Just as my hand nears his face
he moves away like time

Back on my knees
I resume my place
fearing he'll leave my life
then pray that I might see him again
But... he moves away like time

A Mother's Prayer *by* Camille Stone Younger

As a mother, complete and total adherence to the belief in the power of prayer is the practice that has strengthened me. There are times when I find myself praying even when I don't know why I am praying; but I'm so glad I have developed a prayer life. Little did I know just how much I would have to call on prayer to ease my worries and mend deeply entrenched wounds in my life, and the lives of my children.

I found myself grieving for a son who wasn't dead. I asked God one day, 'why are my childrens' lives messed up when I have finally gotten mine together?'

Prayer was sorely needed due to what happened on June 9, 2007, a day that would change my family forever. My youngest son witnessed his father's violent death because his father had made up in his mind that he wasn't going to lose another family. So he went to his wife's home to kill her and the children. However, she managed to shoot him first. From that night on my youngest son, who was spending the weekend, was never quite the same.

Although it's understandable that his life would be different, nothing prepared me for the coming events.

After that tragic night in 2007, my son felt he shouldn't grieve for someone he had no relationship with. Grief is different for everyone and my son refused to participate in the process. He started hanging out with people that were not his usual friends and getting into trouble. I found myself grieving for a son who wasn't dead. I asked God

Author and son

one day, *"why are my childrens' lives messed up when I have finally gotten mine together?"* Then I began to pray because I didn't know what to do and in all honesty, nothing else would do short of prayer. So I began...

Heavenly Father I thank you for life, health, and strength. I bless you for your grace and mercy. God take care of my children. Strengthen them and lead and guide them by your will and not mine and not theirs. Protect them in all things even when they are wrong. God, the same spirit you blessed me with please grant them a spirit that is greater than mine. Anoint them with your holy blessings, peace, joy, and love. Keep them by your power. In Jesus name I pray. Amen.

It's been over six years now and my sons are doing well. Developing a prayer life in the midst of life's challenges will strengthen your faith and relationship with God. The lessons I have learned in my prayers are: I can do nothing without God; and that I am not alone no matter how difficult the situation. Prayer is a deeper level of communication with God that I must continue to do without ever ceasing. So I will consult prayer without fail, because prayer has never failed me.

Tenacious!

A Mother's Story of Trials, Tragedy and Triumph
by Aisha Renee Hall

In 1932, the year of my mother's birth, slavery was over, but had been replaced with an oppressive sharecropping system that greatly impacted her family. Lonnie Hill, my grandfather, worked a small plot of land he rented in return for a portion of crops he harvested. When the white overseer demanded that he work on Sundays, he moved his family to Dallas, a place where life was no easier. This was particularly true for my mother who attended school, worked 40 hours a week and was expected to give her paycheck to her father.

When my mother's father was arrested for allegedly shooting a white man, my mother said that, "It was my happiest day." However, because her mother swore that she didn't know where her husband was when she was questioned, the authorities put all of her children in foster homes, including my mother. Placed with a middle-class lady named Tommy Walker, who took in as many children as her heart and home could hold, I came to know her as my grandmother and a woman of generosity who encouraged my mother to attend college.

I was born to Vernice Marie Hill and Joseph Von Brown in January 1957, and the fact that my parents never married had a profound effect on me.

My mother majored in Nursing until her third year of studies when she met my father, a spiritualist preacher who laid his robe down when he witnessed my mother's beauty. When he learned that my mother was pregnant, he said he could never marry, due to his status. Despite being rejected, my mother continued to attend his church until a jealous *"wannabe"* stabbed her two inches from the heart in her sixth month of pregnancy, but my mother survived, and I came anyway.

Seeking Fatherly Love

I was born to Vernice Marie Hill and Joseph Von Brown in January 1957, and the fact that my parents never married had a profound impact on me. Early on my mother recognized my tenacity because I loved to dart back and forth across the freeway as a child, which resulted in a whipping from my grandmother and a promise to never do it again. I also sent numerous letters to my father at my mother's urging to cope with his absence. Although he never responded, my love and desire to be with him never changed, leaving my mother perplexed about why I cried about someone I didn't really know. Yet, my mother sent me to his church every single Sunday until I was 12, which was the year he died.

As a leading community activist in the '60s, my father had been arrested numerous times and died in jail of a heart attack, according to newspaper reports. However, the black community believed that he died at the hands of the police. My mother assured me of the following concerning my father, *"(His) body is gone, but his spirit is with God and he can always see what you are doing,"* which for the time appeased me.

It felt strange not having my father to write to. I wanted him to love and be proud of me, so I vowed to write a book about him; I reasoned that if my father saw something in my mother and loved her, and I took on the same qualities she had, he would also love me, even though he was in heaven.

A Mother's Descent to the Abyss and Back

Around the time of my father's death, my mother began to act weird. She believed that she invented the nuclear bomb, was a member of the Choctaw tribe and was owed 40 acres of land personally promised by General William Tecumseh Sherman in 1865. Then there was the day she wrapped butcher paper around the house with the words, *"ALL NIGGARS AND CRACKERS STAY OUT!"* Humiliated, I met her at the front porch with my head down. All the kids were laughing, and cars slowed down in front of our house to view the spectacle. When I looked up at my mother I was as angry as I could be.

"Don't you dare think of taking it down either!" she snapped, reading my mind.

The next day someone threw an egg at the poster causing my mom to chase the person down with the longest knife she could find, barely missing the offender. The police took Mama to a psychiatric ward. Thereafter, she was admitted to the hospital for a year. In her absence my brother and I stayed with my aunt until I got tired of her whipping my brother with electrical cords for stealing extra food. So I told him, *"Go get some more of that cornbread, Johnnywayne!"*

Diagnosed as schizophrenic, I prayed to God that I would not catch it; and learned not to be embarrassed when she went through one of her General Sherman phases that I lovingly called, "Her crazy phases."

"Boy, I'm gone whip your ass! Just let me put the rest of this back in the oven," my aunt threatened. *"Go take all your clothes off!"*

I don't think so, I thought. That's when I hit my aunt right over the head with the largest iron skillet I could find! Knocked her out! Then I grabbed Johnny, took the money on my aunt's dresser and caught the first city bus out of there to my grandmother's house.

When I was sixteen, Mama's sanity returned and she was well as long as she took her medicine, which I diligently monitored. Diagnosed as schizophrenic, I prayed to God that I would not catch it, and I learned not to be embarrassed when she went through one of her *General Sherman* phases that I lovingly called, *"Her crazy phases."*

I was allowed to court when I was sixteen and I had my eyes on, Pudding, the neighbor boy. However, I knew that our home was unsuitable for company. So I got a job, purchased a complete living room set on lay-away and began courting Pudding for a short time before I fell hard for his cousin. My mother hated the new relationship when she found out that he had children from more than one girl. And she let me know it.

"Do you think your dad and I wanted you to settle for the first boy you laid eyes on and the first job you landed? God has bigger and better things for you if you just go after it. If you and that boy were meant to be together, he will be here when you come back. You need to be in somebody's college or in the military."

Since she said this literally every day I didn't know if she was crazy or in her right mind. However, she praised me; telling everyone how I had worked and bought a brand new living room set. *"Your dad would really be proud of you,"* she added, as I looked up in agreement.

After high school I had no idea how to get into college. My grades were not the best due to all of the jobs I held. So I joined the Air Force in 1973. Shortly thereafter I met my husband, Henry who I held to two promises: The first was that I visit the beautician bi-monthly and the second was that we travel. I promised that I'd obtain a college degree and go to Africa with him. A year later when we had the most handsome twin boys, Kereenyaga and Kamau, my mother emphatically pleaded for me to, "*Stay in college! Don't quit until you are finished!*"

By my senior year in college I was taking 24 units, working three jobs, and pregnant with my third son, Jamaal. My mother was there to help and ensure I didn't quit college. In March 1980 she smiled proudly when I graduated from California Polytechnic University at San Luis Obispo. By that October she passed away. Her best friend conveyed that my mother used to say, "*If I can live to see my daughter graduate, I'll be happy.*"

The Depths of a Mother's Unconditional Love

Both my husband and I kept our promises to each other completing our educations and moving to Africa after the plant where I worked closed. Due to the efforts of a good friend, I was offered a school superintendent position over three schools in Monrovia, West Africa.

As I looked at Kereenyaga's lifeless body in the hospital, I kept waiting for him to get up. I felt numb and cried every day. Kamau may as well have shot me.

It was amazing living where our last son, Kareem was born. Unfortunately, financial reasons led us to relocate to Sacramento, California, where Henry grew depressed because his dream was to live in Africa. After much contemplation, we eventually divorced and worked as harmoniously as possible for the sake of our sons.

Jamaal and Kareem stayed with me and Henry kept the twins, who were sixteen. Then a year later, the unthinkable occurred. My youngest twin, Kamau shot his brother, Kereenyaga. As I looked at Kereenyaga's lifeless body in the hospital, I kept waiting for him to get up. I felt numb and cried every day. Kamau may as well have shot me. Calls and condolences came from all over the U.S. because the incident garnered national attention. During a television interview Henry was asked, *"What are the chances of a twin killing his twin?"*

In the aftermath I went into hiding, crying alone to keep my other sons from seeing me, but now I was a single mom who had to keep going. Even though I wanted to quit work, work was my saving grace. I used it to try to erase the pain and seized any opportunity for overtime. I also started a Rites of Passage organization for young girls, married again and had a daughter.

Still in denial about the tragedy of my sons, my life spiraled and my second marriage dissolved after 11 months. Visiting Kamau in Folsom Prison was just as difficult as seeing my dead son because I felt as if I'd lost both boys. Like my mother, he was diagnosed with schizophrenia and sentenced to twenty-five years to life. As I write this story, Kamau has served twenty-five years.

Taking Nothing for Granted

In December 2000 I noticed a lump on my breast that the doctor dismissed as nothing serious. However, three months later the lump was protruding from my blouse. I had stage 4 breast cancer. By this time I was a "Born Again" Christian who tried various treatments, concoctions, chemotherapy, radiation and then removal of my left breast. But my underlying faith was in Jesus Christ.

Every day, I count my blessings and thank God for the abundance...

Through pain and tears I prayed until the cancer was gone, but I contracted congestive heart failure due to the chemotherapy. However, that was 15 years ago and today my daughter is in college, Jamaal graduated from Aeronautical Mechanic School and Kareem is a plumber.

I'm married to a wonderful man who spoils me. We both are ministers, who love to experience new things and take nothing for granted. Every day, I count my blessings and thank God for the abundance, and every Christmas, we fill our home with gifts to give to others as God has given so much to us.

Author (center), with her family

GRETNA'S GOLD *by* Sadie Haley
(as told to Anita Royston)

Sadly, at the time of publishing, Mrs. Sadie Haley passed away. She was a local treasure to the town of Gretna, Virginia where her father and his brother bought 200 acres of land that she lived on for nine decades. When her Uncle Boulden died, her father sold all but 18 acres, "to get things straight," according to Ms. Sadie.

"When I was born nobody went to the hospital," Mrs. Sadie Haley recalled. "My (paternal) grandmother, Lucinda Miller, was the midwife who delivered me into this world and I lived on the same mountain for 92 years!" Ms. Sadie experienced a full and vibrant life and lived long enough to share her story with the world, and oh how blessed are those who came to know her in the small community of Gretna, Virginia! Now legions of others around the world will know of her rich life and homespun wisdom. What she revealed when she sat down with co-author, Anita Royston of *Our Black Mothers: Brave, Bold and Beautiful*! only a few months before her death, is golden, just like Ms. Sadie.

A Different Time — A Different Life

On a warm and beautiful Thursday afternoon, Ms. Sadie settled into Anita's favorite chair in her cozy living room, poised and engaging. With a sharp memory, and a twinkle of mischief in her eyes, her stories of a bygone era sprung to life like a lively painting replete with bright colors and characters restored to another time when life was slower, simpler and sweeter. Ms. Sadie recalled how her daddy worked hard and they grew tobacco, corn and sorghum for molasses and attended revival meetings. Then she settled into conversing about the days of old, her family members and the memories that she shared that would last for generations.

Life in the country was different from other places except you had to say yes'm and no'm. We called elder white folk Mr. or Mrs. and we called all elder black folk Aunt and Uncle. And we all got along ok.

With pride and strength in her voice, Ms. Sadie simply, but patently repeated, *"I lived on this mountain for 92 years!"* Then she took over. My mother's name was Louise Dodd. She was born on May 4ᵗʰ—not sure of the year, but she died in 1965. My maternal grandmother was Margaret Dodd. My dad's name was Chris Miller. I had seven siblings. My mother had four children. Her sister had three children ages ten, six and eighteen months, when she died. Though first cousins we all grew up as sisters and brothers. We didn't realize we were cousins until we were near grown.

People didn't talk all that much to kids. My mother never thought it was important to tell us. My sister, Margaret learned how to get out of going to the field by sewing. Momma would go to town and buy the cloth and she would stay in and make all our clothes. They would buy clothes for Daddy and the boys in town.

Life in the country was different from other places except you had to say *yes'm and no'm.* We called elder white folk *Mr. or Mrs. and* we called all elder black folk *Aunt and Uncle.* We all got along okay. I used to hear the old folk talk about slavery time a lot — about how they worked them so hard. It has been so long. I hate to try to tell it now. They talked about how they had to work so hard or get beat but I don't want to mix up the stories.

School Days, Amos and Andy and Mary Foster

Like everyone else in the area I went to Mt. Airy Elementary School. The school was located right below the church and cemetery. In those days one teacher taught all grades. Elementary was first through seventh (grade). Over the years I had Mrs.

Josephine Green, Alvin Green's mother, and Mrs. Burnise Miller as teachers. In school Mrs. Green taught the 23rd and 24th Psalm. I never will forget those verses. My favorite song was *Amazing Grace* then and now!

We had mules, horses and guess what? Daddy never owned a car. We rode the horse and buggy to church and walked to school.

After school we would sit around and look at the radio when we had time. My favorite was *Amos and Andy* and *Mary Foster*. That was a story we would listen to everyday. We loved the stories! When we came home from school we would study our lesson. On rainy days in the spring of the year, the grown boys got to go to school. During the rest of the year unless there was rough weather, they had to help their daddy on the farm. We went to school the last of September through May. And all children had to stop to help with the crop.

We had mules, horses and guess what? Daddy never owned a car. So we rode the horse and buggy to church and walked to school, which was about four or five miles away. I got my first car in 1948; it was a Chevrolet. Don't remember the model.

On days that the water was up high we had to walk across the river on a log. I remember if we came out after school and the snow had melted, the water would be swift under there. So they cut down a great big tree where the bridge was and then took the horses to pull it across the river with a chain and fastened it to a tree. My oldest sister would make us put a stick in our mouth crossways to balance ourselves so that we would not fall in and drown. She would walk us across one-by-one holding our hand, then go back and help the others.

Give Me that Old Time Religion

I have seen a whole lot of changes in the church from the time I was a girl to now. Been going to the same church, Mt. Airy a long time. I went to Sunday school and one time we stood up and I got my Bible verse together. They cut the verses out cause it was taking a long time. Things change. I figure you always had time to say a Bible verse. When Church Revival was going on my mother would stay at the church which started at 1:00pm where there was singing, preaching and testifying. We also had a Mourner's Bench[1].

The preacher, who was the only one with a car, would come up the road one night seeing girls and boys holding hands and the next night he would say something about it.

When we had Revival, daddies worked in the field and the women and children would walk to church during the day for the meeting. We would stop at that big tree by the church and take off our walking shoes, put on our Sunday shoes and go on to church. No one would mess with them. Coming back we would sit down and put our walking shoes back on.

The old women would stay because it would be too much for them to walk back home then come back for night service. Even after we went home to milk the cows, gather eggs and go back, those women were still sitting under the trees with their bonnets on waiting for their food. By 9:00pm church would be over after dark. So we all walked together. The road would be full of us. Mrs. Rice' brother would walk my sister all the way home and walk all the way back along with the Green boys and the Clarks too. The preacher, who was the only one with a car, would come

---

[1]*Mourner's Bench — is a bench for mourners or repentant sinners it was placed at the front in a Revival meeting.

up the road seeing girls and boys holding hands and the next night he would say something about it.

Love and Marriage

I was married twice. First time was in 1934. We had one child, Dorothy, but my husband and I divorced when she was two years old. That marriage didn't hit on much because we never did settle down in one house together. I stayed with my parents who kept their mouths out of it. The world is too big to be tied to somebody you can't get along with. If you can't make it with em... bye! So I made up my mind to divorce and didn't care much what anybody had to say.

The world is too big to be tied to somebody you can't get along with. If you can't make it with em... bye!

Next time I married it was to Earlie Haley in 1948. It was a whole lot different. We were married till he died in 1985. He loved church, was a teacher in Sunday school, choir director... loved his ballgames, but church was first in his book. His favorite team was the Dodgers with Jackie Robinson. He never played but he loved to go to the country ballgames all through the summer on Saturdays.

Earlie was easy to please. Anything I would put on the table he loved except his favorite which was 'thicken' gravy. I couldn't make it to please him so he would put grease in the pan, stir in flour, water salt and pepper and help himself.

An Enterprising Woman

I worked in Bassett Furniture for 18 years. I left at 5:30am in the morning and returned at 7:00pm at night. I would come in, wash clothes, cook dinner, go to bed and get up to start all over again. I also used to help Mrs. Lovelace down at the store. We would sell a stick of bologna and put it in the bread and people would buy it quick as we could make it. We sold hot dogs and chicken too. Didn't fool with hamburgers!

Ms. Sadie Haley

The Diamond was down 40 where neighbor Earl Cooks' house is between there and Mr. Lovelace's house. Mrs. Lovelace store was there too. They sold a line of groceries. That's how I got started. After helping her, I helped Mrs. Francis Monroe in a store in Mt. Airy next to Gene Gold's house. After she stopped, I took it. My husband helped me and our store became Haley's Sandwich Shop.

There were three stores then. Mine was the only black owned store but everybody shopped there, black and white.

I sold plate lunches. Folks bought hotdogs, hamburgers (sold them that time around) fish and chicken sandwiches. I would cook me a ham and sell that whole ham. I did really well. I allowed credit and I got a book at the house now showing where people still owe me for gas and sandwiches! There were three stores then. Mine was the only black owned store but everybody shopped there, black and white. By the time I hit the bed it was time to get up. When I stopped the store I was a teacher's aide in Riceville and Mount Airy. I run the store till my daddy got sick.

After I quit I worked for Alvin then I worked for somebody else and been in the store business for a long time.

Ain't Nobody's Business but Ms. Sadie's

On Friday and Saturday nights after church, folk would come to our café which had a juke box. Sometimes you couldn't find no place to park. (Although) folk didn't dance they'd love to sit around and enjoy themselves. One of my favorite songs was B.B. King singing, *Ain't Nobody's Business!* I wasn't much of a dancer myself but I LOVED to do the *Slow Motion*.

One of my favorite songs was B.B. King singing, Ain't Nobody's Business! I wasn't much of a dancer myself but I LOVED to do the Slow Motion.

One time we went to a birthday party down in town and Earlie called off the dance steps, "Swing your Partner." One of the deacons found out and called him in. Earlie was told that it wasn't right and that he knew better. Some of those old folk was something! They probably were swinging their partner their self!

Lessons Learned—Lessons Shared

When I was asked what black woman most influenced my life I have to say, my mom. She told me to, *"Always respect old people and be kind to everybody. Keep your mouth shut and listen. You can learn more by listening than running your mouth. If anybody else is talking, keep your mouth closed." I tried to teach my daughter like my mother taught me, to respect elders. I learned her how to work. Now she can sew and never sit around depending on nobody for what you can do for yourself.*

One Sunday recently, I had to ask a question of someone. I stood there a long time but had to touch her on the shoulder and interrupt. Even though I was grown and Momma was long gone, I knew I was wrong and felt like I would still get in trouble, because I went against my Momma's teaching. I tried to teach my daughter, like my mother taught me, to respect elders. I taught her how to work. Now, she can sew and never sit around depending on nobody for what you can do for yourself. And above all (I taught her) don't forget her church and Sunday school. She paid attention and respects me today!

I can look at my daughter, and if she gets to talking too much, she will cut it off. She got married, moved to Martinsville and worked for DuPont. She retired from there. She is very successful. I am very proud of her. I also thought everything my mother cooked was good too.

Mother Wit for a New Generation

Ms. Sadie left women with insight that could only come from a matriarch who has lived life well. As she completed her story, she stated, *"The happiest time in my life was with my last husband. Yes, those were my happiest days. He was nice to me."*

The saddest time was when I lost my momma and daddy. It was sad when I lost all of them. You never get past that sadness. With the help of the Lord you can get through it but it never leaves you. You can never get over it. I try to treat everybody nice. I hope when I pass from this life people will say that Sadie Haley was nice to everybody."

Take care of self and respect yourself... If you don't know how to cook, you ain't doing nothing!

As a word of advice to young women, Ms. Sadie explained, *"To have a good life, take care of yourself and respect yourself. When you get a boyfriend pay attention to everything. When they tell you they love you make sure you know where you're going. Go to school and learn how to work so you can take care of yourself. Learn how to cook and feed your family. If you don't know how to cook you ain't doing nothing! When you go to church learn to dress decent. Now it might be old fashioned but don't wear short dresses and flip flop shoes like you going to the bar. Last but not least be sure you dress like you know where you are going!"* which Ms. Sadie clearly exemplified. And yes, as she hoped when she passed, others did think she was very nice, very nice indeed!

Ms. Sadie's daughter and son-in-law

Living by God's Plan
By Nora Lee Jefferson McGee

When submitting this story I was asked to mention what I want people to say about me when I'm gone. Well when I' m gone I want people to tell the truth or just keep their mouths shut.
— Nora Lee Jefferson McGee

It Is Better to Be Humble

It was Mama Brown, the local midwife who delivered me and all of the babies in our community. I was born, Nora Lee Jefferson on December 22, 1934 to Annie Spann Jefferson and Leroy Jefferson in Leflore County, Mississippi on the Fort Loring Plantation. My name was derived from my mother's middle name, which was listed in the family Bible as Noah, although she was called Annie Nora most of her life. Born on October 17, 1915, my mother was the second of Leroy Jefferson's eight wives. Now, Leroy Jefferson is a story all on his own!

My grandparents figured prominently in my life. I referred to them affectionately as Mama and Papa. Although nowadays, I hear a lot about grandparents raising grandchildren like it's something new, it was a natural thing when I was growing up.

My grandparents figured prominently in my life. I referred to them affectionately as Momma and Papa. Although nowadays I hear a lot about grandparents raising grandchildren like it's something new, it was a natural thing when I was growing up because I lived with them in the country as did my parents when they were leasing land during the Depression. Although my grandfather talked about working the leased land, it sounded like sharecropping, except he did everything like a farmer such as buying the seeds and paying the owner. As a matter of fact, he leased everything, including his cars until he lost his money by trusting the banks, which restricted his visits to only a certain day of the week. This occurred because a white man once told Papa, *"If you can dip your face in a flour barrel you can get your money,"* which meant that Papa couldn't get his own money out of the bank because he was black.

As a child, I recall walking four miles to school until my cousins joined me and we'd walk the rest of the way together before they eventually moved to Missouri. After school my job was to go home, eat the baked yam that was prepared and waiting for me, put on my tennis shoes and jeans and go to the field to help Papa who had had a stroke while sharecropping. Since he couldn't work as much, Mama who didn't work in the field would carry him water and I would pull his sack. Then I would weigh and record the results of the sacks Papa had filled.

It is difficult to separate Momma from Papa because the two of them poured their beliefs into me as one. Alma Alice Alberta Josephine Smith-Spann, who was my maternal grandmother, influenced me the most. She taught me by word and example to be a homemaker and how to deal with people. She never had to raise her voice but could get things done with a look and kind questions. To be neat and present myself with quiet authority were important lessons she imparted. She always sang *Even Me* and sometimes I can still hear her humming the words as if it were yesterday.

I was always reminded by my grandparents to, *"Keep a song on my heart and a scripture in my mouth. Remember to be humble. The Bible said it is better to be humble and exalted by others than to exalt yourself and be humbled by God."* My joy of reading came from seeing my mother read love stories and medical books, and Papa reading the Bible. I think my nosy curiosity caused me to read, read, and read anything I could get my hands on. I love to read and to this day I journal daily.

Where My Real Story Begins... Love of Family Never Ends

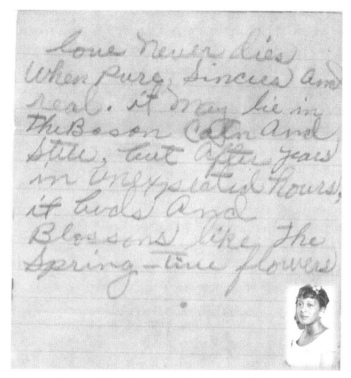

Poem written by my mother, Annie Spann

When I started school at age six in Clarksdale, Mississippi; my parents separated. Mom and I went to Greenwood, and my father stayed behind. My mother, who was a hairdresser, graduated from the Addie B. School of Hair Culture. Then she started her own school where she taught others how to fix hair.

After a hard day of working in the white folks' house cleaning, washing, ironing and taking care of her employer's kids, (while the mother of those kids worked), she fixed hair. Madear, (an endearment for Mother Dear, which is what I called my mother), was very popular in those days and charged $1.75, and those who could not afford to pay brought in a chicken, eggs, butter or whatever they had. I guess bartering was the same as going to the store to spend the money. My mother even taught a student in exchange for room and board.

As the years of childhood passed, I met a soldier when I was 15 during the time of the Korean War. At 18 I married him and loved him and our 10 children dearly. Now that's where my real story begins. On February 3, 1953 I wed Josephus McGee, Sr., Joe was our eldest child, and then came our first daughter Anita.

We lived for a time across the street from my husband's parents, Mack and Callie McGee and my husband's little brother, Calvin in Greenwood, Mississippi. Then two more children were born there and of course, I had a midwife, Mrs. Mattox who charged $25.00 for her services. When you told Mrs. Mattox that you were with child and you wanted her to deliver the baby when the time came, she would ask, *"Have you been to the doctor?"* You had to go see a doctor and come back and tell her.

In those days only rich black people or people with health problems went to the hospital to have babies. Those were the days prior to the selling of feminine items so you started getting lots of newspapers, split a sheet in half and put newspapers in it. Then you'd sew them up, folded and put them away; then waited. People would give you baby clothes so you would be prepared. You put the clothes under your bed and continued to wait.

Despite having a family, I wanted to go to the field like everybody else that didn't work. But my husband wanted me to stay home. He would say, *"Taking care of the children, me and the house is a big enough job."* And the children kept coming. My husband gave me an allowance of $5.00 a week and my cousins talked about me because they thought it was childish to get an allowance.

Eventually, I found opportunities to work outside the home until one of the children would get sick, then of course, I went back to my first job as Mother (smile). Additionally, I enrolled at a University where I was trained to go into homemakers' kitchens to show them how to stretch their budgets and save, since most of them had a lot of children.

Instead of buying instant cocoa, we used powdered milk and cocoa! Gleaning what was left after picking the orchards was also encouraged. I also sold fashion frocks and Avon make-up door-to-door. Since I learned to sew from my grandmother and mother, I once entered a radio contest and won a sewing machine because I was the first caller who correctly identified a certain song. With a yard of material for a quarter, I made Anita cute little dresses. Essentially, I learned to help my family as I helped others.

Author (left) with her mother (top row), maternal grandmother (center) and author's three children: on the left is Josephus Jr., on his grandmother's lap is Israel, Anita is front center. Author's brother, Freddie, is on the right.

As a lifelong learner, I managed to take correspondence courses and enrolled because I didn't finish high school. So I took typing and filing (clerical) and completed several courses. I even went to a business college. They didn't ask if I'd finished high school and I didn't tell them. I got other certificates as well, signing up for anything that fit my schedule. One of the institutes where I received a certificate sent me out for a job. However, I lost that opportunity to a white man who had a high school diploma. So I went to Adult School and discovered that I only needed two or three credits to get my own diploma. Although I graduated I didn't want to walk across the stage because I was more satisfied with the knowledge I had acquired because I loved to learn!

Mississippi Born, California Bound and Life in the Country

After living in Mississippi for 22 years, you might want to know how I got to Sacramento, California where I lived from 1957-2008. After the Emmett Till[2] murder, which occurred in Money, Mississippi, about 8 miles from where we lived, there was a lot of unrest going on. A lady came by when it was raining and asked, *"Where is your husband?"* Naturally I thought he was at church only to find out that he was marching around the court house where the white men who killed Emmett Till were jailed.

As soon as our daughter, Felecia, was born on June 8, 1957, I got rid of everything and when she was 15 days old, I climbed aboard the Illinois Central with all the children and began our trek to California. We learned later that my husband had been moved to number one on the Ku Klux Klan's hit list in Mississippi. So staying was clearly not an option.

---

[2]Emmett Louis Till was an African American youth from Chicago, Illinois who was born on July 25, 1941 and was brutally murdered on August 28, 1955 about a month shy of his 15th birthday. While visiting his relatives in Money, Mississippi, he was allegedly killed for flirting with a married white woman (21-year-old Carolyn Bryant) who owned a small grocery store in the small town of Money. Bryant's husband, Roy and his half-brother, J. W. Milam took Till from his great-uncle's house where he had been staying.

Three days later, Till's body was discovered in the Tallahatchie River,. He had been beaten, shot through the head, and one of his eyes had been gouged out. His death made national news. Pictures of Till's ravaged body were shown in magazines, as his heartbroken mother insisted on an open casket to let the world see what had been done to her son. Despite occurring sixty years ago, Till's story continues to reverberate. Source: Wikipedia, Ebony Magazine.

Protest of any kind by black citizens could lead to eminent death by hate groups. So my husband, who worked at South Side Market as a butcher and manager, received enough warning signs from others who dropped by the market and convinced him to get out of town, and quick! Not surprisingly he came home one afternoon and said, *"I'm going to leave."*

Then he packed a suitcase, caught a Greyhound bus and headed for Sacramento where he moved in with his brother Richard and his wife, Sora, who were living at Mather Air Force Base. Due to my condition, (I was pregnant with a midwife in place), I stayed behind with the children. The store owner, Mr. Cheu Hoy who treated my husband like a son, came by every day to check on us. If I needed groceries or anything he and his wife took care of it.

As soon as our daughter, Felecia was born on June 8, 1957, I got rid of everything that was non-essential and when she was 15 days old, I climbed aboard the Illinois Central with all the children and began our trek to California. We learned later that my husband had been moved to number one on the Ku Klux Klan's hit list in Mississippi. So staying was clearly not an option.

When I was asked if I could re-live a part of my life and change it what would it be? I believe that every place I've been and what I've gone through was a part of God's plan to get me where I am today...

Our other six children were born in California. And in hospitals! When our sixth child, Timothy was born in 1961 he only lived seven months. He had asthma, but no one at that time knew about the severity and harmfulness of second hand smoke from cigarettes, and our home was constantly filled with it. Even doctors were known to have a burning cigarette between their fingers while examining you. Thank God for the United States Surgeon General who proclaimed the dangers of second-hand smoke!

Our oldest son, Josephus Jr. was killed in 1979 shortly after his 27th birthday. His death certificate listed the cause of death as, *under investigation*. I wish a Cold Case unit would find out what really happened so closure can come as his death was under suspicious circumstances.

Years later, after the oldest children left, my husband and I went to school. Thereafter, I became a teacher and received doctorates in theology and Christian counseling and was ordained. Little did I know the troubles and persecution ahead for myself being a preacher lady, and for my husband for having the audacity to allow women in the pulpit where he served as the pastor! Of course, there was the added persecution for supporting and encouraging his wife to preach.

After 53 years of marriage and 10 children, my dear, sweet husband went to be with the Lord in 2006. I miss him every day! Several years after his death I had a stroke and continue to struggle to regain my ability to read and write, which are a few of my favorite things.

When I was asked, if I could re-live a part of my life and change it what would it be? I believe that every place I've been and what I've gone through was a part of God's plan to get me where I am today: —living in Virginia, going to Mt. Airy Baptist Church, and being surrounded by a wonderful group of friends who I didn't know just 10 years ago.

As for my children, I would like for them to be happy and continue to make memories. For there will be times in life where memories will comfort and bring a smile to your heart when you are feeling down. So reflecting on my life, I would say, *"No, I wouldn't change one thing. God has been good to me, and I thank God for the ability!"*

Author with her husband, Rev. Josephus McGee, Sr.

A Mother of Sons, the Farmer's Wife and One Smart-Ass Grandma

by Sunda Taylor Meyers

My story began on a hot Sunday evening in August when I was born as the third daughter to Alfred Charles Taylor and Elma Butler Taylor. My mom was expecting and praying for a son, and had even picked out boy names. So imagine her disappointment when they told her, *"Mrs. Taylor, you have a small baby girl with good lungs."*

My Aunt Betty said, *"Pepper (my mom's nickname), it's ok, we'll just name her Sunday, and one day she just might be a singer."* Well, when recording my name on my hospital birth certificate, my name was spelled "Sunda" and recorded this way at the Bureau of Vital Records. Now how can you misspell the first day of the week? Apparently, somebody didn't attend church or maybe they were mad because they had to work on the weekends! I have been called *Sonny, Sunshine, Sunday-Monday, Cousin Weekend*, and the list goes on.

My mom taught my oldest sister how to cook and do laundry. She taught my other sister how to clean and decorate.

Growing up was pretty rough for me because I was left-handed, and nearsighted. I started wearing glasses at an early age, broke them often, and had to wear them with tape! Now you know I was the butt of many jokes in the community. I know my sisters were embarrassed, but they learned to cope.

Author, aka farmer's wife, on the right, with husband

I was quick-tempered, and would fight in a heartbeat! Nobody bothered the Taylor girls.

My mom taught my oldest sister how to cook and do laundry. She taught my other sister how to clean and decorate. I was told to help my dad in the yard, so I learned how to push a lawnmower and swing a switch blade. I also learned how to change a flat tire! It was cool doing boys' work. My mom eventually had three boys, so as they got older, I taught them what I knew. My dad was in the Service, so we did our share of moving and traveling.

I was always a bookworm (still am) and a nerd before the word was invented. I was part of the group that integrated schools in my area, and I was not about to let some of those red neck teachers give me flak. I was a smart ass. I knew it, and I was the first black student to make and stay on Honor Roll. I even told one of my teachers, who insisted on marking my grades down, *"I'll just get the guidance counselor to change my grades."*

While I was still in high school I made my "bucket list": Niagara Falls, Grand Canyon, Hawaii, Rio Grande, Las Vegas, Alaska, Bahamas, New York City, etc. At the age of 17 I started college and studied hard enough to get scholarships! My dad was in night school at Norfolk State, my oldest sister was in day school at Norfolk State, my other sister was at a community college, and I insisted on getting away from them all! So I went 35 miles away, across the Virginia state line to Elizabeth City State College.

Somewhere between junior high school and high school, my dad became an ordained minister. My roommate in college was also a preacher's daughter who was not allowed to date, wear pants or makeup. When she discovered I dated, wore pants and had makeup, it was like opening up a new world to this girl. She went wild borrowing everything I had! She started hanging out, skipping classes, and I never saw her again after the first semester!

Well, I met a young man from Nigeria named Monday, and everybody suggested we get together. Then we could name our children Tuesday, Wednesday, Thursday, Friday and Saturday! But Mr. Monday had a last name I could not pronounce or spell, and he was allowed to have several wives. I can share clothes, but not my man.

Well, I met a young man from Nigeria named Monday, and everybody suggested we get together. Then we could name our children Tuesday, Wednesday, Thursday, Friday and Saturday! But Mr. Monday had a last name I could not pronounce or spell and he was allowed to have several wives. I can share clothes, but not my man! I did, however, meet a young man who was a Math major which is what I majored in. He was very serious, smart (at least I thought so), a member of Alpha Phi Alpha Fraternity and handsome (yum!). We talked and studied together and he told me he was from a little town called Gretna.

I become excited because I used to live in a little town, which was a suburb of New Orleans, Louisiana by the same name. Wow, it was so nice to meet somebody from that little town! Needless to say, he was from Gretna, Virginia. Although I have lived in the Tidewater, Virginia area for years, I had never heard of Gretna, Virginia! Well, we got married and reside there.

Author, husband and sons

I have two boys who are world travelers. I have always wanted boys. In fact, I prayed for boys. I never learned to do girlie, frilly things, so a daughter of mine would probably have worn blue jeans and a wig because I never learned to comb hair! My boys are ten years apart.

My mom said my brother and I (we are exactly 2 years and 3 days apart) got in a fight, and I declared that *if I ever had kids they would be ten years apart.* God does listen to our request, so be careful for what you ask for. I have one granddaughter that lives with her parents in Indonesia. She is one smart cookie! But she can't help it; she has a smart, serious grandpa (Poppa Nut) and a smart ass granny (Nana Sunda) and her parents are geniuses.

My husband and I are both retired. I worked for 22 years for the Department of Treasury (IRS) and I had a blast. The years flew by and I had never considered retirement until I got the manager from hell. I took all kinds of courses, signed up for training, and became a certified instructor for new hires. My husband taught middle school and high school for more than 34 years, and had a military career for more than 34 years. He still substitutes at the elementary school, but is a big time farmer! He thinks I am a farmer's wife, which I probably am, considering I have learned to can veggies, make jellies and jams and make homemade biscuits. Now if I can just make homemade ice cream and learn to drive a tractor, I will have earned the title of a true blue country girl!

Volunteering for our church and the area food center keeps my husband and I busy. And date nights are every Tuesday. Most of the time we are either dressed alike or in the same colors. Lord knows we have had our ups and downs, but after almost 45 years together, who in the world would want either of us?

I love to travel and one of my most memorable trips was to Chicago where I got tickets to go to the *Oprah Show!* Although I didn't get any gifts it was awesome. Over the years our travels have taken us to several historic sites and destinations, some which include the Negro League Baseball Museum, Bishop T.D. Jakes Potter's House and Dr. King's grave. Since retirement, I have crossed off a few places on my "bucket list," which keeps growing while another dream has come to fruition.

As I mentioned before, my Aunt Betty lamented that I might become a singer. And so I have. I sing a little and enjoy doing funerals because the deceased can't hear me, and the grieving family is too emotional to care. Through it all I thank God that our lives have been well spent!

Bygone Days, Lifelong Memories
by **Doris W. Lovelace**

I was born in 1942 in a little rural area called Vernon Hill, Virginia to Ruth Jones Wimbush and Frank Gilbert Wimbush, both deceased. My father, who was born in 1911, was 63 years old when he died. At the time I thought that was old, but now that I am in my early seventies, I don't think that way anymore. My mother was 93 years old when she died. Now that's old!

With two siblings, a brother, Herman, who is the oldest and a sister, Adell, the youngest, I was the "middle child" and I don't know if that's good or bad. It seems that I was always in the "middle" to settle spats when my brother and sister misbehaved. My mom would always ask me, *"What happened?"* and I had to decide which one to tell on.

The night I was born, my mother was home alone with just my brother. When my dad came home, (we didn't have telephones then) I had already arrived and Mama had done the necessary things to keep me alive, but he still went and got the mid-wife to make sure everything was okay. I guess you could say that I'm very fortunate to be alive.

Author

At a young age, we moved to another rural area called Keeling, VA where we lived in a big two-story house that had a porch that separated the living area from the kitchen. When we first got a radio, I would listen to it and run back and forth to the kitchen to tell my mom what the radio announcer had said. We read and did our homework by oil lamps, but when we finally got electricity we were so happy. It was as if someone had given us a million dollars! In regard to refrigerating our food to keep it cold, we had an icebox which the "iceman" would supply with a block of ice about once a week. It usually melted before he came back around again. We would put our buttermilk in the spring to keep it cool until lunch time.

After we were baptized, I peppered my mom with questions about the things I could and couldn't do now that we were Christians because I was afraid that being a Christian would mean taking away all the fun things in our lives.

We grew up in a Christian Bible believing home. My dad took us to Sunday school every Sunday and church once a month when worship service was held. All three of us children were baptized at the same time in a creek about a mile from the church.

Although I wasn't scared to be baptized, it was the minnows and bugs skimming along the top of the water that I was afraid of. We had to go across a dirt road to a church ladies' house to change clothes. After we were baptized, I peppered my mom with questions about the things I could and couldn't do now that we were Christians because I was afraid that being a Christian would mean taking away all the fun things in our lives.

We Are Family

Despite our Christian upbringing, my brother was still mischievous and at times, he picked on my sister and me. He didn't like for us to play with his things while he was away with my father. So he locked the spokes on his bicycle to keep us from riding it while he was gone. *"But guess what?"* We found the key and rode it until we thought it was time for him to come home, then we locked it back up and put it in the very spot he had it. All and all, we are very close now and get along fine.

In those days, my brother and I had to walk through the woods about a mile to get to the school because there were no buses then. That came later when my sister started school. I would be so afraid of snakes and bears that I would be walking on my brother's heels almost. By the time my sister started school, I had taught her to read all the reading books I had including the *Sally, Dick and Jane* series.

My sister and I talked about school, our boyfriends and our hopes and dreams for the future. Near our last home, there was a spring where we drew water, as well as a big rock that we sat on and talked about everything under the sun for hours. Sometimes we'd stay so long engaged in conversation that Mom would have to call us to come and bring that water home!

If we were working in a field that was along the school bus route, we would hide behind a tree or something when the bus came so our friends wouldn't see us working.

Although my mother had only a fifth grade education, she learned a lot by reading magazines and books that we used to get from a white lady that lived up the road from us. That's when we couldn't afford books and I guess my love for reading developed during that time.

My dad completed the third grade, but he was a very smart man in my view. He could read the Bible and take a car engine apart and put it back together again. People brought their cars to him to repair. He had a chain that he called a chain horse that he hooked to a large tree and used to hoist cars up so he could get underneath to work on them. If he ran into a problem that he couldn't figure out, he'd run in the house and look in his big black "mechanic book" until he found the answer to the problem.

My dad was a Mason, and he thoroughly enjoyed it, especially when they initiated other men into the organization. He would go throughout the house reciting the Masonic rituals, so much so, that my sister and I could recite just about as much as he could. I don't think he was supposed to do that, but my dad had a habit of letting people know just how much he knew.

If We Leave, We're Never Coming Back!

Sometimes we would have to stay home from school to help my dad when he planted corn. We had to carry the corn and fertilizer in buckets as he opened the rows with a plow pulled by a mule. If we were working in a field along the school bus route, we would hide behind a tree or something when the bus came so our friends wouldn't see us working.

My children have brought me much happiness, and yes, sorrows. We have had our ups and downs, but through it all God has been a constant presence in our lives, and He has brought us through many trials and tribulations.

We raised tobacco, corn, wheat and hay on the farm. It seemed that every rock and dirt clod was in those fields. Chopping grass from the cornfield was exhausting; and I also had the job of milking the cow. I didn't mind it so much unless the cow had lain in manure and her udder was covered by it. Then you had to go back home and get a rag and soap to wash it with, making sure to get everything off. My sister and I made a vow that *if we ever left the farm, we would never go back!* And we didn't.

As time passed, I grew up and got married in 1960 when I was 18 years old. I graduated from high school the following year. Just like my mother, I have one son, who is the oldest and two daughters. We raised our children in a Christian home and we took them to Sunday school and church and always taught them to obey and rely on God for all of their needs. My children have brought me much happiness, and yes, sorrows. And it is the dark moments of our lives that will last so long as necessary for God to accomplish His purpose for us.

We have had our ups and downs, but through it all God has been a constant presence in our lives, and He has brought us through many trials and tribulations.

Author on left, with mother

Something Special about Sydney
by Joslyn Gaines Vanderpool

Author's daughter

As my biological clock was steadily ticking away, I wasn't certain if I wanted to be a parent; yet the thought of missing the chance caused me to reevaluate what I really wanted. Adoption was an option too, but then at 36, I discovered I was pregnant.

Unfortunately, my child didn't survive which solidified one thing: I knew without a doubt that I really wanted to be a mom more than ever after the loss of my firstborn. That experience punctured my soul and left me reeling for someone precious to nurture and raise into adulthood.

Urged by my obstetrician to have a child as soon as possible due to my age, my husband and I, once jubilant, expectant parents were hesitant because of our tragedy. Then, it happened, we were blessed with a second daughter when I was 39, and this time she was staying!

Some assume that the impact of a child's death in infancy is less devastating because no relationship has been established, but I can attest that it isn't true. All the dreams I visualized about my life with my child were planted as soon as I knew that she existed. Now there would be no walks on the beach strolling arm-in-arm, no tea parties, proms, graduations, birthday parties and secret mother-daughter conversations. Everything was extinguished with that one last breathe our beloved daughter took on April 18, 1996.

Urged by my obstetrician to have a child as soon as possible due to my age, my husband and I, once jubilant, expectant parents were hesitant because of our tragedy. Then, it happened, we were blessed with a second daughter when I was 39, and this time she was staying!

Author and daughter

Sydney entered our lives as a force. She cried voraciously and had lungs as powerful as a lioness. Sleep seemed elusive for all of us. I loved motherhood. Oh true, there were days when I was ready to resign. I even hung out at grocery stores for solitude and purposely drove by our house to avoid a cranky Sydney, but I always came home to bail my husband out and revel in the delight of having, holding and loving my child.

Something's Wrong, but We Don't Know What It Is

Throughout Sydney's young life, there were comments and comparisons about which milestones she had reached. She crawled on time, but backwards, (which I thought was amazing) and walked at 14 months. I had a sense that Sydney would blossom at her own pace; yet I couldn't ignore her crying jags and constant agitation. Doctor's visits revealed a healthy neural-typically developing child early on. So there were no worries, except she didn't talk much as she got older.

The mystery about Sydney deepened when public outings became too much to manage. We always left events early and only went to buffet style restaurants because Sydney was too anxious to wait for our order at other restaurants and was prone to have massive meltdowns. So I warned my husband, *"No seconds or there will be hell to pay!"*

Sydney at age nine

After several tests Sydney was misdiagnosed with Pervasive Development Delay, which is on the autism spectrum, and then it was Attention Deficit Disorder before she was finally correctly assessed as being autistic. Along with her autism came digestive issues, extreme anxiety and sensory processing disorders and debilitating, non-abating fears.

Once Sydney reached puberty everything changed drastically from being a well-behaved child, to full on aggression.

Sixteen years later, Sydney, though showing signs of improvement, still fears drowning in toilets, being sucked out of planes, tripping on escalator steps, slipping through cracks on the ground, and encountering crowds, except at theme parks where the rides calm her down. She freaks out when someone coughs or there is a startling noise. Looking at people's faces, which seem distorted to her and being stared at, are common fears as well.

Sydney sleeps with the light on because she is afraid of the dark. She also plays her radio day and night to drown out any noises, and someone talking too much is distracting. Also, the thought of certain foods touching upsets her, and she can't tolerate wetness on her face, so I've learned to settle for rubbing noses with her instead of kisses and giving and receiving bear hugs. It takes a great deal of coaxing, strategizing and patience to encourage Sydney through what terrifies her.

Sydney does find relief with car rides, playing in sand, going to the ocean, relaxing in the pool or Jacuzzi and swinging which causes her face to light up when she slices through the air endlessly content.

An Odyssey Begins in Earnest

Our odyssey with autism, which greatly impacts families, has included odd stares, unsolicited advice and misunderstandings about the disorder. Due to Sydney's unusual behaviors we have had to ask doctors to write letters explaining our daughter's condition and give instructions to teachers and respite workers about how to work with Sydney.

Once Sydney reached puberty everything changed drastically from being a well-behaved child, to full on aggression. Sydney ripped her clothes, punched holes in walls, broke windows and appliances, hit us and teachers, upended desks at school, slapped her head repeatedly, screamed at the top of her lungs for hours, and swiped at others when she was upset. During three hospitalizations, which lasted for a few weeks at a time, it took six adults to hold her down on one occasion, as well as the administration of sedatives and a strait-jacket to control her rage.

Sydney's teacher told me that, "The other children think that your daughter is kind of weird." At that moment I felt invisible, like a piece of the wall, as if the teacher forgot I was a mother who was sensitive to her daughter's feelings.

Sydney's school history has been uneven. She's attended eight schools in ten years. At age eight, it was proposed that Sydney get a Certificate of Completion for high school because no one knew how to teach her or saw her promise. I countered, *"She's only eight. There are at least ten more years to educate her,"* but it was like a forgone conclusion that she wouldn't improve.

Preschool for Sydney was one of her best educational experiences. It was taught by a Christian based, multi-racial staff with an African American director. Although they didn't know what was up with Sydney, they saw that she was special and smart, and adored her for being who she was even though they told me Sydney wore one of her teacher's out.

When Sydney was in kindergarten the day care program couldn't deal with her disorder and we had to take her out of the program. Finding appropriate afterschool care for Sydney was impossible and my husband had to stay home to watch her. Sydney's teacher told me that, "The other children think that your daughter is kind of weird."

At that moment, I felt invisible, like a piece of the wall, as if the teacher forgot I was a mother who was sensitive to her daughter's feelings. So there was awkwardness between us that was bridged when I asked the teacher, who had never taught an autistic child before to help her students embrace Sydney's differences. I even bought a book for her teacher about autism.

The teacher really started trying to help Sydney and the other children invited Sydney to their birthday parties and included her in activities. The teacher even offered to teach Sydney how to swim at her home because being in water soothed Sydney.

By the sixth grade, Sydney was called *"too shy,"* by another teacher. And I wondered if the teacher knew that autism is a disorder where communication and social interactions are difficult. By ninth grade, Sydney was asked to leave summer school because her behaviors were too challenging for staff to handle; however, they were brought on by the chaos and unfamiliarity of the classroom environment.

We are still being denied some of the services Sydney needs to learn by her school district. Recently, a requested placement in an internationally recognized residential autism school was rejected. Yet no one could say why? So I wondered, *How can a child learn when she is crying and refusing to go to school daily? How is a child learning when she cannot communicate her needs to her teachers and hits her head repeatedly? How is a child learning when she worries incessantly about being punished in class about a disorder she's doesn't know how to control? And how does a child learn when there is no curriculum to address her specific needs?*

Over the years we have paid thousands of dollars and visited educators, physicians, neurologists, gastroenterologists, psychiatrists, behaviorists, therapists, legislators, and specialists who all have deemed, Sydney's case as "complex." So I scour the internet researching the disorder and writing letters, making calls, arranging meetings; and without a doubt, praying second-by-second.

For the Sake of Sydney, or for Our Sake?
The Fight Goes On

As the window of transition into adulthood is rapidly closing for Sydney, we want to ensure that she will have a quality life. For all that we have done for Sydney's sake like the behavioral interventions, the art, dance, and music therapy sessions, as well as the attempts at Special Olympics, Girl Scouts and socialization groups; Sydney truly has done so much more for our sake. It is a dream to hear her say, "Love you, Mom!" when many parents with autistic children have never heard their child utter a single word. She truly is one smart and clever cookie!

I am still finding some of Sydney's handiwork, such as drawings under the curtains, and I also found rows of neatly packaged feminine pads on the back dashboard of my car, which I had been driving around and parking for hours all over town, clueless that Sydney had put such personal items on public display. When I finally discovered them one afternoon, as I approached my car from the back, I was at first mortified and then amused! Sydney innocently explained, *"I thought they were little pink pillows, Mommy."*

Then there was the time when Ms. Sydney put dominoes, red plastic monkeys and popsicles sticks in the disc drive of my computer. And at a meeting when I rummaged around my purse to find something to write with, the only thing I had was a blue crayon. When I tried to comb my hair it was full of peanut butter which I discovered after it was in my hair, and when I needed to pay for coffee, all I had was *Chucky Cheese* tokens and a handful of sand! All courtesy of Sydney, of course!

During Sydney's African dance classes, she moves like a fullback and then in an instant, she demonstrates the grace of a gazelle. The pictures Sydney draws are wonderful, and the fact that she used to believe I was 10 years younger and weighed at least 30 pounds less satisfied my ego!

Through Sydney's eyes, we have no imperfections and she loves us faults and all. She gives us pause to think and reflect on important questions like why is *"Red, red?"*

It's true that many of Sydney's issues have overwhelmed us, particularly when she announces that, "I'm going to be atrocious!" Or there was the time when we had to remove her toys because she was using them as weapons.

Unaware that we were the culprits (aka: the thieves), she called 911 and told the police that her Barbie dolls and books were stolen. Most recently behind the babysitters' back Sydney called 911 again because she was constipated. When we told the gastroenterologist who had recently performed the surgery to relief Sydney's constipation, she couldn't stop laughing.

Diagnosed nearly 12 years ago, we are still challenged by Sydney's disorder. Adapting, adjusting and being proactive are our credo even when our concerns are summarily dismissed. It's Sydney's desire to be happy and the promise that she has shown that keeps us fighting for her sake.

Sydney insists on going on dates with her father and me and doesn't want to accept the fact that even moms and dads have to get away. She was so determined to keep us from going out, that she asked if she could call my doctor and tell him, *"Mommy is okay and doesn't need a break."* There are days now that she will concede that we need a break, and will offer to give us some time to rest but not much.

Sydney constantly laments, *"I want a life that is full of sunshine and rainbows. I want to be a confident and independent woman, Mommy! I want friends, but I don't know what to say to them. I am afraid that they will be disappointed in me."* It is impossible not to try to do all you can when Sydney looks at you with that beautiful face and ask, *"When will I get better?"*

We know that she is almost there and it won't be too long before she finds the sunshine she has been seeking because she has already filled our lives with volumes of it, despite the heartaches.

Diagnosed nearly 12 years ago, we are still challenged by Sydney's disorder. Adapting, adjusting and being proactive are our credo even when our concerns are summarily dismissed. Just the other day, Sydney said, "I feel invisible in my classroom, not seen by anyone, not knowing what to say." So it's Sydney's desire to be happy and the promise that she has shown that keeps us fighting for her sake.

Since our first baby died, this is the first time that I have reflected on all I thought I would forever miss. True, I can't do those things I dreamt of and imagined with her; and that will never change, but then came Sydney for our sake. Thankfully, her autism has not prevented us from having dozens of tea parties, frolicking on the beach, strolling arm-in-arm, going to her freshman prom, celebrating her graduation from 8th grade, enjoying trips to theme parks and sharing both serious and silly conversations. Sydney has made us laugh… Oh luscious, precious motherhood! Thank God it didn't elude me!

SO WHAT'S A MOTHER OF A SPECIAL NEEDS CHILD TO DO?

As mothers, we are often the rock and glue for our families, but rocks can crumble and glue can lose its staying power. Even though I have found joy in mothering a special needs child, I know that it is a demanding position that can impact your health and chip away at your sanity and relationships. Then there is the problem of isolation because you feel like no one truly understands what is happening. Sometimes you have to dig deep to find help because it isn't always readily available and it can be expensive. I choose however, to stay positive and as hopeful as I can. Some days I am barely hanging on, but I am still here and what follows is what I have learned:

Love your child unconditionally and know every child has something unique or special within. Giving your child permission to be who she is: Revolutionary!

The way Sydney expresses herself is profound and at times very funny. We play word games, take hikes and bake cookies. Discussions about history and life fascinate her. Also in Sydney's case the use of silly words and singing songs expands our ability to connect.

Ask for and seek help.

Find a developmental pediatrician to determine the correct diagnosis for your child. Get more than one opinion. Then seek agencies and associations that focus on your child's disorder to find resources. There are autism, mental retardation, epilepsy, ADD and other groups that might provide invaluable information and help for you and your loved one.

Additionally, there might be support groups in your community to help you cope and agencies that can help pay or defray some of the costs for services for your child. Check into county agencies and your local school district for assistance. If that doesn't work, find disability advocacy agencies, and even an attorney, particularly if you are being denied services or given inadequate services.

Have expectations of your child and maintain them if they are realistic. But, don't try to win every battle, because it isn't always worth it. Be flexible on some things.

It's life, so live it even though there is heartache and hardship, find a way out of the box sometimes by being hopeful. Do the things your child can do no matter how simple.

Get your child engaged in the world.

Sydney enjoys being in her room a lot because it is safe, and we enjoy the quiet. However, withdrawing keeps her from having much of a life. So we go on family outings in order to bond and try to engage her in activities with others. So make it simple like a picnic, car ride, going out for ice cream or going to the beach.

We've learned to go to quieter venues to avoid meltdowns. And, we incorporate what we all like to make it work. When we need a respite worker to join us we bring one along to watch Sydney or we go away ourselves and leave Sydney with a trained respite worker for a few hours.

Make sure to take breaks and get some rest because any form of parenting is stressful, but special needs children often require a lot of attention. Maybe a family member or friend can babysit sometimes. There are some churches that offer programs for families with special needs children that allow parents to have a date night.

There are also day and evening babysitting agencies for children under 12. We used to take our daughter to those programs, but rely on a respite program that is paid for by a state agency that hires individuals who have been trained to work with special needs clients in their homes so parents can escape for a while to rest, go to dinner or to run errands.

Another idea is to actually lie down before you fall down! Although our respite hours are limited, (we received 90 hours in a three month period but no overnight services), my husband and I often visited no thrill hotels to sleep and relax for the eight hours we are allotted per respite visit because we are so tired.

And sometimes we splurged on ourselves, so it was great to order room service, read the paper and chill without anyone screaming. Sometimes I'll spend the entire night to rest and my husband will go home after the eight hours.

If you can, maintain your marriage and/or other key relationships.

The divorce rate for couples with special needs children is purportedly higher. The needs of the child can be so demanding that it often morphs your partner or other family members' needs. Friendships can be tested as well. So have special times just for you and your child's sibling(s) and join a friend over tea or coffee. My husband and I saw the difference in our relationship after being married 11 years without any children (carefree and close), and how we have struggled to find time for one another post children.

We are finally going on monthly "date nights" now, but it used to be only one date a year because we didn't want to burden family and we didn't know who else could handle our daughter. Our 28 year old marriage has been sorely tested, not just because of our child but also due to other issues. Sharing responsibility and working on finding common ground is key. Since my husband has Multiple Sclerosis he does what he can. Sometimes he has to give more and sometimes I do. There is imbalance at times, but we talk it over and realize that we really have to find a way to live another day because the love is still there.

We have to be truthful and expressive in what we need from each other, and have found ways to lean on each other to make it work for both of us and Sydney too. Discovering what drew us together in the first place, and not talking about Sydney when we are out on a date is a good thing. We are looking forward to some really great times ahead and still plan to do those fun things now because it is critical to love and live like there is no tomorrow.

Seek out therapy.

There are various types of therapy, which could be art, writing or dance therapy. Or meeting with a professional counselor or a parent mentor who is going through, or who has gone through what you are dealing with. From-time-to-time I have reached out to other parents for advice and resources and I have a few friends with special needs children who I can relate to.

Consider day camps or weeklong or weekend camps for your child.

There are specialty programs for both disabled children and adults that allow families a chance to take a break. There are even programs for the siblings of special needs children who also need attention and a chance to have fun. If affordability is a problem some programs offer scholarships or your state regional center might help with costs. Make sure to apply early.

It is okay to admit you cannot do it all.

Without help you could literally die. That sounds dramatic, and it is. I called and met with legislators, doctors, educators, behaviorists, etc. to help my child and worked a demanding, full-time job. I paid out-of-pocket for expensive treatments and struggled to take care of my daughter and disabled husband while handling the mortgage alone. All of it nearly killed me as I suffered a major heart attack a few years ago.

Before the heart attack, I was trying to find a case management team for my daughter and a break for myself, because my burden was very heavy. So after that traumatic event, I was forced to go on catastrophic leave for three or four months and it was so beneficial.

The thought of going back to work was terrifying because I couldn't let all the pressures and work load wear me down again. When I realized that it was becoming too much for me, I went on a second leave to try to head off another health crisis.

Sometimes you have to let go and let somebody else carry the torch.

My sister stepped in when she could, and when we asked for assistance, but we really never wanted to ask for help because she had her own life and family. Since our daughter's situation has become too complicated, we have decided to send her to a residential boarding academy for children with autism.

About a year ago when we were constantly under siege due to Sydney's violent outbursts (she still has them, but less frequently) it was suggested that we try an out of home placement. We were tentative and no placement was found for her so there was a sigh of relief at first because we were unsure whether we could let go of her.

Today is a different story. We know in our heart that stepping back and allowing Sydney to soar under the tutelage of experts is the best thing we can do for her. She'll get the 24/7 consistent and structured care and an education that addresses her autism related challenges.

With the right focus, we believe that Sydney can reach her fullest potential. My husband and I will continue to offer love, nurturance and visits; but we also know that our high levels of stress will most likely improve, as our daughter's life improves and she gains the discipline and skills it will take for her to live a more independent and successful life.

Find time for you, and your dreams and passions. And remember, you are more than someone's Mommy.

Though motherhood is a critical role with a range of ups and downs, women have to realize that it is okay to do other things that will enrich our lives which may not only be good for us, but for our children too. To be continually stressed and overworked does not make for a healthy and happy mother. So to continue to grow and discover all facets of who you are has major benefits for all.

Find an outlet that excites you even if the time you give it is minimal.

Seek out a moment for you and dance again, so to speak. Don't allow anyone or any societal norms guilt-trip you into believing that you can't. There was a period of time when I kept receiving emails at work about a woman's business and publishing group, which I kept deleting. Then one afternoon, I decided to actually read the email, and it was an action that would transform my life.

Within a month of reading that email, I flew out to Dallas, Texas for a conference and came back restored and energized to write. I immediately joined forces with a colleague, Anita Royston and began the process of writing, *Our Black Fathers: Brave, Bold and Beautiful!* which took us to places we never realized we would go and taught us invaluable lessons about how transformative life can be if one has faith and believes in the possibilities that abound.

I also started a business that I plan to expand within the year. And I have already started writing a play which I have always wanted to do because the poetry within me was starting to die.

Last, laugh when you want to cry. But cry when you have to cry.

Despite my taxing situation, I went to a couple of overnight pajama parties and played laser tag with my grown friends. We laughed to our heart's content, while my husband babysat. Last fall he was in a singing group for his own relief and sanity. For us laughter is therapeutic, but remember—there are other forms of therapy that I mentioned before.

Try to find any semblance of balance and let go of those things that are adding too much to your load. Prioritize and say 'no' when you should, which is something I am learning. Remain hopeful, create joyful memories and inject humor whenever possible. Seek quiet space. Pray, if you believe and even if you don't (everyone needs something). I did and I have found some answers and more hope along the way. And most importantly, when you're tired, rest to renew.

Sydney, before autism diagnosis

Section Two

Mama Said... and Mama Did!

PJ, Mama and the Case for a New Pair of Shoes
by Percy Taylor

Author, young PJ

I am the youngest of five children. Like most northern black families in the early 1950s, both parents worked to make just enough money to pay the bills, give a little money to the church and cook a chicken dinner on Sunday (During the week we ate vegetables from our garden and turkey neck-bones or pig's feet for meat). My mother, Lillian Taylor, ran the household, which continues to be common of black women. She made sure that food was on the table, we had clothes to wear and that our chores and school work were done. Not surprisingly, she was the judge, jury and warden for delivering swift punishment for our transgressions.

There is a poignant memory about my mother taking us on a shopping trip to buy me a new pair of dress shoes for church. Not only did I have a hole in them, but it had worn through two cardboard handcrafted insoles placed in the bottom of my shoes.

My sister recounted that on this one particular Saturday morning we waited for a bus to take us to 14th Street and Broadway in downtown Oakland, California. Only a few people were out shopping that early. So according to my sister's account of events, my mother let me run on ahead of us to look at the large selection of shoes in the window display case at *Big Bob's Shoes*.

"Come here, Mother. I want to look at these shoes!" PJ pleaded.

"Okay," she said hesitantly as she watched PJ's eyes slowly scan the shoes on display. He pointed to a pair of black shoes with pinhole designs on the front of them like his father's shoes.

"Nooo those shoes are too expensive for a little boy like you," Mother protested.

The next shoe store we went to was *Little John's Family Shoe Store,* which had a sign in the display case that read, *"Half off of All Children's Shoes on Discount Rack. Self-service. NO REFUNDS."*

Mama grabbed PJ's hand and started for the door. *"Sit over there,"* Mama said, pointing to a chair near the register, as she started walking stridently towards the children's discount rack. PJ and I watched her slip into the crowd of people. A few minutes later she emerged with a pair of brown, square-toed, lace-up-shoes similar to the ones she bought him last year. She handed him the shoes.

"Try these on!" she cheerfully urged.

PJ began frowning at the shoes while struggling to get them on.
"They feel tight," he groaned.

Mama's tone turned stern, *"Try them on!"*

As soon as PJ started walking he began to limp.

"PJ, what's the matter with you?"

"The right shoe hurts my foot."

"PJ, come here! There isn't anything wrong with those shoes!"

The salesman, eyes darted back and forth from PJ to Mama, back to PJ, then to the floor to hide his smile. I was standing behind Mama so she couldn't see me trying not to laugh. Without saying a word, she proceeded to squeeze, push and mash on this pair of shoes just like she did with the others.

By the time PJ reached her she was already down on one knee, reaching for his right foot and squeezing the front of the shoe to see if his toes had enough room. Next she felt the sides of the shoe to see if they were wide enough. Finally she felt the top of the shoe to see if the fit was too tight. She did the same with the left shoe to see if she could detect any difference.

Satisfied that the issue had been resolved, Mama surmised, *"There isn't anything wrong with these shoes except you don't like them! Try walking in them again!"*

Reluctantly, PJ tried to walk in them again, however, it was slower this time, and the limp was still there.

"Stop limping!" Mama implored.

"I can't," PJ whined.

"Boy, sit down!"

As PJ took his seat, Mama went back to the shoe rack hoping to find another pair of shoes his size but she couldn't find any. When she approached PJ, he looked at her sheepishly. She was unsympathetic as he put on his old shoes and we continued to search. It wasn't long before we reached *Spencer's Shoe Store* where shoes of all styles and colors were on exhibit in the window display case. This time it did not take PJ long to find what he was seeking.

"I like those shoes!" PJ shouted, pointing to a pair of black, round toe, lace up shoes in the store window display case.

"So you do?" Mother replied cautiously, noticing the price tag and immediately assessing that it was a little more than she had intended to pay.   A jolly salesman with a bald spot on the top of his head bounded in.

"May I help you, Madame?"

"Yes. My son would like to try on the black round-toe, lace up shoes in the window."

"What size does he wear?"

"Three and a half D."

When the salesman went to the stockroom to retrieve the shoes, PJ looked at Mama longingly.

As soon as the salesman returned with the shoes, he placed them on PJ's feet.

"Try walking in them, young man."

PJ complied, walking without any apparent limp.

"Well, how do they feel?" the salesman queried.

PJ walked up and down the aisle once more, and looked at his shoes before walking toward Mama.

"Mama, how do they feel?" he asked, with a tinge of hopefulness in his question.

The salesman, eyes darted back and forth from PJ to Mama, back to PJ, then to the floor to hide his smile. I was standing behind Mama so she couldn't see me trying not to laugh.

Without saying a word, she proceeded to squeeze, push and mash on this pair of shoes just like she did with the others.

"They feel fine," she said in a soft voice.

"They feel fine to me too!" PJ chimed with a big grin on his face.

Then we all smiled.

"Well, I guess we'll take them," Mama told the shoe salesman. And we did….to the delight of PJ.

PJ's resourceful, loving mother

Five Feet of Courage
by Ruth Mitchell

I am the eighth sibling from the family of ten. My mother, Charlener Gilyard, tilled the cotton fields from sunrise till sunset in order to provide a place for myself and nine siblings to live on the plantation for a small fee, food, water and shelter. A woman of strength, courage and charm, she taught us about having self-respect and pride. Most critically, she assured us that we are as important as anyone else.

Coming from a life spent in a cotton field of empty promises that offered no path to prosperity, my mother, who was born on May 26, 1929, achieved only a tenth grade education. However, she firmly believed that attaining an education was the key to our success.

When making a point that might not have been understood, she would use choice words that she emphasized such as, "Girl don't just have book smarts, have some common sense to go with those books."

In our every endeavor, Mother tried to provide encouragement, even in some ventures that she may not have agreed with because she envisioned better for us. Nonetheless, she continued to pray, believing that God would take care of us.

Every bit of five feet, my mother was powerful and showed kindness and good gesture toward all that she came in contact with. But when it was time to make things happen because she felt she was not being treated fairly or justly, she would turn on the switch and put things in order. I learned so much from her which included her charm and mother wit, which are ingrained in me. When making a point that might not have been understood, she would use choice words that she emphasized such as, *"Girl don't just have book smarts, have some common sense to go with those books."*

From being whopped to praying, I appreciated my mother and all she gave me. Her inspiring character has transcended to the next generation, as all my children are educated and leading successful lives. I thank my mother who will always live within me. Her story, which is a cherished memory that I will share with her grandchildren and great grandchildren, will be preserved for a lifetime as a template of true love, determination and success.

Author's mother, a woman of courage

TRUE GRACE
by **Kimberly Biggs**

That's My Mama, and She's Alright!

In February 2013, the most devastating news rocked my world and that of my family's. My mother, who had just turned 83 years old, had been diagnosed with a Stage 4 rare cancer. No one in the family knew what to do and the reactions ranged from anger to extreme sadness. For me it was the hardest news I have ever received and it brought me to my knees.

"Did Pam get some food?" I laughed through my tears because that was so typical of my mother to come out of major surgery taking care of those she loves. All I could say is "That's my mama and she's all right. Thank you, Father God."

The day of the surgery some of us arrived at the hospital at 5:30am for the 7:00am scheduled procedure. Shortly after 10:00am, the surgery began and the mood in the waiting room was light, with gentle joking among those of us who were praying and hoping for a successful outcome. I had brought school work to occupy my time and took a test while waiting.

Six hours after the surgery started, the doctor came out and called for the family. I knew he was going to give us good news.

"We removed the tumors from her face. For her to be 83 years old, she came through the surgery like she was in her forties." I knew that this was due to her taking care of her health all her life.

When I walked into the recovery area the very first thing out of my mom's mouth was *"Did Pam get some food?"*

I laughed through my tears because that was so typical of my mother to come out of major surgery taking care of those she loves. "All I could say is *"That's my mama and she's all right. Thank you Father God."*

My mother's always been that way. For as far back as I can remember she has taken care of everybody.

Call her Mother, Friend, and Kindred Spirit

Eleanor Elizabeth Marshall is the mother of five children, 17 grandchildren and 33 great grandchildren. She is the matriarch of our family, as well as our rock and pillar. No matter what, she's always there for us and has been instrumental in teaching me so much about being a woman and a mother. Growing up as a bookworm in an upper middle class military family, I fantasized about being as smart and as beautiful as my mom who bought me books that captivated me. She and my grandfather introduced me to black authors, poets and history! Despite our differences as adults, she was and still is my best friend.

I feel blessed to have a mother I can call on the phone and say to her, *"Girl!!! You're not going to believe what this fool did!"* Or tell her a funny story about someone that will have her cracking up. We can talk about almost anything and sometimes she just tells me to *"Shut the hell up, Kim!"* when I speak my mind, and she doesn't want to hear what I am saying. I just laugh and sometimes I cry because I want her to understand what my heart is saying and she doesn't, or maybe just doesn't want to accept what I am saying to be true.

I fantasized about being as smart and as beautiful as my mom. She was and still is my best friend, despite our adult differences.

I learned the meaning of true friendship from my mother, who packed up the car with groceries every month and traveled to her friend's house. Upon arrival, my mom cleaned and then cooked a delicious meal for all of us afterwards. Non- judgmental and loving, she just wanted to help make life better for her friend and her family if only for a weekend.

When Mom and my dad were getting a divorce, she was hurt by his actions. My father remarried and when he became ill with renal failure, blindness and diabetes, he was left in Colorado with his young son. My mother went and took care of him, making sure he had what he needed to get healthy. She arranged for him to get regular haircuts and shaves and cooked for him. Most notably, she spent time encouraging him to take care of himself as best as he could under his circumstances. I tell my mom that my father was the love of her life, and despite everything, they became good friends again before he passed away.

Understanding the power of prayer was also a significant lesson from my mother. When I had to have an emergency C-section with my last child, I was scared because I was told that both I and my child were in danger. Without my mom by my side, I refused to go into surgery until she finally arrived, which would be the first time in my life I heard my mom pray out loud. Her prayer was so strong and powerful, that my fears were alleviated. And as with my other children, my mother was the first one to hold my new baby girl.

The depth of a mother's love has been shown to me through the examples mentioned and the multitude of sacrifices my own mother has made for her children. I believe that she gave up her dreams to take care of her family. Even though she has her own health issues, my mom, for the past 20 years has taken care of my sister who has Multiple Sclerosis and is incapacitated from the waist up. I can only hope and pray to be a fraction of the woman my mother is...

My Biggest Cheerleader

The day my mother called herself a monster broke my heart. The cancer altered her physical appearance which caused her to get very angry at people for staring at her, especially little children. I explained to her that people stare out of curiosity while repeatedly reassuring her of her beauty. *"When I look at you, I see the beautiful spirit that is and has always been inside you."* This was evident when my mother was attending a fragrance fair that we were late for.

My mother always smells delicious! She also takes pride in her appearance, and dresses with her own unique sense of style, donning funky tights and socks that you wouldn't expect of an "old lady." As we entered the room, the presenter stopped, waved and called out, enthusiastically.

"Hi Eleanor!" Everyone turned and stared because they wanted to know who my mother was. So on that day, she was treated like a celebrity!

I wish every little girl could have a mother like the one God blessed me with. I can only hope that I have made her as proud of me as I am of her.

Aside from her outer beauty, what my mother truly exhibits has been true grace, pride and dignity as she faces the fight of her life. I have had a hard time accepting my mother's choices concerning her illness and even in the midst of her own fears, she calmed mine with words that left me no choice but to accept and respect her wishes.

I can't express how much I love my mother. She has been my biggest cheerleader my entire life, giving me opportunities to learn about character as a Girl Scout and financially funding my non-profit, as well as encouraging me as a child to start writing poetry and short stories. I wish every little girl could have a mother like the one God blessed me with. I can only hope that I have made her as proud of me as I am of her.

Although writing about my mother has been difficult, I wanted to share a story of courage and inspiration about a woman who has survived life's ups and downs, and can still smile about it. If you were to look up the definition of the phrase "true mother's love" in the dictionary you would find the name, Eleanor Elizabeth Marshall with a beautiful heart next to it: mother, friend and mentor.

Author's beautiful mother, Eleanor Elizabeth Marshall

A Remarkable Woman with an Uncommon Name
by Peter Vanderpool

"Keet (Keith), Pam, Patrick, Patricia, Peter…dinner time!" Those are the words of my mom who had a no nonsense manner of getting her children's attention. She chuckles when she reminisces about our allegiance to obeying every word. *"Like five little ducks in a row de would follow me,"* Hildred Vanderpool explained. *"If I say go right, de would go right!"*

While growing up, Mom hovered over us like a mother hen, watching her chicks. She brought us up to know right from wrong, to respect others, be kind to animals; and most significantly how to conduct ourselves like ladies and gentlemen. An unforgettable force, my mother is a true matriarch and a model of perseverance.

Love, in our household was dispensed in the form of the tasty meals that my mother still prepares. Although we were poor, we never went to bed hungry. With full command of the kitchen, she attentively created meals fit for a king or queen with only the basics. A dash of spice here and there and Mom produced exquisite dishes such as curry chicken and potatoes, hot simmering pepper pot, black pudding, and rolls made from scratch. All are delicacies that have filled our family with comfort.

Both my parents worked hard and my mother, who is a remarkable woman, was fiercely protective of her children and would do without for our welfare. She saw to it we had the best education she could afford, and a home of comfort, which for nearly a decade, she diligently saved for.

Author on right, with his remarkable Mom

Immigrating to U.S. —author (l) with twins, Patricia and Patrick

At 4:00 pm daily when I was growing up, as a part of the British tradition of tea time, Mom would sit down with us to enjoy homemade tennis rolls (which are essentially biscuits) and of course, a cup of tea! During those days Mom was the one who stayed at home with us and in doing so, supplemented my father's salary, as a seamstress.

Born in Georgetown, British Guiana on November 22, 1925, my mother has persevered with dignity, strength and faith. She received her uncommon name after her father read *The Trials of Hildred.* Upon the loss of her parents at a young age, she was cared for by her grandmother, and when she passed away her Aunt Dorrie, (Ms. Dorothy Bourne), a public school teacher and a strict disciplinarian stepped in and raised my mother to be an educated, honest, respectful and trustworthy young woman.

In 1951, my mother married my father, Barrington Vanderpool. Lasting more than 60 years, their marriage is still going strong. Mom continues to be my father's inspiration and the love of his life. As a matter of fact, they hold hands on the porch and enjoy each other's company. Together they have raised five children, (Keith Barrington, Pamela Eugene, twins, Patrick Oliver and Patricia Alice, and me, Peter Stanislaus), weathered many storms including their own health issues and the devastating death of my sister Pam, who passed away of renal failure in her twenties.

Answered Prayers

My mother had always prayed for a way for her children to leave Guyana to have a better future. And by immigrating to the United States we gained that opportunity to start a new life. Even though the educational system was good in Guyana during the time we resided there, in order to get a university level education, it was imperative to go to England, the U.S. or Jamaica. So leaving the country they knew and loved was one of the greatest sacrifices my parents made for our family. And that opportunity presented itself when my Uncle Carl, who already lived in the U.S., sponsored my father, who secured visas for the rest of us to come. My father left Guyana first to make enough money to bring my mother to Washington, D.C. Then they both worked together for a year to get the children there.

My mom has raised children, taken care of her husband, cooked joyfully for family and friends, and is as amazing as ever! "Yes I got good kids and we've been blessed. And I tank God for it!"

My mother, who is a remarkable woman, was fiercely protective of her children and would do without for our welfare. She saw to it that we had the best education she could afford, and a home of comfort, which for nearly a decade, she diligently saved up for.

My mother's prayers were answered and the move from Guyana to the United States has provided progress and prosperity for the family, as she had hoped. My mom has raised children, taken care of her husband, cooked joyfully for family and friends and is as amazing as ever! *"Yes de are good kids and we've been blessed! And I tank God for it!"* my mother states. And I thank God for her: my brave, bold and beautiful mother!

Author's Parents

Matrilineal Reminiscing
by **Dr. V.S. Chochezi**

Shades of Grace

As her 100th birthday approaches, thoughts of my grandmother are frequent. Though she now dwells with the ancestors, we speak her name and remember her life, which in the ancient African tradition invokes her spirit. An African proverb suggests *that as long as her name is remembered, she lives.*

My grandmother Grace was in her eighties and experiencing some senility when she made her last visit to California. As we drove past open fields, after picking her up from the airport to go to my mother's house she casually mentioned leaving the reservation and going to school. *"This reminds me of when I picked cotton as a little girl growing up in Mississippi,"* which was a revelation that caused me to swerve off the road because it was the first time I had ever heard about her picking cotton! Stunned, I looked at her intently, momentarily forgetting that I was behind the wheel. After regaining my composure, I set the car straight and we continued on our journey.

In her younger years, it was revealed that she liked to ride on the back of the motorcycle with a hot guy at the wheel going fast while she hung on tight. And she had a short fuse, once shooting at a man who visited the house looking to date my mother after she warned him that she did not like the idea.

A young Grace

My grandmother seemed oblivious to the fact that she had almost caused a major accident on Interstate 80. She continued explaining that while attending school off the reservation, she was not allowed to speak the Choctaw language, and that when she would do so, she would be beaten. Again, I gripped the steering wheel firmly. No swerving this time, but it was difficult to maintain control!

Really?

I had heard from other family members that we were part Choctaw. Not surprisingly, probably every black family has heard they were part Indian. My mother remembers her grandmother, Irena "Pinky" Rosenbur, reverently and mentions that she usually wore two thick braids hanging down to each shoulder.

In black and white photos, she stands straight-backed in a floral patterned dress with a serious expression on her face. Her hair appears to be combed out and tucked up in a roll in front, resembling those I've seen of women with natural, thick, kinky hair that has been blow dried and styled. Though I'm sure there were no blow dryers back in my great grandma's era. By all accounts, my great grandmother was a very dark skinned woman, so I don't know why they called her Pinky.

Although my mother thought her grandmother was part Choctaw, other family members said it was actually her grandfather who was part Choctaw. Pinky married Benjamin Harris whose ethnicity is difficult to ascertain.

From the one photograph I've seen of him, he appears white, not Native American. And even so his name doesn't suggest that heritage either, but no one seems certain. Either way, I had some inkling that we might have some Native American ties, but I had never considered that my grandmother might have lived on a reservation at some point in her life.

When we finally arrived at my mother's house I told her about the conversation, and how my grandmother said she stopped speaking the Choctaw language, because it was so heavily discouraged in her youth. My mother was incredulous because she also had never heard the story. My grandmother did have memory slips (though she was lucid most of the time) my mother had trouble believing the tale.

Giving Grace

Grandma Grace was neither the oldest, nor the youngest of her many siblings. She was fair skinned, some would say red boned, while some of her siblings were jet black. She had a straighter grade of hair and was very attractive by most standards.

When I was younger, I would fly from California as an unaccompanied minor to visit my grandma on her farm in Maryland. While there I hung out laundry on the line, collected the potatoes she hoed, shucked corn, snapped peas, plucked chickens, and gathered eggs for breakfast.

I spoke to any of the folks driving by who always honked and expected you to at least wave. I also watched Grandma when she canned peaches and made jam. She even made ice cream from snow!

Apparently, Grandma took many secrets to her grave. I still don't know if her mother or father were part Choctaw, whether she ever picked cotton, lived on a reservation or once fluently spoke the Choctaw language.

I always thought of my grandma as being old. I don't recall her as youthful. She wore glasses and visited on the phone with her friends, laughing and talking. But in retrospect, she was actually very active. She sewed, crocheted, cooked, and helped take care of the farm animals, and her husband and family including the grandchildren and her church family. Grandma Grace was adamant about everyone in the household attending church every Sunday, which was right across the street from the farm. We sang in the choir and I attended 4H club.

I don't recall ever hearing my grandmother curse or honestly, even raise her voice in anger. I saw her make wine, but don't recall ever seeing her drink. My grandma, a pig farmer, always seemed confused and a bit put off when I would say, "Grandma, my mom said I can't eat pork, and I shouldn't straighten my hair. " Grandma Grace never spanked me and though it was clear she didn't always exactly approve of my upbringing, I don't recall her ever chastising me. She would encourage us repeatedly to *"Quit jumping on the bed and behave!"*

Forever Grace!

After my grandmother's burial imagine my surprise when family members got together and told some pretty unbelievable stories about my sweet, hardworking, beautiful, and pretty much saintly Grandma Grace! Initially, I was certain that I had misheard, and that they were most assuredly discussing one of my aunts or great aunts. But no – my mom assured me that they were referring accurately to my grandma.

In her younger years, it was revealed that Grandma liked to ride on the back of the motorcycle with a hot guy at the wheel going fast while she hung on tight. And she had a short fuse, once shooting at a man who visited the house looking to date my mother after she warned him that she did not like the idea. Once, they said she even gave her husband a thrashing when he came home drunk and was too inebriated to urinate properly in the restroom. After that, I was told that he never drank again.

I miss my grandma's patient, calm demeanor. For me she seemed to have a very uncomplicated outlook on life and appeared happy and satisfied living on the farm, supporting her family and her community.

Apparently, grandma took many secrets to her grave. I still don't know if her mother or father were part Choctaw, whether she ever picked cotton, lived on a reservation or once fluently spoke the Choctaw language. I do know she was born in Mississippi, never attended high school, raised half a dozen children, embraced more than a dozen grandchildren and held a strong belief in God.

Still, hearing about different sides of her personality and earlier periods of her life really gave me a new perspective on the idea that people can change and you never *really* know someone.

I miss my grandma's patient, calm demeanor. For me she seemed to have a very uncomplicated outlook on life and appeared happy and satisfied living on the farm, supporting her family and her community. She brought my mom into the world and we give thanks that we have been fruitful and multiplied.

Writing about my mother for this anthology leads me to the realization that she has personally touched six generations. She knew her grandmother, lived with her mother, came into her own identity, birthed and raised me, helped me as I raised my daughters and now she is helping to shape the minds of her great grandchildren.

My great grandma Pinky passed the matriarch torch to my grandmother, and now my mom wields it responsibly, showing us how it should be done at 70. Indeed, my mom recalls her grandmother and I remember my grandma as being bold, brave and beautiful and I am happy to share that memory and this story with my children and grandchildren. Great grandma Pinky and Grandma Grace... as long as we remember you and call your name, you will live on in our hearts and minds.

Ase!

Four Generations

Beautiful Line
by Staajabu

She didn't finish seventh grade and became a mother
at the age of 13 but no doubt my mother, *Miss Grace*
had the potential to be a chemist, carpenter, meteorologist,
mathematician, or artist because she had the cleanest,
best looking laundry in all of Foggy Bottom

She made her own lye soap, mixed just the right amount
of bleach and borax in the wash water and just the right amount of
bluing in the rinse to make our white clothes sparkling white and
if the white clothes were that clean you could rest assured the
other clothes were spotless!

An old wringer washer, an old wrought iron
wood burning cook stove, two six-quart boiling pots,
a scrub board, two huge zinc tubs, three laundry baskets
and a garden hose equipped her back porch laboratory
Every Saturday morning right after breakfast
she already knew the temperature, wind direction,
how many loads could be washed and hung by sunset,
and if she had enough clothes pins to hang them all

She wiped each clothesline with a rag, checked the
clothes props she had made from scrap pieces
of wood to be sure they would be strong enough to hold
each line, especially the ones with work clothes
Whites were hung first, next light colors, then dark
shirts, skirts, pants, socks, underwear, towels, bed linen
and blankets were hung together connected to each other
by clothespins on five lines giving the appearance of dancers

holding hands flapping and frolicking in the breeze

Until I was tall enough to hang clothes, I played
in the back yard helping to pick up dropped clothes pins
pretending the pins were people, listening to grown
folks conversations between her and neighbors
whose yards abutted to ours about babies, men, church,
school, the white folks they worked for, what number to play,
dream books, who was sick, who died and Nat King Cole

The women exchanged recipes, offered condolences
or congratulations and more than once I
heard one of the neighbors comment
when mom had gone inside to check the pots on the stove,
"Grace, sure do hang a beautiful line." "Um hmm,"
the others would reply, and I with my clothespin people
sitting in the grass under freshly washed clothes,
beamed with pride and felt very loved

A Faithful and Fearless Mother
By Ruby H. Robinson

He's got his eyes on you; he's got his eyes on you… My Lord is sitting in the kingdom with his eyes on you. I would not be a liar. I'll tell you the reason. I'm afraid my Lord might call for me and I wouldn't be ready to die. He's got his eyes on you, He's got his eyes on you…. my Lord's sitting in the kingdom with his eyes on you.

– Lyrics to one of my mother's favorite songs

A blessed event occurred on May 20, 1900 in Gretna, Virginia. My mother, Mrs. Nannie Elizabeth Miller Haley was born to the parents of Mr. Jack and Mrs. Elizabeth Callands Miller. They had 21 children, and were hardworking, God fearing people who were members of a prominent Baptist church.

Author's mother:
Nannie Elizabeth Miller Haley

At the age of 21, my mother married my father, Reverend Pruden H. Haley and they soon started their own family. They had 18 children and I am number 17. My mother was a strong woman who was not afraid of anyone. She didn't smile a lot, believed in nipping things in the bud and wasn't hesitant about speaking her mind when she felt she was right. However, she was one of the nicest people you could ever meet and would do anything to help anyone.

My mother was devout in her belief, but when she was introduced to holiness, "A more perfect way," according to Acts 18: 24-26, she changed her membership, and received the baptism in the Holy Ghost with the evidence of speaking in tongues. For this she was ostracized, called a Holy Roller and even crazy. But she wasn't deterred. Blessed with the gift of healing, she always carried a bottle of blessed oil in her pocketbook.

People from miles around sent for her. And many were healed through her prayers and laying of hands, like the man who was in a coma and returned to consciousness. There was a woman who no longer needed surgery because her condition disappeared after Mama prayed for her. One of her grandson's had a terrible speech impediment.

The young man stuttered so much, it would take almost a minute for him to complete a sentence. He would even hit himself in the chest to make his words come out. When my mother laid hands on him, he was healed instantly. I also remember my mother actually praying for our car one day, when it wouldn't start, and you guessed it: the car started. PRAISE GOD!

God dealt in many ways with my faithful and fearless mother! On a bus trip 400 miles away to visit another sister in Chester, Pennsylvania, my mother forgot to take the address.

One Sunday morning in August, 1950 my mother awoke and began pacing the room. *"I need to go to Lynchburg,"* she firmly stated. Yet, in those days, you didn't just up and go to Lynchburg because such trips had to be planned.

My father couldn't console her, so she asked my sister and brother-in-law to take her. When they objected, my mother declared, *"If nobody will take me, I'll walk!"* And she actually started walking. At that point, they accommodated her. Upon arrival, my other sister who lived in Lynchburg fainted when she saw Mama at her door. As it turned out, she had just received news that my oldest brother had been fatally stabbed. I'll never forget my father weeping and clinging to my mother. After he heard the news, he was never quite the same.

God dealt in many ways with my faithful and fearless mother! On a bus trip 400 miles away to visit another sister in Chester, Pennsylvania, my mother forgot to take the address. Since she had never traveled alone before, and we lived in the segregated South with no telephone, all of us were extremely worried and afraid for her.

Mama didn't even know what my sister's husband real name was because we had been calling him by the nick-name that my sister had given him. After she got off the bus Mama asked a couple of people if they knew my sister and brother-in-law. When it was apparent that no one could help her, she prayed and all at once the address suddenly popped into her head. Until the day she died, my mother never forgot that address.

A Place of Our Own

My mother made a mean dew berry pie and chicken dumplings that my father absolutely loved! She also canned all of the vegetables and fruit we planted, which was a source of pride for some of the women in our community who talked about how many jars they'd put up. Being tobacco farmers, we worked hard; and for as long as I can remember we always owned our property.

Being tobacco farmers, we worked hard; and for as long as I can remember, we always owned our property. We lived on a farm in Markham, Virginia, where there was racism.

We lived on a farm in Markham, Virginia, where there was a lot of racism. So when my parents heard about a large beautiful farm in Midway, Virginia that was being auctioned off, they settled on an offer and prayed on it. The property, which had a small tenant house and family cemetery was 199 acres and had always belonged to white people.

On the day of the auction, my father went alone, and nobody made a bid after his bid, despite the auctioneer taking a break and resuming. It was crazy because the property was three times the price that my dad purchased it for. Little did anyone know that my father, who looked white, was really black.

When someone asked, *"Who bought the farm?"* The response was *"Some white man from Markham bought it."*

So the misconception about my father lingered, until he moved in with his clearly black wife and children. That's when strange things started to happen like the disappearance of our cow that was found dead in a ditch the next day. Despite the misfortunate happenings, it was God that blessed us with that property.

Wildness, Whippings and Worry

When I was in high school, I started to look at the boys, and they started to look at me, and my mother was looking at everything; and didn't miss anything! Like all teenagers, we wanted to go dancing and to basketball games.

I was a *Daddy's girl* and the youngest of three teenaged daughters still living at home. So my mother was hesitant about me hanging out with them, but my daddy, who allowed our older brother to drive us would say, *"Let her go, Nannie."* And she did, but we had a curfew of 11:00pm.

Being a little bit on the wild side, I didn't always comply with my mother's curfew, often weighing the fun time I was having with a potential whipping for disobeying. When my sister and I went on double dates, it seemed like the fun would just be getting good when my sister would say, *"Come on Ruby, it's time to go!"*

I couldn't wait to get home to receive my whipping so that I would feel better. But much to my horror, my mother didn't whip me or even say anything to me. She just had a hurt look on her face. I thought "Wow my mother doesn't love me anymore."

I knew if I was late I'd be in trouble but I figured the fun was worth it. Sometimes my sister would try to wait in a certain place for me, but if I didn't come in ten minutes or less, she'd leave. When I arrived home, Mama would be waiting for me in the stairway in the dark, and whip me all the way upstairs.

There was an unforgettable incident when my mother forbade me to attend a Halloween party with my brother, Willie and our friends. Hurt, I retreated to my room with one of my Modern Romance books when I heard my brother tap on my window to sneak me out. It was the worst time I had ever had because I felt guilty. I couldn't wait to get home to receive my whipping so that I would feel better.

But much to my horror, my mother didn't whip me or even say anything to me. She just had a hurt look on her face. I thought *"Wow my mother doesn't love me anymore."* I told her later, that of all the whippings I received, her silence was the worst punishment. She assured me that she loved me dearly and really blamed my brother more, because he was older.

Our Driving Force to the End

Mama loved to drive, but more importantly, she was our driving force. Despite many attempts to get a license at the Department of Motor Vehicles, she never received one. However, she obtained a Learner's Permit, which she renewed every few months. Although my father teased her, it didn't bother her in the least.

Some of my mother's driving mishaps included the time that she accidentally drove the car across the road into the woods. After retrieving the car, she got right back in and continued to drive because she didn't want to lose her nerve. And she didn't! But some family members did!

The older I get, the more I remind myself of my mother who I learned so much from. I've learned that you love all of your children, but you can't treat them the same, because they're different.

One day, while driving with my brother beside her and a couple of my sisters on the back of a green truck, Mama careened down a hill toward a bridge. The ones on the back jumped off with the truck in motion. When we heard the screams and commotion, my father and the rest of us ran down to investigate. The siblings who jumped off were really bruised and scarred up. The ones that stayed on weren't hurt, but the experience really led to them needing to use the bathroom REALLY bad!

The older I get, the more I remind myself of my mother who I learned so much from. I've learned that you love all of your children, but you can't treat them the same because they're different. From raising us, to being at the birth of most of our children and participating in the lives of her grandchildren, Mama was there. And I intend to share with my grandchildren some of her sayings. When she heard something that was really crazy, she'd say, *"Child that took the rag off the bush!"*

The last conversation I had with my mother was on New Year's Day, 1983. We never talked long. During the conversation, she said, *"I don't want to be a burden on anyone. I don't want to suffer."*

"Mama, I don't believe God will allow you to suffer. You had 18 children and I think that is suffering enough."

Because my husband and family used to drive across country every other year, I recall telling her, *"You know this is the year that we'll be coming home."*

"I hope I'll be here."

"Where else would we be?" I playfully replied.

"Well, I might be gone home to be with God."

"Mama, I hope not, but if you are, I promise you I will meet you there one day."

Mama awoke Sunday morning and couldn't get out of bed. She was taken to the hospital, and by Tuesday she was gone. She passed away on January 4, 1983, outliving my beloved father by a little more than 20 years. At her death my mother had 13 living children, 50 grandchildren, 52 great grandchildren and four great, great grandchildren.

I couldn't help but remember all the things that my mother had done over the years for other people, and I know without a doubt because of my mother, God did not, has not, and will not ever forget her child.

THANK YOU, MAMA. I LOVE YOU!

My Enraptured Melody
By Francene G. Weatherspoon

Music is My Life

Author at piano

While my dad was deployed in Korea in the early 1950s at the height of the war, Mom and I lived with my Grandma Mable in Georgia. Although we weren't rich, we had a spinet piano on which my mom played gospel songs, hymns, pop tunes and classical music. The spinet was a small piano manufactured in the early 1930s. During the Great Depression, people had little money and could ill afford a normal upright or a grand piano so the spinet served as an alternative. Our spinet has been in the family for more than sixty years and still is bringing music into our lives.

When my mom sat at the piano, the keys readily responded to her gentle touch. I would stare in wide-eyed wonder as her long, skillful fingers graced the keyboard, gliding easily from note-to-note.

My mom played beautifully...so beautifully that I wanted to play just like her. Sitting real close to her on the piano bench, I was enraptured with the melodic sounds emanating from the piano. When my mom sat at the piano, the keys readily responded to her gentle touch. I would stare in wide-eyed wonder as her long, skillful fingers graced the keyboard, gliding easily from note-to-note.

On the other hand, when I played it didn't sound like anything remotely familiar to the songs I heard at church or on the radio. Although my mom read music, it seemed to be something I didn't need to do. To my four-year old mind I knew that I could mimic what she did if only she would move over. I would practically push her off the bench. It seemed to me that if only I could only feel the warmth of the keys, I would be able to play just like my mom. There was one problem: by the time I touched the keys they were ice cold.

Life Lesson: *Nothing comes easy. It takes great effort to learn a task or to perfect a skill. It doesn't come by "osmosis."*

"That's not the right note!" my mom admonished from the kitchen when I was off tune. It was not easy for an eight-year old to practice piano lessons amid the competing voices of her buddies who were living it up right outside. *"Hey, when are you coming outside to play? Aren't you done yet?!"* they wailed during my numerous piano lessons. They of course, were having the time of their lives, engaged in baseball, skating, board games, four-square and all sorts of fun events. As for me, I was missing it all!

Although my dad was stationed in several states throughout his military career, somehow, my mom was ALWAYS able to find a piano teacher for me. Some were very strict; some were elderly, and some I simply came to love. Despite the challenges of arriving at a new air base, my mom networked and talked with many others in order to find a music teacher for her daughter.

Life Lesson: *If you want something in life you have to persevere and not let new surroundings and/or new people thwart your efforts. Be sociable and enlist the help of others in meeting your goals.*

The Beauty of Our Blackness

Author and mother 1952

My earliest remembrance of my mom's fierce *black pride* surfaced when I was coloring. *"Stay within the lines and color the faces brown and the hair black!"* she implored.

"Why?" I asked, curiously.

"The characters on the page should look like you." I had no further questions. That was all the explanation needed for a five-year-old.

As early as the 1960s, I received a walking doll named, *Wendy* for Christmas. I often wondered, *where on earth my mom found a black doll, particularly in Japan, where we were stationed?!"* Who knows? Wendy was my pride and joy. She was beautiful and had long, silky black hair. Although she was fairly stiff, she could walk if you held her by the hand and strolled with her. As of this writing I am 62 years old, still have Wendy, and have never owned a white doll.

Like other kids of our generation we thoroughly enjoyed watching the television show, *The Little Rascals.* It was comprised of black and white neighborhood kids who were very poor. However, my mom thought that the black kids were stereotyped with pearly white teeth, bushy hair, and large rolling eyes. While we thought it was funny, my mom saw it as racist and she did not want us exposed to it.

She was highly incensed to see black children portrayed in that fashion and to see her very own daughters laughing was intolerable. Despite her objections, we would sneak and watch it when she wasn't at home. But one day, we were so engrossed in an episode that we didn't hear her come in from work. She immediately rushed into the room and practically wrung the knob off of the television. And that was the last of the *Little Rascals* for us!

Breaking away from my mom, I headed for the fountain. No sooner than I had depressed the button to dispense the water, my mom came up to me and snatched me back, saying that that water fountain was for "Whites Only."

Remembrances of Racism

In Mississippi, I attended a segregated public elementary school in the late '50s. At the time, I had no point of reference that things should have been different. I had no idea that schools should have been integrated with white and black children being educated together and attending the same school. That knowledge was to come later.

I recall one day my mom and I went downtown to Dillard's Department Store. While our money was welcomed at the store, we were not. On that sweltering day I spotted a drinking fountain and ran to get some water. Breaking away from my mom, I headed for the fountain. I no sooner depressed the button to dispense the water when my mom snatched me back, saying that that water fountain was for *"Whites Only."* She pointed out the other water fountain (next to it) and explained that it was for *"Coloreds."*

Hmmm…the fountain for whites was a clean stainless steel fountain with ice cold water; and the one marked for "Coloreds" was a white porcelain basin with warm water. I remember this because there was condensation on the outside of that stainless steel fountain. As a child I couldn't figure that out, still can't and never will. I could only think about how thirsty I was and that there was a fountain of cold water within my reach that I didn't have access to. *What did my color have to do with which fountain I drank from?*

On another occasion, my mom and I attended a Christmas Parade. Several segregated troops of Girl Scouts were marching. My cousin Glynnis was in one of the troops. I asked my mom, *"What is Glynnis?"* And she said, *"A Brownie."* Made sense to me! I immediately pointed to one of the white girls and asked, *"What is she? "A Brownie,"* my mom responded. *Now, how confusing was that?*

Life lesson: *My mom always told me that to be "as good as white folks" you had to be "better than white folks." There are distinctions in life that are unexplained and illogical. Despite differences we must live together and learn from one another. As Dr. Martin Luther King Jr. said, "We must live together as brothers or perish together as fools."*

A Declaration of Independence

My mom has always been a *people person.* She easily made friends (at home and abroad) and has maintained those same friendships through the years. In fact, until her recent passing, the Matron of Honor at my mother and father's 1950 wedding was a dear friend of my mom for over sixty years!

A proud alumnus of Albany State, my mom, with some help from her mother, put herself through college by working an assortment of jobs from a dental assistant to an elementary school teacher. Whenever my dad was stationed at a new base, my mom recommended one of her friends to replace her.

My mom was always the *fashion plate.* While I woke up with rumpled pajamas and sleep in my eyes, my mom was already up and well groomed. No matter how early in the morning it was my mom had on earrings, lipstick and makeup. I have pictures of her always well-coiffed, wearing beautiful clothes.

When my dad proposed to my mom he told her that he would take care of her and that she wouldn't have to work outside the home. I am told that my mom responded, *"I appreciate that, but with your military salary, you can't take care of me in the way I've grown accustomed to."* So my mom worked outside of the home all of my childhood years until her retirement. But she also encouraged me to complete school and get a *good job* so that I could earn my own money. She said, *"When you have your own money you can spend it as you like."*

Life lesson: *Depend on no one. Don't be beholding to a man to take care of you or tell you how to spend your money. Be independent so that you don't have to ask his permission. Always keep money set aside in the event that you need it.*

Words to Live By

As of this writing, my mom is 87 years young. She's seen a lot, and as a result, there are many who come to her seeking advice about life issues. My mom tells it like it is and they still come back for more!

She has ingrained the following words to live by: *When you can't please anyone else, please yourself. Don't be reliant upon others, learn to entertain yourself. And get up doing something; don't sit around. Be productive!*

Talented and bright, my mom follows every single one of those tenets she speaks of without fail. I only hope that I will be half the woman she is. *Love you, Mom!*

Author with mother, and one of her treasured dolls

My Mother, My Rose

By Sandy Holman

A rose, a rose that you adore - A rose, a rose and many more
A rose, a rose to take you ashore and lead you to the Mother's Day Door!

The first poem I wrote for my mother in the third grade...

My Protector to the End

Author (right), with mother

As I lay next to my mother in her bed, music I wrote for her played in the background. I placed a stained glass angel against her cheek, clipped a lock of her coiled hair, recorded her labored death rattle, and snapped a last picture of her sunken face with my cell phone.

Then I whispered in her ear, *"You can leave this world and I'll try my best to keep our family together."* Afterward, I wailed like a wounded animal, primal and raw. It was the first time I was alone with her for weeks and I absorbed the last wave of heat from her body. It felt like a dream.

When my sister returned to the house from running errands, I knew it would be my last time seeing "Ma" alive. After I left and went to my dad's house which was less than 10 minutes away, I received the call that she had passed. I knew she did not want to die in front of me.

Arline Doris Holman's 72 years of life were full and vibrant. Although she was a country girl at heart, she possessed a city attitude that fueled her zest for living. A proud member of Christ Apostolic Church, she loved serving people and God. Holiday meals were legendary and she had an open door policy, welcoming the world into her home.

An old-school mom who believed in discipline, my mom did gamely participate in an intimate discussion about sex when I queried her about the topic as a teenager.

My mother was a nurse who told patients the truth when they needed to hear it and she was adored by doctors. To family, she was the mom you didn't mess with and all six of her children knew not to challenge her. She commanded respect. As an adult, I spoke to my mom daily and spent time with her weekly. We talked about life, loved eating Japanese food, and laughed at anything funny. I enjoyed seeing her giggle and when she was relaxed and having fun, it was priceless and deserved. After all, she had raised six children and dealt with all the complications that go with that accomplishment.

The lessons I learned from "Ma" were many: *Go to church and rely on God* (we would be in church for hours) – *Stay in school and go to college - do things to help people - learn to cook and clean - Work hard - Go after your dreams and love and forgive people.*

An old-school mom who believed in discipline, my mom did gamely participate in an intimate discussion about sex when I queried her about the topic as a teenager. I asked her everything too and she laughed uncomfortably as she answered every one of my questions. She affectionately called me "Crazy Thing" or "*Sandy Mandy*" and was extremely proud of me. In the last months of her life, "Ma" revealed that I had never caused her any major concern and I relished hearing that fact.

A Woman of Valor, Wrapped-Up in Homemade Ice Cream

I still marvel at the toughness my mother modeled, especially when dealing with her health and ultimately her death. She was the bravest woman I have ever known. My mother created a sense of joy in her life, even though she had much to worry about and faced many challenges.

Author, with mother, on wedding day

Did you have any regrets in life, Ma? I asked. For which she boldly answered without remorse, *"No! I have done everything I wanted to do. I wanted to get married and I did. I had children, and I became a nurse. I lived all my dreams."*

In a nutshell, my Mom was her homemade ice cream all sweet and delicious—her southern-style mac and cheese all warm and comforting. Her exquisite gumbo, full of flavor and variety, and her roast beef hash, all solid and fulfilling.

When I asked my mother if there was anything she wanted to tell her loved ones when she passed, she spoke about her funeral, which she had basically planned. *"You read a poem; have your sister sing a song. I want chicken, green beans and side dishes."* Knowing my mother, I should not have been shocked, but I stood at the side of her bed speechless. My Mom, who was not a passive woman, made things happen even if it was tough.

In a nutshell, my Mom was her homemade ice cream all sweet and delicious; her southern style mac and cheese—all warm and comforting. Her exquisite gumbo, full of flavor and variety,. and her roast beef hash, all solid and fulfilling. She packed a "punch" which was unique like the drink she was famous for and was legendary like her pound cakes. She was my sweet potato pie and I was lucky to eat her for breakfast, lunch and dinner. Her essence, particularly all the beautiful parts of who she was, resides in me and is my just dessert. When I envision her, it's like a white and yellow hummingbird whizzing by, and when I sit near her seat at her church I hear her whisper in my ear and it dawns on me, *all is well*.

A rose, a rose, that you adore - A rose, a rose and many more
A rose, a rose to take you ashore - And lead you to the Father's Door...

Dedication on a memorial bench
in honor of my mother upon her death

"Sister Moma"
by Anita McGee Royston

The Master Teacher and the Magical Gift of Learning

Author's Moma (right), with beloved Uncle

When I think about my Mother, Nora Lee Jefferson McGee, I see a beautiful quilt and a coat of many colors, I see understanding, celebration, organization and God's will, among other wonderful things — not necessarily in that order. I fondly call my covering, Sister Moma. Let me tell you a bit about my mother.

In addition to being my friend, she is — perhaps above all — a master teacher. She can't help it. She believes that everyone, if they apply themselves, can learn and can do better through knowledge when they are gently approached with knowledge.

Her children had to learn because she loved us and knew what the world does with ignorant people. So we were eager to learn because our teacher could see things in her mind and paint a picture with words so colorful and vivid that we could see what she saw.

At eighty, Sister Moma is still a strong, quiet and awesome character, whose life is a great story. I learned from her how to comb and style hair (I am the oldest of five girls so I had plenty of fun getting out of work by doing the easy things. She got me again! I learned to iron clothes, which I didn't mind because the television was on one of the four local stations. I also learned to wash diapers and cook without measuring ingredients.

To my undying gratitude, she also taught me that reading books was enjoyable, and writing my own stories was great fun, too. Some nights at reading time, Sister Moma, who was always writing stories, would read them to her spellbound audience of children.

As a result, I spend many hours a week today in the library reading, completing assignments, and working on projects such as this one with Joslyn: *Our Black Mothers, Brave Bold Beautiful!* She's in California; I am in Virginia and connected through the many services offered by the Gretna library.

I love reading, because Sister Moma made it fun. She unlocked our minds with reading because it was enjoyable for her and that filtered down to us.

My daddy (Josephus McGee, Sr.), was a gospel preacher /pastor. Moma is one, too. Being preacher's kids ("PKs") meant all of us were expected to be (1) saved, (2) successful in the Lord, (3) active participants in most areas of church work, and in today's grand phraseology, (4) positive role models. Of course, we tried to be all of those things, and more, especially in the public! If we misrepresented our home training in public the good church folk would wonder how our daddy could run a church when he couldn't even run his own home!

Anyway, one Sunday Daddy preached a sermon, which is a tradition in black culture from times when most people, excepting preachers, could not read. Its purpose is to motivate people to accept Jesus Christ as their redeeming savior from sin and restore their relationships with God the Father. Members who like what the preacher is saying voice their approval with a resounding *"Amen!"* Others who may be unmoved look at their watches. On this particular Sunday morning, Daddy, who had two jobs, told of the time when he stayed home from work. *With ten kids and a wife, I guess he needed to.*

"Everything was fine, until the children finished cleaning the kitchen," daddy recalled. We children had already learned in practical ways how assembly lines function *(You probably thought we learned from Lucy and Ethel? Wrong! It was Sister Moma.)* One child washed the dishes, another dried and put them away, while another swept the floor, as the grown-ups retired to the living room. Daddy continued preaching, something like this:

Suddenly, like a rushing mighty wind, the children ran upstairs, and they came down with books, while my wife began pulling down the shades and turning on the lamps. No one spoke a word. It was strange to witness. Then each one sat in a spot that must have been assigned. They opened their books and began to silently read.

My wife looked like she had wings, as she floated from one child to the other, asking in a voice I had not heard before, 'Where are you now? What are you doing?' The children answered with excitement! They thought they were the character they were reading about!

Of course, Daddy was not used to being home during the evenings so he had no clue as to how Ms. Nora's program went. I thought it was perfectly normal. I love reading because Sister Moma made it fun. She unlocked our minds with reading because it was enjoyable for her and that filtered down to us.

Moma had us say words, comprehend them, imagine what the story characters felt and get behind the words into the all-important meaning of the story. She taught us that all life is a story and written stories were great adventures. She told us that with an open book in hand we became *armchair travelers*! She would tell us in that mystical voice of hers that *"you can be whoever you want to be and go where ever the story takes you!'* She gave us an escape from uncomfortable moments through the gift of reading!

Reading was fun because the stories we read were as good as or better adventures than the stories on TV or the movies because our imaginations propelled them. And it is better to imagine being chased by bad people than be actually chased by bad people! I believe that the problem with illiteracy today is that people teach reading like they teach people how to do chores.

A gentleman told me that recently a teenager told him that when he is told to read, he just says the words but if someone asks him to explain what he has "read" he doesn't remember and has to read it again. This separation means reading teachers and parents are not doing an effective job teaching reading and comprehension. The two go together like air and breathing. I think that children should be taught like Moma taught us. I thought everyone was supposed to know how to read before they went to kindergarten and never understood why my teacher made a big deal out of "everyday things."

Didn't everybody's mother teach them to read? I learned much later that they did not!

If reading teachers and parents today taught reading like Sister Moma, illiteracy would drop like a bad habit. Good teachers have a special talent for creativity. I must say in the hindsight that sixty years on this earth has given me, Sister Moma had a fair degree of cleverness in her quilt and coat of many colors, too.

Cup Rice, a Broad Imagination and a Grand Scheme Equals Love

During summers, sometimes Sister Moma would have us make dish water in a big pan made like a wash tub. If we washed the dishes fast and finished the kitchen while the water was still warm and soapy, we could take the tub outside in the yard, dip our hands with fingers to thumb in the water to make a circle of giant bubbles that would float in the air! *Hooray!*

It wasn't until I had children of my own that I figured out her scheme, if you will. Of course, I never used such schemes with my own children. No. Never! *Wink, wink!*

One thing I did do with my children was to introduce them to what was known to us as *Cup Rice*. I loved coming home for a lunch of *Cup Rice*. Sister Moma would take a tea cup and pack it with cooked rice, turn it over and place the compacted rice on a plate, remove the cup, and then drizzle brown gravy over the rice! It looked *like a mountain or erupted volcano!*

My children loved it too, and I told them I enjoyed it as a child. Later, I asked Sister Moma how she came up with the idea. Her answer floored me: *"Sometimes all I had was rice and a little flour and sometimes peas."* I smiled and learned yet another lesson—no matter what the situation, you can escape through a tunnel called *imagination* so that your children never have to stress.

Additionally, that creative thinking is an example of how black people, more specifically mothers have survived by taking a little of what's left and making it into something special and beautiful.

When she said, "You're gonna find yourself getting up from under the couch," I didn't think that was physically possible, because I didn't think adults exaggerated the truth. How could I get knocked beneath six inches of space between the couch and the floor? Bet I didn't ask.

With Sister Moma, little words became big, special stories. Then stories became bigger mysteries. Then the mysteries left me dumbfounded and confused by her one liners used to make a quick point when she was not pleased with our behavior. When she'd say, *"I'll knock you to kingdom come!"* I had no way of knowing how she could knock me to the Kingdom of God in heaven but I didn't want to find out.

I saw myself flying like I'd been shot out of cannon straight to the Kingdom past the singing angels. Dumbfounded and confused because we were taught that God was coming back on a cloud to get us and she was threatening to with one hard knock, send me there herself. Sister Moma was connected.

When she said, *"You're gonna find yourself getting up from under the couch,"* I didn't think that was physically possible, because I didn't think adults exaggerated the truth. *How could I get knocked beneath six inches of space between the couch and the floor?*
Bet I didn't ask.

Other proverbs were *"Do you want the angels to take your name out of the lamb's book of life?"* (I believed she had the power to have that happen. *And then what?)* Kids nowadays might ask, *"Can you really make that happen?"* Or she'd say, *"You're on my bad list"* or *"I hope you have five children just like you!"* (I did!) And the worst, which required no decoding, was: *"Wait 'til your father gets home."* That one turned out to be the least scary of all because Daddy had a real soft spot, at least for the girls.

He was playful. Sister Moma was quiet, and she meant business. They had great balance.

A Simple Superb Life in the Midst of Human Incivility

When you grow up in a working class family like mine, your favorite activities involve simple, uncomplicated things, like cooking, family quilting, storytelling etc. Back in those wife-homemaker aka *housewife* days, Sister Moma was a wiz at creating things like banana pudding, egg salad, yeast rolls and so forth. She was a great gourmand before all of those TV cooking shows became the rage they are now.

She always absorbed new ideas from her many cook books as well as recreated fancy dishes her mother taught her after living the high life with her progressive siblings in St. Louis when she became of age. Oh could she set a table! After all, she is a native of Mississippi, and from a delta town between Vicksburg to the south and Memphis, Tennessee to the north, the capital of Southern cooking. It is implied that *If a woman from Mississippi could not cook, she was not worthy of her heritage.*

When I was in the first grade, I was given the honor of taking our classrooms' baby mice home in their own shoebox for the weekend. After school was dismissed on a Friday, I showed them to Sister Moma and she was apoplectic!

There were other simple but exciting activities Moma provided such as our New Year's Eve cookie baking contests. The big kids would stay up late to see which of us could out bake the other. Daddy would come home resplendent in his waiter's tuxedo from Sacramento's fabulous *Antinena's* Restaurant and greet us in the morning with a movie stars autograph and party favors.

Another uncomplicated good time was church. I recall the sheer joy of Daddy taking us kids to church so Moma could stay home and rest. Afterward, I greatly anticipated coming home to an immaculately clean house with good smelling food and the sounds of Nat "King" Cole, Frank Sinatra or Perry Como wafting through the house. During Daddy's dinner prayer, however, which was MUCH shorter than Sunday morning breakfast prayers, the music was turned down.

When I was in the first grade, I was given the honor of taking our classrooms' baby mice home in their own shoebox for the weekend. After school was dismissed on a Friday, I showed them to Sister Moma and she was apoplectic! *"Why would you bring rats home? What if those things get loose? Take those things back to school!"*

Sister Moma didn't seem to care that it was Friday and the teacher was long gone. School was out. What was wrong with my sister? So I sat on the back porch and figured out a solution. Without telling Sister Moma, I disappeared back over to school and found that the custodian was still there. He helped me put the mice back inside their family aquarium in my class so they'd be okay. When I got back home, Sister Moma seemed happy. *What would she have done to those cute baby mice? They weren't rats!* Although Sister Moma and I didn't agree on the mice incident, she always came to school to encourage her children, particularly at the primary grade levels.

However, I learned much later that when she would come to junior high PTA meetings at our predominantly white school, Joaquin Miller in Sacramento, California, white parents would shun her by moving to the other side of the room. She said her feelings were so hurt that she stopped going. California was not the promise land it was presented to be!

At the time however, Daddy would be there because I was in band and orchestra and loved it when they would come and hear me play the violin and clarinet.

It was tense. Things we saw on TV; the way our people were being treated there, were being relayed to us before they made TV from Grandma's letters.

At the breakfast table during the week when it was just Sister Moma and us kids, she would update us on world history. We learned about Fidel Castro, and Batista, Fidel Castro's predecessor in Cuba; and, of course, the civil rights movement in the South. My mother would read our maternal Grandma's letters from Greenwood, Mississippi, where I was born and raised until my Dad had to leave when I was three.

At the time, we lived less than ten miles from Money, Mississippi, where the Bryant brothers were being held for the brutal death of Emmitt Till, a 14-year-old-black teenager from Chicago, Illinois ,who was visiting relatives in Mississippi in 1955. Till was killed for allegedly flirting with a married white woman. Her husband and brother-in-law murdered him, and everyone knew it. That's how brazen Mississippi brutality was then. Moma told us stories about how black people handled the situation surrounding the youngster's death that I've not yet read about in a history book because the old excuse was, *not now.*

When Daddy became the number one target on the *Ku Klux Klan hate list for his anti-racism protests in front of the jail, he was in imminent danger and couldn't stay in Mississippi. So he departed for California to live with his brother, Richard, and his wife, Sora. The rest of us arrived by train later to join him and embark on our new life.

After we left Mississippi, Grandma would say in her letters that when black voters arrived at polling locations, the registrar would ask them silly questions like *'how many beans are in this jar?'* or *'how many bubbles are in this bar of soap?'* to disqualify black people from registering if they didn't "know" the answers.

It was tense. Things we saw on TV; the way our people were being treated there, were being relayed to us before they made TV from Grandma's letters. Police dogs, attacking innocent demonstrators both white and black, and cops wielding Billy clubs on children; and vicious racist governors like Ross Barnett of Mississippi, George Wallace of Alabama and other bigots were boldly spouting their hateful rhetoric!

These forays into adult business were structured accordingly because my parents believed that children should not get too much information concerning that which was deemed to be *"grown folks"* business. I believe that today, too. *You don't fill up a car with jet fuel because it is not a jet. Likewise, you should not fill up a kid with grown folks business because a kid is not a grown person.*

Something to Live For

Moma always says, *"You must always have something to live for."* I think that life lesson is the key to her being a brand new octogenarian. Last December she turned eighty! I saw her lose my brother, Timmy to an asthma attack in 1961, when I was seven. Eighteen years later, her oldest child Joe, was killed in a suspicious automobile accident. And nine years ago, her husband of fifty three years, whom she tirelessly and lovingly attended to after a debilitating series of strokes and other ailments, passed.

Though the pain of each of those occasions was immense, she came through each with God's amazing grace and a determination to live!

Moma always says, "You must always have something to live for." I think that life lesson is the key to her being a brand new octogenarian. Last December, she turned eighty!

She remains the lady because she has something to live for: seeing her loved ones again at the *Family Reunion*, as she said in her book, which she had already prophetically written about...*the family reunion to come!* She is child of the past, the present and the future—a spirit child, living for something forever! She is, **Sister**

Moma, with the emphasis on "Moma." Although I remember so much more, I will close on this note: *Moma I love you and I rise and call you blessed!*

Author on right, with her mother

Author's mother on right, holding up sign

Section Three

Pioneering Women

Born Free
by
Dr. Melissa Cadet

An Expected Way of Life

Little Gertie, High School Queen

The air felt like a warm curtain of moisture that you can almost touch. Like a fine, nearly invisible mist, tiny droplets form and meld against your skin, making you sweat. No one escaped bayou heat. The oppressive curtain of air blanketed the small town of Donaldsonville, where this story begins. It is nestled in the bayous of Louisiana about 25 miles from New Orleans. In the 1930s the town was little more than a whistle-stop where those of color toiled for the rich who owned the plantations and major retail stores.

If you were female and colored ranging from off-white to black, you worked as a domestic in one of the homes of the rich and would be famous. Famous or not, they were the kings of the town and they were feared, respected and unquestioned. Questioning meant trouble; resisting led to dismissal and loss of income from the homes of the rich and would be famous. So, most women of color toiled in their homes and raised their children because that was the expected way of life.

"Why can't I have my own home?" asked Gertrude Verette, who was a very tall, young mulatto woman with Indian blood, high cheekbones and silky black hair; so long it reached her waist and curled softly around her angular face and pointed nose. Gertrude, also known as "Gertie," was likely a Chitimacha Indian

descendent. The Chitimacha was a group of indigenous people who lived along the Mississippi River before European colonization. While Gertrude never questioned her Indian ancestry, she was afraid to speak about her white heritage. Some deep-rooted, perhaps negative experience rendered her incapable of discussing this part of her lineage.

If you were female and colored ranging from off-white to black, you worked as a domestic in one of the homes of the rich and would be famous. Famous or not, they were the kings of the town and they were feared, respected and unquestioned.

Gertrude came from a long line of women who worked as domestics in the town. Most lived in shanties near the larger plantation homes. In 1906, Gertie was 18, but she already had ten years of experience working in the plantation-style homes. She knew domestics did not work regular hours because they were always on call to the white family that employed them.

Gertie toiled for hours washing clothes by hand, hanging them out to dry, cooking, cleaning, and nursing her plantation family's children back to health when they were sick even if that meant staying up all night without sleep. She lived with little pay, but wanted more. So, she started to read and teach herself as much as she could whenever she could get her hands on a few books.

As she improved her vocabulary, diction, and professional manner, she 'progressed' and received special treatment from the family she cared for. She didn't know who her father was, but she knew she was a treasured household fixture. For many women of this period, this privileged treatment was enough but Gertie wanted a life and children of her own.

A Dream Come True

The Lemon's Department Store was the biggest one in the region. *Coloreds* were not allowed to shop there or mix and mingle with the white staff—except for one, Mr. Clifford LeBlanc, a short, stout, dark-skinned 'Negro' with a brisk walk and air of confidence. Though he did not have the title, he was the underground right hand of Mr. Lemon himself. He was Mr. Lemon's trusted chief operations officer, supplier, manager, chauffer, confidante, and boy Friday.

When Mr. LeBlanc did Mr. Lemon's work and carried out his requests, he not only had clout, he empowered others. Everyone called him "Mr. LeBlanc"—even the white folks. He was well-liked and well-respected especially by Gertie who watched him with admiration.

Most importantly, Mr. Lemon gave Mr. LeBlanc a house in the "up-town" part of town, where only whites lived with a formal parlor, elegant dining room, and a fig tree in the back yard.

One day, Gertie officially met Clifford at a small "sock hop" dance back-of-town by the bayou. They danced and talked for hours even though people teased and mocked them because Gertie was over a head taller than Clifford and wafer thin compared to his short, teddy-bear shaped frame. They were an odd, but very poised and polished couple full of shared plans, hopes and dreams.

When they married in their mid-twenties, people from all walks of life and colors of the rainbow attended. Most importantly, Mr. Lemon gave Mr. LeBlanc a house in the "up-town" part of town where only whites lived with a formal parlor, elegant dining room, and a fig tree orchard in the back yard. Gertie's dream came true and she raised five children in that house while keeping her domestic job.

Gertie's oldest daughter was born on her birthday in December 1930—a grand surprise so treasured that Gertie named her daughter after her, Gertrude LeBlanc. Little Gertrude loved the house with the grand piano, large southern-style porch at the top of an elegant stairway, and large claw foot tub so big you could swim in it! Ms. Gertie —as she was now called—pampered her daughter and taught her about her heritage and her importance in the community. Like all mothers, she wanted the best for Little Gertie and all of her children.

Little Gertie attended St. Catherine's High School, became one of the girls basketball team stars, and the Belle of the Ball elected as the prestigious St. Catherine's High School Queen. Very much like her mother, Little Gertie had aspirations too. She wanted to see more of the world than the small town atmosphere of Donaldsonville allowed. She watched her older brothers enlist in military service and travel to foreign places. Her beloved older brother, Reginald served and died in the Korean War but the bond between them would last well after his death.

Not My Daughter: Breaking the Grip of Oppression

One day, Ms. Gertie stomped into the house highly upset. She argued loudly with Mr. LeBlanc who had a habit of sitting on the porch smoking a Cuban cigar. The cause of the ruckus stemmed from Ms. Gertie's argument with her employer who demanded it was now *"high time"* that Little Gertie also work in the home of the employer's daughter helping her to raise her children.

Ms. Gertie was so furious, she stormed out without saying goodbye to the kids she cared for. They knew their beloved Ms. Gertie was uncharacteristically upset and followed her halfway home trying to console her without understanding the cause of her rage. Realizing this, she cooled down and walked them both back home assuring them she would continue to care for them and their family. But, Gertie did not want her daughter to become a domestic. In her mind, Little Gertie was born free of those slave-like requirements. She would not stand for this forced conscription.

As soon as little Gertie graduated from high school, she was expected to assume her domestic post—a post she loathed. Yet, she did not want to cause turmoil for her parents and their stature in the community.

Mr. LeBlanc was also enraged, but conflicted about the best course of action to follow. If Little Gertie did not work for Ms. Gertie's very wealthy employer, he was certain he, or Ms. Gertie, would lose their jobs. Their employers had assumed that their children were supposed to follow in their footsteps.

As soon as little Gertie graduated from high school, she was expected to assume her domestic post—a post she loathed. Yet, she did not want to cause turmoil for her parents and their stature in the community. Despite their acceptance into the white neighborhood and living in their own house among them as friends, they had only broken the surface of the color barrier. Weren't the LeBlanc children born free?

Gertie and Clifford stalled while they figured out what to do. Little Gertie's high school graduation was fast approaching. As 1947 High School Queen, the very attractive and petite Little Gertie had shed her nickname and was known simply as Gert. She stood 5'1' and like her mother, had long, silky hair cascading down her back.

One of the young men from Lowery's Training School, Joseph Lawson, caught Gert's attention. He was graduating and joining the Navy; and promised Gert he would take her away from the situation. Much to the surprise of Gert's parents, he announced that he would marry their daughter and take her with him on his military assignment on the West Coast. Gert accepted the proposal and averted the dilemma for her parents and for herself.

In 1951, Gert started a new life in California free from the control that threatened to enslave her, and engulf her dreams. By making this decision she broke the stronghold and legacy of dominance and oppression that had governed her family for years. Although she was born free and knew it, fate intervened to ensure that she was truly able to forever live free and be free!

Postscript: Gert's beloved brother, Reginald LeBlanc died in the Korean War but the bond between them lasted well after his death. He lives in the hearts of Gert's children who loved listening to their mother's stories about their Uncle Reginald. One of Gert's greatest joys was discovering that one of the statues in the National Korean War Veterans Memorial located on The National Mall in Washington, D.C. is a replica of Reginald.

The Memorial is in the form of a triangle intersecting a circle. Within the triangle are 19 stainless steel statues designed by Frank Gaylord, each slightly larger than life size (between 7 feet 3 inches and 7 feet 6 inches), representing a squad on patrol.

When Gert saw the larger than life statue of Reginald, she wept. Like her mother, Gert had five children and one child was born in December. She named him Reginald. However, he missed the shared birth date of his mother and grandmother by eight days!

Homemaker Extraordinaire:
A Genuine Pioneer

by
Fannie Callands

Resourceful, soft-spoken and wise define the loving legacy of Mrs. Cornelia (Nean) Coleman Callands; the woman with a gift to tap into the wisdom of God and the ability to advise younger women concerning relationships and raising children. When it came to her own children she had keen motherly instincts. The first time one of her daughters went to the beach, Nean saw a vision of her child surrounded by a large body of water even though her daughter didn't tell her mother about her beach trip.

There were times when Nean used an idiom to emphasize a point like *"A mule's head is longer than yours and he doesn't know everything,* or *every crow thinks his own is the blackest."* Due to Nean's intuitive spirit she was kept informed of possible dangers in life facing her children.

Charged with caring for her father, younger sister and four brothers, Nean never received a formal education due to all of her responsibilities.

On Valentine's Day, 1920, Nean was born to Matt (Buster) and Mary Coleman. Her mother, Mary died shortly after child birth and Buster remarried. He and his second wife had four children, but when she died, Nean, who was the oldest girl, became the home maker and surrogate mother. Charged with caring for her father, younger sister and four brothers, Nean never received a formal education due to all of her responsibilities. However, through persistence, curiosity, patience and the teachings of older women in the community she learned the necessary life skills needed to become a productive and responsible adult.

When Nean married Talbert Callands on Thanksgiving Day, 1939 she continued doing what she knew best, and together they raised eight children. Without access to modern conveniences, Nean was a woman who knew how to do it all. An excellent cook, noted for her fried chicken, chocolate cake, baked bread (aka "hoecakes"), and country ham gravy, she had a knack to stretch food. There always seemed to be enough to eat even with the arrival of unexpected dinner guests.

Nean also was a great gardener who grew beautiful flowers and a bountiful vegetable garden. As an outstanding food preserver she canned an assortment of vegetables and fruits, including pickled cucumbers, peaches and pears; and she canned pork sausage and tender loin. When it came to washing clothes, Nean made her own lye soap and boiled clothes in a cast iron pot over an open fire to remove stains. She even churned butter and gathered wild food stuff like nuts, berries and greens.

Anything but a Patchwork Life

A patch of discarded material was magically and painstakingly transformed to a work of art when Nean Callands touched it. She could design clothes and make home furnishings and quilts from mere scraps. Her sewing skills were developed to the point that she could see an outfit on someone and from memory recreate the outfit for herself or her girls. Many of the quilts and curtains that decorated her home were her creations.

And from all of the work she did in raising generations of family members, Ms. Cornelia Nean Colbert Callands, made a life for so many with so little, and ended up creating an enduring masterpiece designed with love.

From garments her children had outgrown, she would cut pieces of fabric into squares, rectangles, triangles, or even diamond shapes. Then she would color coordinate them and sew the pieces together forming different patterns. She repeated that process until enough pieces were sewn together to form a full size quilt. And from all of the work she did in raising generations of family members, Mrs. Cornelia Nean Colbert Callands made a life for so many with so little, and ended up creating an enduring masterpiece designed with love.

Ms. Fannie Callands

Of Sweet Tea and Quilts
by **Dera Williams**

I am honored to submit my story about my mother, my grandmother, traditions and the importance of telling our stories. Of Sweet Tea and Quilts speaks to our fragile, yet empowered existence as mothers.
— *Dera Williams*

"Did I dream you told me you were going to retire?" my mother queried for the third time in the last two hours.

"No, it wasn't a dream. Dera is retiring next month. She told us last week," my sister, Florence, replied, looking over at me and shrugging my shoulders.

"But you're too young to retire. What are you going to do?" Mama asked peering over her glasses with a look of intensity.

I sighed and composed myself before I spoke. *"No, I'm not too young, Mama. I told you what I plan to do."*

"Well, I think you're too young. And what was it you said you're going to do?" She asked puzzled. I looked over at my sister and shook my head.

As of late, this was a typical **conversation when speaking with my mother regarding just about every topic. While in relatively good health, despite turning 88** last April, her mind is becoming frail. Repeating something to her that I had just told her five minutes prior was not unusual.

Florence reminds me that Mama's short term memory is almost nonexistent. While that might be true, she surprises me sometimes when she casually mentions something from her childhood, or recalls an occurrence that happened 20, 40, or 60 years ago.

Time is fleeting, and I am feeling the urgency to get all the stories, more from my mother, aunt and the other elders.

As the family genealogist and the keeper of stories for my family, it is a wonderful gift when my mother reaches back to the furthest corner of her memory and reveals one of those gold nuggets of stories past. Stories of family history are what inspire me to keep searching for more clues to add pieces to the unknown puzzles that are still missing so I can write and share them with our family and the world.

Arkansas Strong and Deep, California True

My mother and I both were born in Arkansas, she in 1926 and I in 1951. Like so many African-American families of the south in the 1950s, our family migrated to California when I was two years old. So I was a California girl true; I ate the tortillas that my childhood friend's mother made and swam in the recreational swimming pools at every opportunity.

But my family's roots run strong and deep in the Arkansas soil and our summer visits were the high points of my life. It was in Arkansas where I drank gallons of sweet tea or "sun tea," so named because a big bucket of tea was brewed in the backyard under the burning sun.

On the porch of my grandmother Otelia Rowland, I heard family stories, embellished ghost stories and adventures of Mom and her siblings. Grandmother would sit in her favorite chair, laughing at my uncles and admonishing, *"Stop telling those lies to those chil'ren."* Then reach down for her coffee can to spit tobacco and continue either sewing a garment or piecing a quilt. *"Hand me that blue thread, baby. Now I think this would be pretty with the North Star pattern."*

Mom told me about the quilting parties the ladies had in the country which were usually held year round on a Wednesday or Thursday afternoon. Piecing quilts, pulling together their scraps of fabrics, bickering good naturedly over what pattern to use and catching up on the local gossip and their families' lives was the usual routine.

Afterward, the women would break for a short repast of leftover collard greens and cornbread, finishing off with brown-edged tea cakes fresh from the oven and tea. Depending upon the weather, it might be hot tea mixed with milk and sugar or in warm weather; sweet ice tea, a staple of the South.

Piecing Together a Memory

Mama traveled back to Arkansas to visit her mother and to confer with her siblings. She came back with a quilt that Grandmother had made.

Grandmother Otelia often visited us in Oakland and taught my sister and I how to crochet and knit and to embroidery pillowcases. I remember her as full of life, but as time passed, there was talk of Grandmother's failing memory. Finally in the early 1990s, by then a great-grandmother, Otelia was diagnosed with Alzheimer's, a disease that robs one of memories.

Mama traveled back to Arkansas to visit her mother and to confer with her siblings. She came back with a quilt that Grandmother made. After opening it up I was surprised to see the crooked lines and unmatched pieces. This was not the work of my grandmother who was fastidious about her sewing; but a quilt made by a woman who had been robbed of her talents.

After Grandmother's death, Mom began the task of reconstructing her quilt. She took apart and tore out threads and worked painstakingly to piece the quilt the way her mother would have had done if she not been ill. Finally, it was finished and restored to a beautiful piece of art, something Grandmother would have been proud to call her own.

The quilt became a legacy and a story was born of the mother who recreated her mother's quilt. Mom is still an avid quilter, still holding down the quilting bee at her church; faithfully attending every Thursday afternoon. There are fewer members, **most** elderly but determined to carry on the tradition. They decide on a theme for the year and make a joint quilt as well as work on their individual projects.

Last year, Mom saw a pattern in one of her quilting magazines of a quilt of the U.S. States. She ordered the pattern and went about choosing fabric and collecting scraps for this large project. Almost every time I went over to her house, she was working on the quilt, one state at a time.

"Well, I finished Arkansas," she said one day beaming. She held it up and I saw the intricacy of the work. I thought, but didn't say out loud, *Wow, I wonder if she is taking on too much?* Her dementia had gradually increased in the last two years. But I also saw how determined she was to finish it. Some days I didn't see her working on it and would mention it to her.

"Oh, I've been tired," or *"My arthritis in my hands is bothering me,"* but then a few weeks later I would walk in and she would be down on the floor, brow furrowed as she maneuvered the cloth to get it just right. I had never known Mom to work so long on a quilt and I worried that it was taking so long.

Carrying Generations into the Fold

Last June, I went to the Alameda County Fair and attended the quilt exhibit and admired the many quilts that were displayed by local quilt artisans. It occurred to me that while many of the quilts were outstanding, my mother's quilts were of equal value and skill or in some respects surpassed the handiwork displayed in those glass cases.

A few days later, I stopped by Mom's and I asked her about the progress of the states quilt. She said she was close to finishing it. I asked to see it and she went in the back and we rolled it out. It was beautiful, intricate and detailed.

"Emma has been helping me," she said, referring to the head quilter in her group. *"I have to finish the last two states and then send it to the woman in Kansas to stitch the outer edges."* She explained that with her arthritis, she couldn't do the finishing.

"Mama, those quilts at the county fair were nice, but there was nothing that resembled this. Let's finish this quilt and next year we are going to enter it into the county fair exhibitions."

"Do you think it's good enough?" she asked, with doubt in her voice.

"It sure is. This is a masterpiece. I can't wait to see it finished!"

I was determined to bring my mother's work into the public arena, but sometime later, when I asked about finishing it, she said she had been tired. I knew what I had to do: help my mother finish the last pieces of the quilt. As I prepare to do so, I think of my life, now that I am in my AARP (American Association of Retired Person) years. Will my daughter, Rebecca have to help me finish a task in 20 years?

There are days I forget something walking from one room into another. Time is fleeting, and I am feeling the urgency to get all the stories, more from my mother, aunt and the other elders.

Will I have enough time to write all of the stories of my ancestors that need to be told; to write of the mothers who came before me and told their stories with their hands, weaving tales through the quilt patterns of the old south? What of my young granddaughter, Brooklynn in 40 years? What charge will she inherit to carry on the traditions of her foremothers? It is a cycle built on love of family, where the elders reach back and carry the generations into the fold.

Author's mother and granddaughter

Breaking the Classroom Color Line
by Johnnie M. Fullerwinder

Stepping Up to the Plate—The Jackie Robinsons of Education

Segregation was pervasive in the south and other locales in the United States in the 1960s. Virginia was no different. In 1967 it was considered illegal for individuals who were of a different race to marry in the state. The case of Richard Loving, who was white, and his wife, Mildred, whose ancestry was African and Native American, set off a legal battle because they dared to fall in love. Due to the laws on the books at that time, they were in violation of the law and sentenced to jail. Refusing to divorce, they had to leave Virginia to maintain their marital status.

In 1963, Dr. King was in Danville to hasten the path to racial parity. The city's African American population had grown weary of the discriminatory practices of their town and many engaged in protests to end segregation.

Other racial slights and major indignities like being refused basic human rights and constantly encountering the customary 'Whites Only" and "Coloreds Only" signage which were posted to designate one's place in society was prevalent in many states, including Virginia. Even attending a school that was integrated, as Dr. Martin Luther King, Jr. had envisioned, and outlined so beautifully in his, *"I Have a Dream Speech,"* was just an unrealized vision in Danville, Virginia, but change was in the atmosphere during those tense days and years of legalized inequality.

In 1963, Dr. King was in Danville to hasten the path to racial parity. The city's African American population had grown weary of the discriminatory practices of their town and many engaged in protests to end segregation. By 1966, change was imminent, but far from easy. A plan had been drafted to integrate staff and faculty at George Washington and Langston High Schools.

The candidate selected for this historic mission would have to be strong, patient and committed to the cause of equal educational opportunities. He or she would have to handle the possibility of facing abject racism and be prepared for outright rejection as well. In other words the "test case" teacher(s) would have to be like the *Jackie Robinson* of the classroom in order to break the color line. Such a person stepped up to the plate, no pun intended, and took her place. In 1966, Johnnie M. Fullerwinder became the first African American teacher in Danville to integrate the public schools.

Ms. Fullerwinder started her journey at the then, "practically all-white" George Washington High School. During her career as an educator, she also was a brave, bold and beautiful mother to two children. Her contribution and sacrifices positively impacted the Civil Rights Movement and more critically, children with a simple dream to learn. What follows are her own words about being called to duty.

A Pioneering Woman

"Cry... adjust... endure."

Suppose, as a young African American female teacher, you had been hired to teach in a racially segregated southern city that prided itself on being the Last Capitol of the Confederacy. You were assigned to the city's largest high school with an enrollment of over 2,000. The entire faculty and staff were of a different race than you and the student body was 99.9% of a different race.

Despite the enormity of the challenge and a husband and a very young child at home to nurture, I would not be outwitted.

Unknowingly, you entered the large school alone and found... on that day... you were the only person of your race in the entire building and most of the faculty didn't seem to know you were coming to join them!

With only three years of teaching experience in another state and no prior warning, during what I considered an impressive job interview, I had ended up in this situation... a seemingly school division's "test-case."

Alone, but not Outwitted

Surviving the initial shock and sobering realization that this was reality and not a dream, I wrestled with many unsettling emotions. First among them was the thought, *Should I run for the nearest exit?* As sound reasoning prevailed, quietly, I sat down and observed.

Despite the enormity of the challenge and a husband and a very young child at home to nurture, I would not be outwitted. Possessing a solid command of my subject area, strong religious faith and a determination to defy defeat, I chose to remain on the faculty.

Whoever was selected for this historic mission would have to be strong, patient and committed to the cause of equal educational opportunities.

Holding head and shoulders high, employing the best teaching practices and exhibiting a genuine love for children, slowly I garnered support of both faculty and students. With strong reliance on faith and a supportive husband, who found himself as a 'test case' in another school division, I had raised two wonderful children of my own, along the journey. Both of them earned college degrees and became teachers as well.

I excelled and attained the position of assistant principal, later receiving recognition as *"Outstanding Secondary School Assistant Principal of the Year"* for the state of Virginia. Prior to retirement, I was promoted to District Level Supervisor (K-12) for my subject area of science and mathematics. Over time, bridges were crossed almost unnoticeably as promotions followed, segregation became a thing of the past, and children were educated.

My Multi-Faceted, Multi-Dimensional, Most Sensational Mama!

By April Clark

No Limits, No Labels

Akilah Jaye was born as Janet Clark in Sacramento, California on July 21, 1952 to Jane and Benjamin Clark. Her mother was of Filipina descent and her father was African American. When it came to political correctness in regard to calling one's self African American, my mom said, *"That's so limited. Being called African American limits yourself to just one continent. I'm black. Black can be Cuban, Puerto Rican, American or so much more than just African. Black is global!"*

My mother paid attention to words and their meanings and was especially careful of labels or categories.   When I think of words to describe her: *Mother, poet, secretary, sister, organizer, social worker, aunt, comedian, dancer, spiritual seeker, daughter… I realize she was multi-faceted. She was eclectic!* My mother's sister said Mom was always writing poetry when she was little that she read aloud in church.

Being called African American limits yourself to just one continent. I'm black. Black can be Cuban, Puerto Rican, American, or so much more than just African.

During her childhood my mother had a moment of fascination that caused her serious harm. While my Nanny (my grandmother) and Pappy (my grandpa) were having an argument, my mom, who was a then curious three-year-old, climbed on a stool to look inside of a big pot of beans that were cooking on the stove.

"Get her down from there!" Nanny yelled to Pappy, who quickly rushed over and snatched the stool from underneath her, but his attempt was too late.

My mom was still holding onto the pot and all the hot boiling beans poured over her face and upper body. Panicked, my grandparents wrapped her in a blanket and threw her in the back of the car and rushed her to the hospital. She had welts for the rest of her life and a heavy complex about them. So she always made a conscious effort to cover her burns. I still have childhood memories of my mom sitting in front of a handheld mirror picking at her scars with tweezers.

As a teenager, my mom became pregnant with my older brother, Wesley which angered her mother. According to my mom, Nanny told the cops *"Take her away!"*

For many years afterward the two didn't talk. But my mom, being very resourceful and loveable was adopted by a few families. One family was the McGees, who she married into and became close to. She met and married Joe McGee before I was born.

Despite their short relationship, his family took her in as one of their own and she became a lifelong sister and daughter. When I came along, my mom was surprised about the pregnancy. It certainly wasn't planned. At the time, she was testing out a new religion called Scientology. As an independent, daring, free thinker she was always questioning things like religion. It was part of her life's journey to find the perfect spiritual fit.

The Birth of a Family

Raised apostolic, my mom later attended a Baptist Church. I recall one of the McGee sisters saying she loved when my mom would become "saved" again because she would give her all her old makeup. My mom would completely pour herself into a new religion. I'm not sure what sparked her interest in Scientology in her early twenties but if it wasn't for her seeking out answers there, I wouldn't have been born.

Someone named Phillip Hanford picked my mother up for Scientology classes. That's basically all I knew about him growing up, except that he was white, and nice to my mother. I never had a picture and Mom said little about him. Years later after she passed, my husband found him online.

After a DNA confirmation, I connected with Phillip Hanford, and we met shortly thereafter. I remember emailing him. *"My mother was Janet Clark and attended a Scientology class in the '70s. She passed away and left a gift for a Phillip Hanford. If you are him, then please contact me."* Later, we both laughed when I told him I was the "gift."

I'm not sure what sparked her interest in Scientology in her early twenties but if it wasn't for her seeking out answers there, I wouldn't have been born.

Phillip, my dad, told me the Scientology organizers gave him my mother's name and address as one of the participants to pick up for the class. They quickly became friends and attended the classes together. After their brief love affair, then break up, my mom discovered she was pregnant, which he never knew about.

For many years, my mom was considered the black sheep of her family, but made her own family along the way. From her chosen family she developed a sense of community and gave back generously, starting LACE (Local Artists for Charity Events) when I was a teenager. She passionately put her heart and soul into that non-profit agency, working there after her daytime state job writing grants, doing events and organizing artists.

The Last Ride

By the '90s my mother's birth name was not acceptable to her anymore. She renamed herself "Akilah Jaye." Akilah meaning, "wise" and "Jaye" for all the "J" names she had been called over the years (Jane, Janet, Jeanette). Close friends and family were invited to the funeral of Janet Clark, and the birth of Akilah. When I walked around town with her, people would call out *"Janet!"* or *"Jeanette!"* and she would ignore them. *"I buried her,"* she would say, to my embarrassment.

Owning her motorcycle was like being a teenager again. On the last day that she rode, she exhibited a youthful exuberance...

The final chapter of my mom's life included a move to Napa, California after running for state assembly woman. Despite her loss she received close to 4000 votes. In 2000, she began taking motorcycle lessons and bought her first Honda after getting her permit. Owning her motorcycle was like being a teenager again.

On the last day that she rode, she exhibited a youthful exuberance, as I followed behind her in her car. We had lunch together with all her other biker friends and afterwards she grabbed me by the shoulders and looked in my eyes. Smiling radiantly, she said, *"I love you!"* which was the last words she expressed to me and the last time I saw her alive.

My mom died immediately on impact in a head on crash with an automobile. The night before the tragic turn of events my mother won a Humanitarian award for bringing all types of people together. The funeral honoring Akilah, according to one who witnessed it, was "a snapshot of what the United Nations would look like if regular people were on the board. There were Hells Angels, motor cycle clubs, Asian, black, white, Hispanic,

Gays Lesbians, Baptist, Pentecostal, and adults and children of all ages.

All you could do was smile because the audience was reflective of (Akilah's) global heart. So she lives eternally due to her work to unite all people from all walks of life of various hues, and diverse backgrounds. Beyond being multi-dimensional, multi-faceted and multi-cultural, she was most of all my mother!

Author's Sensational Mother

Trailblazer:

From Military to Motherhood
–A Life of Service

by Jeri Marshall

"If you can't raise the child, then what's left?"
-- J. Marshall

My mother, Odessa Smith Taylor Marshall was born black, brave, bold and beautiful! Her life's journey is a testimony that embodies the color of strength, the courage of change and a legacy that is merely stunning.

*Author's Mother, Odessa
before military and motherhood*

Sometimes I Feel Like a Motherless Child

Life started for my mother, Odessa Smith Taylor Marshall, in the rural area of Stantonville, Tennessee in 1923. What she has accomplished epitomizes Ralph Waldo Emerson's quote, *"Do not go where the path may lead; go instead where there is no path and leave a trail."* Although Odessa's path began in a family deeply immersed in ill feelings of abandonment, she always embraced her own family. More importantly, she has left an undeniable trail of service to her country and to her children.

Odessa's care rested in the hands of her extended family, a not always comprehensive network of relatives, which was the way of life for many Negro children.

Born out of wedlock to Pearl Smith and Isaiah Taylor, the fact that my mother was considered illegitimate created strife and bitterness between Pearl's mother, Cassie Smith and Isaiah Taylor. Cassie, who Odessa refers to as *"Almomma"* meaning Our-Momma, insisted that Isaiah marry Pearl, but he refused; clearly demonstrating that he had no desires for marriage or fatherhood.

Thus Odessa's childhood was mired in an atmosphere of strained relationships, custody issues and being forgotten by her mother, father and grandmother. The tenuous situation and hard times eventually led Pearl to neglect her responsibility of raising young Odessa, who emphatically states, *"My mother and grandmother abandoned me!"*

Child abandonment is still an issue that tears at the social fabric of our communities. When my mother was a child in the 1920s there were no child protective services or foster care options for children, (although, I am not saying those services are always the best or only viable alternative) regardless of race.

Odessa's care rested in the hands of her extended family, a not always comprehensive network of relatives, which was the way of life for many Negro children. In my mother's situation, she was shuttled between relative's homes in Memphis, Somerville, Statonville and St. Louis, Missouri.

Despite the number of individuals involved in Odessa's upbringing, Louise Wilson-Taylor, her father's sister, stepped in as the primary caretaker for my mother who claims that her Aunt Louise is the only woman she ever called *"Momma."* Since Aunt Louise had raised four boys, she always wanted a daughter and Odessa fit the part.

First to Serve

As a teenager Odessa faced the career path of most Negro women in the 1940s: being a maid for white families. Yet my mother wasn't one to follow tradition; so she chose to pursue her destiny and *"Go where there was no path and leave a trail."* In 1945, America was engaged in World War II and the country had begun to enlist Negro women into the Women's Auxiliary Army Corps (WAAC).

Odessa saw this as an opportunity to move past her current circumstances and chart her own course for life. Although my mother was too young to join WAAC, she and Aunt Louise forged the induction papers. The choice to join the Corps was an act she never regretted. Unknown to Odessa she was taking a path that would allow for her to leave a historic trail for others to travel.

Although the Women's Auxiliary Army Corps allowed Odessa the opportunity to see England, France, Holland and Belgium, there was neither a ticker tape parade nor any fanfare for the 6888th battalion when they returned to the United States.

America, as well as the military was segregated until 1948, and WAAC was no exception. The all colored group of more than 800 Negro women was selected to enlist in the only organization of that nature in the United States. It was the first time in American history that Negro women had a semi-formal opportunity to serve in an auxiliary capacity to the United States Army. So participation in this prestigious organization was for Odessa, and the other women, a chance to experience life and new opportunities beyond America's segregated borders. For my mother, who loved being in the Corps, it was an introduction to womanhood.

The historic all Negro military training facility in Fort Huachuca, Arizona was where my mother was initially stationed to prepare for service in the 6888th battalion. Better known as the *"Six Triple Eight,"* the unit of Negro women was the first to ship overseas under the command of Major Charity Adams, a Negro woman officer. Designated to serve in Birmingham, England and Paris, France, the 6888th's maiden voyage to England was on the Queen Mary commercial ocean liner which was converted into a troop transport vessel.

Due to the fact that all Negro troops trained at the then segregated Fort Huachuca, Odessa had no idea that there were others who served until they docked in Great Britain. Upon arrival she saw uniformed personnel and quipped, *"I didn't know that white people were in the military too!"*

As a teenager, Odessa faced the career path of most Negro women in the 1940s: being a maid for white families.

Although the Woman Auxiliary Army Corps allowed Odessa the opportunity to see England, France, Holland and Belgium, there was neither a ticker tape parade nor any fanfare for the 6888th Battalion[1] when they returned to the United States. This was disconcerting for Negro troops who proudly and honorably served their country but returned home as second class citizens.

After their experiences abroad, members of the *"Six Triple Eight"* battalion entered another chapter of their lives, including Odessa. Her main concern was getting an education, which she eventually did, becoming a nurse in later years. However, she encountered an unexpected diversion by the name of Buck Sergeant Joseph E. Marshall who would alter her course a bit, but not her path.

---

[1] It wasn't until 2009, that the U.S. Government recognized and honored the service and contributions of the Negro women of the 6888th postal battalion. Odessa went where there was no path and left a trail for all Women to officially serve as members of the United States Armed Forces.

There's Something about that Joe!

When Odessa's tour of duty ended in 1945, she attended the Tucker Training School where she met Buck Sergeant Joseph E. Marshall. Their courtship began on a misdirected encounter by Sgt. Joe.

While wearing her WAAC uniform on the first day of school, Buck Sgt. Marshall made the chauvinistic mistake of applying a pinch to Odessa's backside. Of course, she was highly offended and confronted Joe about his behavior. The circumstance of that story has been the cornerstone of their nearly 70 year marriage, nine children, and numerous grand and great-grandchildren.

When I asked Odessa, "What does life hold next?" She reflected on where she wanted, as a dedicated soldier, her final resting place to be.

Joseph Earl Marshall and Odessa Smith Taylor married in 1946, one year after the near disastrous pinch. In 1947 they welcomed their first of nine children, Joseph E. Marshall, Jr. into

Author's father, Sgt. Joe Marshall

the world. Six of their children were born in St. Louis, Missouri before the family moved west to Los Angeles, California in pursuit of better opportunities and the extension of their family with the birth of the last three children.

Today, Joe and Odessa Marshall are both in their nineties and are quick to point out that they are the oldest Negro couple still living who served during WWII.

When I asked Odessa, *"What does life hold next?"* She reflected on where she wanted, as a dedicated soldier, her final resting place to be. *"Have my ashes interred with my son at Arlington National Cemetery. Arlington is the place where soldiers rest and that's where I want to be."*

Although, Odessa was raised feeling abandoned and laments about never having a childhood, her life experiences prepared her to not only give her children a childhood, but a sense of belonging. We were also provided an education and a wealth of opportunities. Currently, seven of Odessa's nine children are still living. Deborah Ann Marshall, Odessa's oldest daughter died of cancer and her third oldest son, Sgt. John Winston Marshall was killed in Operation Iraqi Freedom in 2004.

Quietly blazing a historical trail for future generations to emulate, Odessa has a tremendous legacy within her family; and one ninth of her story has been proudly told. To my mother, Odessa Smith Taylor Marshall, you were destined, and will always be black, brave, bold and beautiful!

Author's mother, Odessa Smith Taylor Marshall

5th Generation Girl

by Tammy "Goody" Ballard

From my mother
To my mother's father
From his mother and father
and their parents-my Great Greats
Lydia and Derry
During a time when couples stayed married
To *Big Mamma,*
4ft 2 and 104lbs still the strongest woman I've known
Bore 12 to help work the fields
From slavery to pickin cottin'
Boys plowin the fields, and butcherin the hogs
Girls out back wringin chicken necks for suppa
And milkin the cows in the pasture

As I stare at their photos on my wall
of those that I see, came the production of me!
5th generation girl
You, breaking down barriers, standing tall—
Living AFFIRMATIVELY!
Eighty-six, my grandfather, got his name the day
a white man spit on him
"Get on your side of the road, ya damn Nigger!"
From him came Effie who at 19
bore Tammy
Oh, where would I be without my
ancestors who paved the way for
me?
From slavery through sweat, pain,
tears, tornadoes
...southern storms!

Author's Great Greats,
Lydia and Derry Shorter

Twelve mouths to feed for at least eighteen years!
Oh where would I be without you?
From segregated schools, protest and hard times
I'll tell you where I wouldn't be…
in college earning my degree
Because of the doors you've opened
nearly dying and sometimes dying for me!
Because of you I've arrived!
For without your struggles
I, as a black girl would not have this opportunity
to spread my wings and thrive!
Oh glory…God bless your souls!
I thank you and love you, dearly!
Because of you….5th Generation can now and forever fly freely!

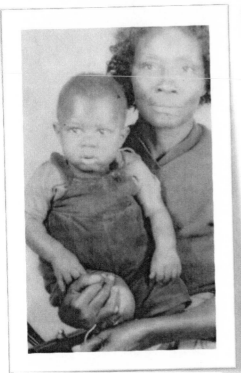

Author's grandfather on mother, Effie's, lap

Author's great grand aunt, Bertha.

Young author and her mother

From PFC to PhD:
The Story of Dr. Allie Harshaw

by Frank Withrow and Joslyn Gaines Vanderpool

Dr. Allie G. Harshaw, USAF

A United States Air Force First and a Testament to Faith

Dr. Allie G. Harshaw once stated if ever a book were to be written about her, she would like it to be titled *From PFC[2] to PhD*. Thus we honor her wishes and pay homage to a great American heroine and mother figure who's modeling of unflinching bravery and courage under fire led many African American women and men to serve their country.

Although Dr. Harshaw might have started her military career with the rank of Private First Class, she rose through the ranks of the United States Air Force to become the first black female Master Sergeant to retire with 30 years of service in 1973. Yet, Dr. Harshaw didn't stop with that accomplishment. This pioneer's life was stellar and truly is a testament to her faith and the old adage of *"When one door closes another will surely open."*

---

[2] PFC—Private First Class

More than a decade before the Civil Rights Movement took hold of America's consciousness; Dr. Allie Harshaw was already blazing a path for inclusion.

Upon her death at the age of 98 in October 2013, a complete stranger who read Dr. Harshaw's obituary was so struck by her life that she wrote, *"I never had the pleasure to meet Dr. Harshaw, but after reading her obituary I wished I had. I know she blazed many trails during her life for women and deserves our gratitude. Godspeed...."*

Smart, quick-witted, and full of laughter and adventure, the daughter of Amanda and Hugh Harshaw was one of 13 children who was born in Lawndale, North Carolina. While in school she was reprimanded for talking and sent to catalogue books in the library when she ran across a copy of *Up from Slavery*, by Booker T. Washington.

Intrigued, she found a card in the back of the book about the Tuskegee Institute and sought to enroll by taking an exam, but needed $50 to buy a train ticket. She arrived in Alabama and her life changed. Eleanor Roosevelt and George Washington Carver, were but a few of the notable individuals who were there or visited when Ms. Allie was a student.

Oh what a monumental legacy Dr. Allie G. Harshaw left for others to cherish, emulate and honor! With a journey steeped with obstacles and triumphs, Dr. Allie did it all including making scrumptious rum cakes, bowling with the Grey Panthers and even travelling around the world on a German freighter when she was 72! *"It was wonderful!"* she excitedly commented after the voyage.

Being a first, Dr. Harshaw is one of many heroic North Carolinians of African descent who made an impact in world History, such as Hiram Rhoades Revels, who became the first black member of the United States Congress. Or the four brave black college students who staged a sit-in at the counter of the

Greensboro Woolworth store in the early 1960s: a place that was off limits to African Americans. Their boldness would further propel the Civil Rights movement into a force that would chip away at the foundation of institutional racism.

The War at Home and Abroad

Before the sit-ins, and protests of the fifties and sixties there was the enlistment of numerous African Americans in this nation's war efforts. During World War II black Americans had to fight on two fronts: The war at home against racism and the actual World Wars that threatened not only freedom in the United States and abroad, but a form of freedom that many African Americans yearned to experience on their own soil.

Arguably no African American military fighting unit was as prominent during that era than the Tuskegee Airmen, a group of fighter pilots who never lost a plane to the enemy during their heroic feats in World War II. Dr. Allie Harshaw would have ties to that legion of men and would win a rightful place of honor for her efforts and life's work on their behalf.

Through the years, Dr. Harshaw took many exams, which she successfully passed in her attempts to advance to officer status in the US Air Force.

More than a decade before the Civil Rights Movement took hold of America's consciousness; Dr. Harshaw was already blazing a path for inclusion. Although she was primed to serve her country during World War II, at the time, the military was very much segregated and doors were not readily open to women; let alone black women. However, Dr. Allie made her mark serving as a member of the newly formed Women's Auxiliary Army Corps which she joined in 1943, a few years after earning her Bachelor's degree at Tuskegee Institute in 1940.

As a physical therapy technician, Dr. Harshaw served the Tuskegee Airmen near Columbus, Ohio. Besides her involvement during World War II she also served during the Korean and Vietnam wars and was stationed at several Air Force bases around the country before transferring to Vandenberg Airbase in California where she retired in 1973.

Through the years, Dr. Harshaw took many exams, which she successfully passed in her attempts to advance to officer status in the US Air Force. However, due to the racial climate of that time, such positions would elude her despite her abilities and the contributions she continued to make to her country.

As a true warrior of valor and faith, she carried on and earned a doctorate in Human Behavior from the United States International University at San Diego, CA and had a long illustrious teaching career with the Lompoc School District.

Hail to Dr. Harshaw: History Maker and Heroine!

Apparently no slights, racial or otherwise would deter Dr. Harshaw from a life well-served. She received accolades, awards and achievements for her exemplary work as a teacher, radiology technician, and for her service in the military. Her story has been profiled in HERSTORIES, which is a tribute to African American women who served in the United States Military during World War II that was compiled by Gladys Carter.

Dr. Harshaw is also included in Voices of World War II: A Lompoc Veterans History Project; she is also listed on the US Women's Military Service Museum's website in an article written by John Bowman of the Ventura Press.

One of the crowning achievements for Dr. Harshaw was when she received a Congressional Gold Medal (the most elite honor given by the United States Congress) in 2007 for her work with the Tuskegee Airmen. It was an award she never expected to receive in her lifetime.

After Arthur Hicks, one of the original Tuskegee Airmen, received a Congressional Gold Medal from President George Bush in Washington, D.C., he was told that Dr. Harshaw would also receive a Congressional Gold Medal. Once it arrived in the mail, Hicks presented it to her in a surprise ceremony during a convention of her college sorority, Beta Pi Sigma in Burlingame, California.

Dr. Harshaw was so surprised about the medal that she remarked, *"At least I was one who got one while I was still alive. Most don't get them until they're dead! I feel very, very honored. I didn't know about it (the award) until they gave it to me."*

Admired by family, friends, military service members and people who never knew her personally, but are amazed by her powerful story, Dr. Allie G. **Harshaw** broke down barriers and opened doors. She is a true American heroine. We all owe her a debt of gratitude for courage and bravery under most difficult times.

Author's Aunt, Dr. Allie Harshaw, an African American first

My Mum, the Major General
by
Pauline Zawadi

When Pauline Zawadi contributed a story about her mum, she provided only a few details. So after a request to tap her memory for more information about her mother, she revealed that her mum raised her to have good manners and was a wonderful role model, and then, which was really amazing, she casually stated that her mum was involved in the Mau Mau Uprising—a bloody rebellion against British Colonial Rule for independence, which raged on from 1952-1960 in their native Kenya. Her mother's incredible story follows:

I really want to honor my mum for being my hero because she is so hard working and focused. Even now at her old age she still has style, class and always perfect memory which would be insightful in recounting her youth in a mission that would forever be crucial to Kenya's history. Surely gifted, my mum is the one who got *"Born Again"* in our family, and through her, my dad, and then me, came to know the Lord in a closer relationship.

My mum is a jewel in my life and has made me the woman that I am today. Just by looking back and seeing what she used to do I am inspired.

Author's Mother, the Major General (right)

When I was born, it was a miraculous birth, as my mum was already around 45 years old. She had given up on having children, but the Lord gave her a dream of a child. While pregnant she took care of herself by taking bed rest until I was born and she brought me up in the best way possible. Unlike other households she was always very concerned about diets and made sure that we ate all sorts of vegetables, fruits, cereals, meats, etc.

My mum is a jewel in my life and has made me the woman that I am today. Just by looking back and seeing what she used to do I am inspired. She was also a disciplinarian and through her I learned the best manners. Other than that, she was enrolled in the Mau Mau Rebellion.

Freeing the Motherland

We come from the Republic of Kenya which is situated in the Eastern side of Africa. I also come from the tribe of Kikuyu which is the majority in the country and this is the tribe that came up with the Mau Mau Rebellion, which was a cause that my mum, Teresia Kanyi, joined in 1952 when she was 23 years. From 1952-1960, men and women came together to fight for our nation against an oppressive colonial British government.

I have seen the normal and the mighty coming to look for my mum whenever they needed an interview of the war and the movement.

My mum earned the rank of Major General which was not given to women, but through her toughness she was able to attain that title. The Mau Mau were hiding in forests, and taking oaths to fight for their Motherland which they felt that the white people were trying to take from them. They had their own handmade guns and machetes.

They also had their own networks which were secretly operated to take food to their comrades in the forest without being noticed and medical supplies, if any were available. Mostly they used the individuals who were employed as nannies, cooks, watchmen to get to their targeted people.

In 1953, my mum was shot and captured by the colonial government and put in an isolation cell in a maximum prison called Kamiti. She was jailed and given a life sentence. During the trial she could be taken to bury the Mau Mau men who were being sentenced to death. She was not even allowed to change her bloody clothes and had to stay in them. After six years of imprisonment, she was released in 1959 by the government.

One thing I noticed, when my mother was telling me the story regarding the Rebellion, was how intent she was on stating how they were so united; if you betrayed them you would be killed. The Mau Mau also had to change their names and used code names for the purpose of secrecy. The code name of my mum was Major General Njeri Muiritu wa Iyego.

The Mau Mau used to sing war songs and even composed a song for my mum, who never betrayed the men on trial. I saw the respect given her when they visited our home after the Independence, even though I was young. I have seen the normal and the mighty coming to look for my mum whenever they needed an interview of the war and the movement.

Today the Mau Mau fighters are still waiting to be awarded some money for the torture, pain and loss they acquired when they were fighting the colonial government. However, my mum will always be a part of a significant event in African history. In January 1960 during a Parliamentary conference; the British government agreed that it would accept a "one person, one vote," majority rule and a freer Kenya would emerge for generations to come.

Testimony to the Spirit of Black Woman
(*circa forever*)

by
Joslyn Gaines Vanderpool

I've heard say we're broken, but we're not buried yet,
Can't seem to put our spirits down for that final rest,
Stomped on our soul more times than we care to recount,
No, we're not broken, not in the ground yet

Slavers snatched our children away from our breasts,
Sold them like water, surprised we would resist
We held them in our memories as we wrung Massa's clothes,
Held them imagined in the folds of our old souls

We've heard that we're ugly because of the broadness
of our nose, we've kept it centered, defined ourselves and rose

We've heard that we're too black, so black, blue-black to be seen,
We've hid our wounded pride, replaced it with granules of esteem

We've heard malicious commentaries mockingly implied,
trained intensely on that we refuse to hide
Objections regarding our fully formed lips, the expanse of our
hips, we won't be broken, erased, eclipsed!

We've been close to broken, but we're not in the ground,
can't be close to broken, if our spirit forever resounds!

Powerful black women (top left – author's great aunt Adela, r. author's great aunt Lovey, bottom left, author's great grandmother Frances, center mother, Ruth, far right, author's grandmother, Mable

A Sacred Inheritance
by Claire P. Taylor

Sometimes when Grandmother Clara looked at my hands she used to say, "Child, you ain't worked a day in your life!" And she was right. I never did. I never worked one day in my life like she did every day of hers.

My mother's mother, Clara Bell Washington Johnson lived 108 years! Born in 1897 in Yazoo County, Mississippi, she was the oldest of 15 children, and her father, George Washington (later Bunch) was born a slave.

A small woman with a mighty heart, Grandmother Clara had a gift so powerful that it transcended a generation and was so profound it greatly impacted my life and showed me an important part of who I am. Delighting in simple things, Grandmother Clara led with love and made other's feel loved. As her namesake, I'm proud to be known by my family as *Claire P.*

Sometimes, when Grandmother Clara looked at my hands she used to say, *"Child, you ain't worked a day in your life!"* And she was right. I never did. I never worked one day in my life like she did every day of hers. In grandmother's early life she and my grandfather, Fred, worked hard on their farm raising cows, pigs, geese and chickens.

Grandmother rose early and after cooking a farm breakfast, she set some pots up for supper and then rode out with the family to pick cotton in the fields. Then she'd ride back early to complete supper so it would be ready when the others came in from the fields. She carried out this ritual every day except Sunday; and worked in the fields through her eight pregnancies until the mid-wife said she could no longer do so.

Go, Grandmother, Go!

After 62 years of marriage, my grandfather, Fred, passed away. For years before he died he grew more and more attached to the land and wouldn't complete any travels to go see his kids and grandkids in other states. He'd get packed, get in the car and would allow us to drive him for about 80 to 100 miles away from home and then he'd inevitably say, *"Take me home."*

Well, we all did whatever Granddaddy wanted and back we'd go. He also didn't want his Clare far away from him so she obeyed and would rarely travel without him because she felt strongly that that was her duty as a Christian wife.

Unbelievably, I had never heard my grandmother sing before! I guess I just missed it. I am the last of six; but I don't know why I hadn't heard her.

After Granddaddy passed, my dear grandmother took her reward because she was up, going and gone, visiting every state where her children and grandchildren lived. She also attended all the family reunions faithfully, continued teaching Sunday school and still maintained her prison ministry. She even fished, walked almost every day and sang in the church choir.

A Most Cherished Gift

My most moving experience with my grandmother involved her singing. We often had dual birthday celebrations because my grandmother and father were born on the same day. At Yazoo City, a classmate of my mother's got up and sang an old Johnny Mathis song she'd rewritten especially for my grandmother. Then members of her church sang. Grandmother was so delighted that her smile lit up the room. Then she got up and said how beautiful the songs were.

"Now I have a song to give you," and she began to sing.

Unbelievably, I had never heard my grandmother sing before! I guess I just missed it. I am the last of six; but I don't know why I hadn't heard her. Two verses into singing one of her favorite hymns, I burst into tears because she must have been at least 95 or 96 at the time and her voice was rich, full and beautiful! You see, I love to sing and at the time of the birthday celebration, I hadn't kept up with it.

My mother asked me periodically what I was doing with my singing. I knew I loved it and people said I sang well but I always wondered somewhere deep down if I really was good at it. It did come easy and brought me joy, but until the moment I heard my grandmother sing, I didn't know it was part of my heritage. That realization went straight to my core and I've never doubted the gift that I share with my grandmother since.

It's precious to me. Not only am I named after her, but one of the things I enjoy doing most in the world, I inherited from her – the ability to elevate my voice in song, a gift that is my most cherished!

The Original Multi-Tasking Mother
by Linda Monroe

Wife, Mother, Professional

From an early age my mother, Juanita Delores Hernandez had an amazing work ethic which was not surprising considering she was born in about 1930 during the Great Depression. I'm not quite sure because she never would say how old she was.

Her parents, Charles Hernandez and Edwina Green, were West Indian. When Edwina died my grandparents, Mrs. Clementina Green and Mr. William Murry Grogan Green raised my mother who might have adopted some of her working ways from her grandfather, a pastor from Jamaica who brought over many West Indians and gave them jobs.

A pioneering woman, my mother longed for more than the typical career choices of a domestic worker or the unskilled jobs that were offered to black women several decades ago which my mother was never satisfied with. So she kept looking for suitable positions, until she found a job as a telephone operator. Excelling in that job enabled her to become independent on her own.

To me, she seemed fulfilled with her duties as a wife and mother, but she never let go of her abilities as a professional woman.

As a young, black working female, my mother soon caught the attention of a young black working male. It wasn't long before they married and my mom had a new career as a wife and then mother, which all happened before she reached the age of 20. With three girls and one boy, my mother demonstrated love and patience with each of us. She spent time reading and talking to us; and allowed us to put on plays and puppet shows. Eagerly setting up the stage, she was also the enthusiastic audience member who laughed and clapped during our performances.

Leading by example, my mother taught the basics in life and modeled for us how to sew, cook, clean, and how to sit and be a lady, according to the etiquette of the time. As for my brother, she taught him how to be a gentleman, a trait he still retains. In regard to my father, mother took care of his needs, which included having dinner done at the same time every day.

With an a great sense of determination, my mother fought and fought until she fought her way up to becoming the first black female supervisor for the JFK Air Mail facility in Jamaica, New York, during the 1970s.

Mother served many different kinds of food and always had a flower garden and my father a vegetable garden. When serving us, she put just the right amount of food on our plates because she didn't believe in throwing food away. So we were expected to eat all our food. She never ate red meat and never ate after evening hours.

Even sixty years after her marriage, she still wears a size 6 and her face is beautiful and unwrinkled! When she went out on dates with my late father, I remember her wearing a flowery off the shoulder sun dress and lipstick, and on Sundays, she wore gloves. Such a fashion plate!

As a disciplinarian, my mother had my father back her up when we got out of line. To me she seemed fulfilled with her duties as a wife and mother but she never let go of her abilities as a professional woman.

The Will to Work: An Unstoppable Fighting Spirit

When we were old enough to attend school, my mother returned to work as a secretary. I remember her practicing every day on that old typewriter. Then she got a job at the post office when we were in high school. I'd hear my mother talking with my dad about the grievance committee because although she typed well, and passed all the tests she wasn't promoted. She also noticed her white co-workers would leave for other jobs but she was still there.

A pioneering woman, my mother longed for more than the typical career choices of a domestic worker or the unskilled jobs that were offered to black women several decades ago which my mother was never satisfied with.

Finally, after many attempts she broke through and was the only black woman at the post office. She kept breaking through and was the first black woman at each move. She had to fight for the right to take the test that would allow her to move up once she passed the exams.

With a great sense of determination, my mother fought and fought until she fought her way up to becoming the first black female supervisor for the JFK[3] Air Mail facility in Jamaica, New York, during the 1970s – a position she held for 30 years until her retirement, in 1991.

My mom is an original, multi-tasking woman even before the word was invented. She had a work ethic which I and my sons have inherited. I thank her for my own determination and fortitude which I needed to continue my studies, my career and most essentially, my life.

---

[3] John F. Kennedy

A Feast for Life
by Macia Fuller

"If I could help one somebody, LORD let me try."

The Early Years: Etiquette, Elitism and Educational Excellence

Bessie Mae Boyd-Royster was born in the segregated quarters of Gulfport, Mississippi on August 8, 1927. She often heard her maternal grandmother, Susie Norris, singing an old gospel hymn *"If I could help one somebody, LORD let me try."* It made a lasting impression.

At the age of twelve, Bessie was sent with her sister Lucille, to Birmingham, Alabama to Aunt Mamie's for a year of finishing school. She was given an education in etiquette and the mores of *Colored* Southern aristocracy. She hated the elitism which kept her from playing with another *Colored* girl she liked because her Aunt Mamie considered the girl to be from the wrong neighborhood.

Even though the segregated schools Bessie attended were poorly-funded by the State, and Colored students were given old books and other supplies previously used by their White counterparts...

*Author's mother,
Deaconess Bessie Royster*

When their mother, Rosa Lee Norris-Boyd divorced, Bessie and Lucille were delighted to join their mother and their younger sister, Lee Anna in Sacramento, California. Although Bessie would greatly miss her grandparents, their influence had taken deep root.

Bessie's home in Sacramento's Oak Park on Third Avenue was very different from Aunt Mamie's two-story, stone home in an elite *Colored* neighborhood with fireplaces in each bedroom. In Birmingham and Gulfport Bessie had been surrounded by people who looked like her and respected her family. She had been sheltered from the racism of the Deep South by the segregation that necessitated that *Coloreds* establish independent and self-sustaining communities, including educational institutions.

Even though the segregated schools Bessie attended were poorly-funded by the State and *Colored* students were given old books and other supplies previously used by their white counterparts. However, they had excellent and committed *Colored* teachers, who made sure their students, especially, the bright and "talented" received the best education possible.

Teachers also infused their students with a sense of racial pride in their accomplishments. Students were also driven to exhibit a work ethic predicated on the belief that in order to excel they would have to work harder and be smarter than those they would compete with for jobs. This gave Bessie and her classmates, confidence in their abilities.

"You may have the whole world to fight outside of these walls but within them we will love and support each other."

In Sacramento, Bessie shared a modest two bedroom, rented home in Oak Park, which is the first suburb of Sacramento. At that time, the residents were predominantly white with only 15 other Colored families in the neighborhood which was reflective of the number of students in her school.

While walking to Sacramento High one day, Bessie first heard the "N" word. She soon realized that her former teachers had prepared her well. She had read more than her new classmates and had already been taught advanced math concepts. Proper English had been drilled into her and writing was one of her strong points. In most of her classes she was the only Negro, as she was referred to in California.

Bessie's hatred of Colored elitism in Birmingham grew to include the hatred of any attitude or behavior that excluded others. When Negro students were denied participation in extra-curricular activities & school clubs, Bessie organized the Booker T. Washington Club so that Negro students would be represented in the Year Book. That was the beginning of a lifetime of community activism and service.

At age 18, Bessie married her childhood sweetheart, Jimmie Royster, who followed her to Sacramento from Gulfport. The couple began their family right away; and Bessie who has always been a strong believer and advocate for quality education for all students, became a life time member of the *PTA serving at several area schools, including those that her children attended.

Besides Bessie's own children; Macia, Stanley, Tyron, Ramona (Mona), Jeron and Danny, her sister's five children were in her home daily and Auntie Mae loved them and continues to love them as her own. Bessie's porch was always filled with neighborhood children who feasted with the family on her delicious food. They learned to respect her strict but fair standards for behavior towards one another. No fighting was allowed especially amongst family members.

Bessie subscribed to the following, which were lessons she repeated, *"You may have the whole world to fight outside of these walls but within them we will love and support each other,"* and *"family is anyone who loves and supports you."* She also strongly believes that *"It is not the color of a person's skin that matters but the condition of their heart."* This belief can be attested to by the many extended family members from different ethnic groups who consider themselves her acquired children and call her Mom.

A Flourishing Future—Catering to the Influential and to "Those in Need"

To supplement Jimmie's salary, Bessie began working for a new caterer in town. Marion Pringle was an accomplished chef and business woman from New York, who recognized Bessie's skills in the kitchen and familiarity with proper etiquette learned in Birmingham. She took Bessie under her tutelage and they became good friends while working for the rich and politically powerful in Sacramento. After Marion was killed in a tragic accident, Bessie was urged by their customers to take over the catering business which she did.

Family members, friends and others needing work were trained and employed in the business. They had to be able and willing to meet her high standards and work under her eagle eye for detail. New people on the job were extra help. Mother made sure she had adequate, trained and tested helpers to do a superior job. If someone new proved to be a hard worker and was able to take snap instructions without getting in the way, they were given other opportunities to work. Single moms and students were compensated well for working hard.

No matter how important or influential the client, anyone who disrespected her or her employees did not get a second opportunity to do the same...

As sole owner of Royster Catering, Bessie was sought after. She provided elegant meals for the special occasions of the most prominent families and politicians in and around Sacramento. Her clients included farmers, ranchers, educators, business men and women.

California governors Earl Warren, Edmund G. Brown and Ronald Regan and Supreme Court Justice Anthony Kennedy, engaged Mrs. Royster's services. Parties, weddings and political fundraisers were scheduled based on Bessie's availability. Her biscuits and extravagant fruit centerpieces became legendary must haves for a successful event.

When one of Bessie's grateful customers asked what he could do as a special thank you for her services; she responded *"I would like to go to lunch at the Sutter Club."* At lunch the customer realized he was the first to bring a black person to that exclusive, private club.

No matter how important or influential the client, anyone who disrespected her or her employees did not get a second opportunity to do the same; not even the pleas of clients in good standing could change Bessie's mind. The parties given for clients never exceeded the love and preparation put in by Bessie, for parties given for her families and friends.

Bessie had only two regular black customers. A young business woman and socialite from the Bay Area and a couple employed as professors at Sacramento State College. Her prices were competitive with other quality catering facilities which precluded many from engaging her services.

*Bessie, second from left,
and author/daughter on the right of mother*

However, Bessie was generous in providing services for free or the cost of the food, for worthy causes. She was always willing to work with a young professional, often giving them more than what they contracted for in order for their event to be a success.

Impassioned Entrepreneur, Cancer Survivor and Advocate for Youth

Author's mother

Having a family & successful business did not prevent Bessie from being active in many civic clubs and organizations. Her commitment to help all the *"somebodies"* she could led Bessie to serve on the Oak Park Mental Health Advisory Board founded by her friend Walter Mae Mikes. With another friend, Stella Brandon, Bessie revived the Oak Park Neighborhood Council to address the inequity in services after white flight changed the demographics of Oak Park from predominately white to a predominately black and Hispanic neighborhood. Bessie also served as State Chairwoman of Women of Business and Industry.

An association with the National Association of Colored Women's Clubs began in 1966 for Bessie, who has also served as the State Chairman of Education and is a current member and past officer of the Camellia City and Viola

Ms. Bessie's catering creations

M. Brooks Civil and Social Club. The Women's Civic Improvement Club and Sacramento Women's Council are other organizations that have benefitted from her membership and leadership.

Bessie was tireless in promoting and fundraising for youth activities. She and Jimmie believed that children should be kept intellectually stimulated and physically exhausted so they didn't have the time or energy to get into trouble. Bessie led Brownies; Girl Scout and Boy Scout Troops; an Oak Park drill team and a girls' softball team. She also chaired Little League meetings for the community and worked in the Snack Shack.

As a member of First English Lutheran Church, the first church in Oak Park to integrate, Bessie taught Sunday school and was one of the first females on the church council. She also ushered and used her catering skills to fundraise for the church. After retiring from the catering business Bessie began classes with Bible Study Fellowship. She completed a seven year course and helped as a sitter for the children of BSF Leaders.

*If I could help one somebody, LORD let me try, h*as often been a refrain on her lips and demonstrated throughout her life. In 2012 Bessie was diagnosed with both breast and lung cancer. After successful surgery and radiation treatments she resumed her life of service.

Currently, she serves as a Deaconess at Kyles Temple A.M.E. Zion Church and is a faithful participant on the church's prayer line and makes daily calls to the sick and shut-in. Today she is often heard singing another verse remembered from her childhood.

There is a burden in my life so hard to bear. But, I promised I'd keep trying if you only let me, stay. I'm willing LORD to go all the way.

Her influence on her children, 18 grandchildren, 14 great-grandchildren and the numerous other lives she has touched is still making an impact which will continue her legacy of hard work, achievement and service.

Ms. Bessie Royster, fourth from the left

And Still I Watch and Pray
By Gloria W. Campbell

Early Days... Happy Days

In the early days of my marriage, my husband, Lawrence Campbell, joined the segregated United States Navy and went overseas to fight for freedom and democracy throughout the world. Except

Author right and herhusband,
Reverend Lawrence Campbell

the U.S. didn't extend those same concepts of liberty to black people. At the time of my husband's return from World War II, *Virginia and the United States of America were both champions of racial segregation and racial inequality.*

Although I attended St. Phillips School of Nursing in Richmond, Virginia to become a professional nurse, which was one of the few professions open to young black women at that time, the other being a teacher or professional seamstress or hairdresser; the Lord had other plans for me.

My husband and I went to Washington D.C. to live with my mother-in-law, and began attending Bible Way Church; though my husband's attendance was rather sporadic. On the other hand, the Lord was dealing with me.

One Saturday, I had a toothache but after I joined the church, the pain went away immediately! I took that as a sign and promised the Lord I would be faithful in attending, but I kept it secret from my wayfaring husband. Despite begging him to go, he did not relent. Ultimately, I gave my life to the Lord by accepting His invitation to join the church.

The black church was the place to be in those days because we could go and be completely
free. Segregation kept us unwelcome at every other social institution.

Our life changed. We had a little apartment and I told my
husband the story of Joseph in the book of *Genesis*. I spoke of his
life as an abandoned brother, slave, and honored servant to
Pharaoh — a man who spurned his unfaithful wife, and was a
champion for his brothers; the twelve tribes of his father, Israel.
And that Sunday my husband gave his life to the Lord! We were
so happy. This was about 1949 or so. Thereafter, we had a son
Larry, Jr. then Philip, and our daughter, Alethea.

In those days we had so many friends who gathered together
to have group prayer. My husband would leave us on Sunday
mornings to usher during church services, and then he took the
street car to come and get us. I was in a women's Sunday school
class and he had 100 men in a class he taught. The black church
was the place to be in those days because we could go and be
completely free. Segregation kept us unwelcome at every other
social institution.

Eventually, we returned to Danville, Virginia where my
husband was led by the Lord to build a church. Mother needed
me so I went to help her. After Larry Jr. was born, I went back to
D.C. and I experienced a series of prophesies: a woman stood over
me at a prayer meeting saying *"March, March, March"*! I had lived
with a Ms. March. Sunday morning the preacher said *"This is the
first day of March."* Something was going to happen in March!

The Revolution of Radio and Race Relations

My husband's voice changed while he was praying. The word was out that we were going to Danville for good. The next thing I knew we were in Danville. We were in a big field on White Street. Larry preached so intently, spitting bugs out of his mouth! Beavers Funeral Home lent us chairs for people to sit on.

We sometimes used the Lee Street School building, which has been demolished. On the field, we did not win a soul, but during the first month in that building we won 16, all the while eyeing a pot-bellied piano in the building. The ministry grew. We were blessed to broadcast over WDVA radio, a white station that let us use the airwaves at night. My husband worked in a hospital and preached at night.

The radio station enabled us to meet scores of people, famous and not so famous. It revolutionized little Danville and made it a hub or center of black progress in southern Virginia...

The real challenge came when the D.C. pastor asked the famous singer Roberta Martin to do my husband a favor. Gratefully, the Lord touched her and others to help my husband's growing ministry. I introduced the Martin singers, the Clara Ward Singers plus her mothers' group to headline a concert in Danville broadcast over the radio. James Cleveland was there, but he was not as well known in the field of gospel music, but he would later become really popular.

Gospel music was a very big deal to black people then because it was our sacred music. So their appearances helped to put our church in a big, popular public spotlight. The concert was so big we had to rent the now nonexistent Langston School to host it.

The radio station enabled us to meet scores of people, famous and not so famous. It revolutionized little Danville and made it a hub or center of black progress in southern Virginia which lit a fuse of dynamite as far as relations between blacks and whites there were concerned. Our progress created tension between us and them, who wanted things to stay as they were. Problems were bound to happen.

Leaving a Legacy of Racial Consciousness: A Man Ahead of His Time

One of my late father's sayings went something like this: *"A donkey won't pull while he's kicking!"* *That meant that if a man just pulls a wagon for another man, he'll never see what else he can do for himself. But if he gets stubborn and kicks, no pulling for another will get done as the donkey asserts his choice not to pull!*

My concern for people was inherited from my father, Elmer L. Williams. He was in the 1920s and 1930s, as people would say in hindsight, born ahead of his time. Leaving a lasting legacy of racial consciousness, he fought hard for civil rights, a rarity for a black man born and raised in the segregated South during perhaps the worst times of racial discrimination in America. Today, people would call folks like my daddy *"a civil rights leader."* Back then we called them "race men" or a "race man," meaning people who publicly stood up, at great danger to themselves and their families, for us. Although people like me were called *"Negroes"* or *"Colored"* at best, and *"niggers,"* at worst, by the majority of white people in Virginia and its neighboring states, my daddy could not be silenced.

This was probably due to his strong personality; in addition to the fact that he was a self-employed businessman, which was uncommon. He owned and operated a transfer business, which is known today as a moving company. With two vehicles and eight employees on his payroll, his business had prominent white people as customers.

DANVILLE, VIRGINIA

Daddy became so successful that he even owned a swimming pool on Highway 29 patronized by the upper class. However, most notably, due to his success and good work in the area of civil rights, his picture was placed in the local newspaper as a tribute. He was self-sufficient and proud of his accomplishments.

Being Daddy's little girl, I used to go with him on his rounds and stand up in the backseat of the car. It was exciting! in those days. My daddy worked tirelessly to get black people to vote in Virginia and United States elections at a time when voting could easily lead to death because of resistance from many white people who believed in the status quo.

Back then, if you were black and did not pay a poll tax, officials would not let you go inside a polling place to vote. *That rule is against the 1965 federal voting rights act now, but then in Virginia and most southern states it was legal and had been for about 80 years! You had to pay a special tax if you were black and you wanted to vote.* 'Can you imagine that today?'

To circumvent the poll tax rule, Daddy would give money to the pastors so they could pay their taxes so they could vote. He also persuaded black pastors, who were leaders of the largest gathering place of our people: the church, to persuade their congregation members to register to vote. As I mentioned before, it was the only place we could go and be truly free, since white people tended to give more leeway to preachers because preachers were on *"the Lord's side"* and a fair number of white people considered themselves Christian.

That was sometimes tough to see, because of the way they treated us. Despite my daddy's and earlier civil rights pioneer's efforts to eradicate the practice of discrimination at the ballot box, it would take many more battles, protests and deaths to bring forth change. Just before the last year of the Second World War in 1944, I lost my daddy. Though I still miss him, I was destined to continue his valiant fight.

A Fight for Right—Continuing in My Father's Footsteps

Major racial inequities in Danville still existed in the '60s like not having the right to vote. It was a crime to go to a place segregated for white people's use only. There was no public park black people could visit due to strict segregation laws which led to jail if you violated them.

Unless a black woman was pushing a carriage carrying a white baby she was taking care of, she could not enter any Danville public parks because they were segregated for white people's use only. The same was true for theaters, schools, hospitals, everything.

Separated things were never equal, which the segregation laws required, and it was why we always got the short end of the segregation stick. We got tired of it!

There were no black policemen or firemen. And what they had that was segregated for them was much better cared for and managed than what they segregated out for us. Separated things were never equal which the segregation laws required and we always got the short end of the segregation stick. We got tired of it!

For ten years, I read announcements on the radio, prayed, raised my boys and settled in as a church preacher's wife, regarded as the "first lady" of your husband's church. Problems started that we could not ignore. After the successful Montgomery bus boycott in 1955 and 1956, students in North Carolina in 1960 started protesting segregation in public accommodations by staging "sit in" protests until they were accommodated or arrested.

My husband got a Methodist and a Baptist preacher to join him and "sit- in" at a F.W. Woolworth's discount store restaurant counter where white people sat to get service. They were not served, and Larry was thrown down the steps by angry white people at Danville City Hall. We were encouraged by civil rights leaders then, including Dr. Martin Luther King, not to fight back. Non-violent resistance to white anger was the approach our leaders were using then to win "de-segregation" and we followed it although *"turning the other cheek"* was very challenging.

Larry was jailed for protesting. He later told me that he saw me at the A and P Market from his jail cell, and hollered out for me but I did not hear him. I demonstrated too and so many people were herded like cattle into a police van and carried off to jail. Jail was a constant part of the protesting cycle: protest, police, clubs, dogs, jail, if you managed to get there without getting beat up, broken up, bitten up, wet up or messed up by the police.

Prior to the march that would be called *Bloody Monday,* we organized, as the Danville Christian Progressive Association or DCPA, and appealed to city fathers to no avail for access to parks and other city entities, as well as an end to segregation and job discrimination by the city. With our requests unmet, we had no other option but to march. So I volunteered. Many teachers and other professionals had to consider job security and thought they would be violent. So they didn't march; however, they gave money, cooked food and helped secure bond for those that were arrested.

When we met with the attorney, Ruth Harvey Charity, she told us that if anyone had any weapons they had to leave them behind before going to jail or things would be worse. Even hairpins had to be removed from girls' hair as they could be taken to be weapons by the police, who were looking for any reason, real or imagined, to beat or kill us and our children for violating what they called *"the Southern way of life."*

At dusk on June 10, 1963, the evening of **Bloody Monday,** we marched 1.5 miles. I joined a group of 48 protestors who walked in an orderly, peaceful fashion and sang civil rights songs like, *We Shall Overcome*, as we made our way toward Danville City Hall. Upon reaching the hill where I could see where we were headed, onlookers crowded on the opposite side of the street. Another block away we saw deputized garbage collectors, national guardsmen and dogs.

When we got about two blocks from the building, I noticed a big fire truck and a radio station car. Upon turning to the pavement of City Hall, police made human chains of their bodies, interlocking their arms. They displayed night sticks, as if they were getting ready for battle. We had a number of designated ministers for each demonstration. The preacher told us to bow our heads to pray as the battle lines were being drawn.

When we got to the church, people were angry and crying. Only the Lord prevented a riot that night.

I was taught to watch and pray so I looked around discreetly and saw firemen unrolling their big, canvas covered fire hoses, *even though there were no fires*. They turned the hoses on full strength, and we were thrown to the pavement and beaten with nightsticks until many were bloodied.

It was a dangerous thing but I knew that I had to get out and advance through the crowd to make my way to a safer spot on the sidewalk. In the mayhem, I saw a little girl unconscious and bleeding. That particular march was just to go to City Hall and pray for the protesters who had been beaten earlier that afternoon.

A brother from the church pulled over in his car and gave me a ride back to the church with the police right behind us. At that time, the car ran out of gas. Miraculously, somehow we got back to the church. There were no cell phones then, and no hair dryers; and I had BIG HAIR, which was dripping wet from that fire hose blast. It was 3:00am before I got my hair dry.

When we got to the church people were angry and crying. Only the Lord prevented a riot that night. We did not deserve to be washed into the gutters like garbage but that is how Danville, Virginia regarded us: like trash, like garbage. We were taken to Winslow Hospital, the segregated hospital for black people, where we were treated and released. Winslow is now a nursing home.

During that summer of 1963, when all of this took place, I was chosen by the group to go to the district court to testify regarding what happened. So I testified before that special commission. The FBI, *which was led by a fellow named J. Edgar Hoover, who hated Martin Luther King, Jr. in particular, and black people in general*, took pictures of my wounds. However, nothing came of it.

Like my daddy, who always shared his blessings, my husband Larry Sr. was a tireless champion of civil rights, a great speaker and a trusted friend and advisor to fellow preachers, who fought to bring freedom, justice and equality to all people. In 1963, he was accused of violating the John Brown Law[4], and spent more time in jail than most: six months.

In an effort spearheaded by Reverend Thurmond O. Nichols, a marker was designated in memory of *Bloody Monday*. It was erected in front of the Danville Circuit Court in 2007, and highlights the period of time when protests where led by Danville's black ministers, including Lawrence Campbell, Sr., Reverend R.H.C. McGee and others to combat widespread racial inequities and segregation. Their efforts and those of many black citizens of Danville, in conjunction with Dr. Martin Luther's King's I Have a Dream Speech and the passage of the Civil Rights Act of 1964 eventually broke down some pertinent racial barriers.

---

[4] The John Brown Law was passed in 1830 after a slave uprising made it a serious felony to "...incite the colored population to acts of violence or war against the white population." It became known as the "John Brown" law in 1860 because it was used to convict and hang abolitionist John Brown after his raid on Harper's Ferry in 1859. (Source: Wikipedia)

An Introduction to Integration and Eventual Change

"Danville was totally segregated from the time you were born until the time that you died." — *Minister Lawrence Campbell Sr.*

The introduction of integration did not come easily or without resistance. When libraries were integrated all of the tables were taken out so there would be no chance or opportunity for blacks and whites to sit at the same table.

As laws were changed, my daughter, Alethea went from an all-black segregated school: Langston to George Washington. She was the only black child in the school; and said that the only other black people she saw were cafeteria workers at lunch time. Letting her go to that school alone was the hardest thing I could do as a mother. I dropped her off and was never late picking her up.

When our daughter's class went on an overnight trip, her father felt she would be safe because the height of the violence from the police was over and all eyes were on them; but I still did not let her go, using the excuse that she wouldn't be able to do her hair.

By 1970, all of the schools in Danville were integrated. It seemed impossible back then but today Danville has changed. Hotels are happy to allow us to have occasions there... *if we have the money, of course!* I remember Dr. King made an appearance at the High Street Church and things have since never been the same. Today, my two sons, Larry, Jr. and Philip hold meetings in the building where we were beaten; Philip is a Danville School board trustee and Larry is a city councilman. My daughter, Alethea, is married, and Larry, Sr. is still busy in the struggle — too busy for grass to grow under his feet.

As for me, I still watch and pray.

Section Four

Heart and Sole Provider

I'm Here
by
Sha Vonn Smith

For You… I'm here, I'm here
Mother I'm here
Have no fear
You don't have to do it on your own… all alone
I grew up for you so I can make it to school, work, church
See it's all for you
I saw what you did and you did it with a strong hand
Did it on your own and I'm proud of you
There was no man
You were too good and proud
When people had their hand out
You never broke your smile
And I love for you
And do for you
I'll cry for you but instead of anger
I still love
I still love
I still love
I still loooove
You
See… you are the truth
And when you're quiet and the lights are off
I know you say
I love you too!

Photo on left: Author on the right, with mother
Photo on the right: Author on the left, with mother

The Blind, Beautiful Faith of a Child
by
Tammy "Goody" Ballard

My momma left me to believe I had the flu when I was 17 and had been hanging around the house for about a week vomiting, but in actuality I would soon be a mommy. Although, I wasn't quite sure what a "mommy" was because I never experienced that particular relationship growing up. Nor had I ever even held a baby or changed a diaper at that point.

Yet, the instant I rubbed my belly, I knew that I would indeed be the best mother I could to the person growing inside me. Immediately I'd fallen in love with my child; and there was no preference whether it was a girl or boy. Eventually I gave birth to three children over the years, but my first precious gift came on July 13th 1990 at 7:13am. I named her Tim'esa.

I was always the "Momma" which I made clear. However life has taught me that it is equally important to listen to children.

Being a mother has been my most cherished position in life. Even now as young adults, my children and I continue to have healthy and positive relationships even though there are constant challenges for everyone during their journeys. While raising my children as a single mom, it has always been important for me to express honesty, love and communicate openly, which happens to work both ways.

I was always the "Momma" which I made clear. However life has taught me that it is equally important to listen to children. Parents often get hung up on a power trip feeling as though their way is the only way, particularly in the old days when kids just didn't have a say.

Yet in this day and age many of us depend on our children for input mainly with things such as all this new technology. I personally had a hard time coming from the era of eight tracks to cassettes and from VHS to DVD's and now iPods! I refuse to have a cell phone.

If You Listen to a Child, You Might *Learn* from a Child

Wise mothers learn just as much from their children as the children do from them. Children need to know they have a voice too. I strongly believe as human beings and children of God we can all learn from one another. At the age of four, Tim'esa and I had recently moved to a new state.

We didn't have a whole lot and the first few days there we only had enough food for her to eat. As we curled up on the floor in the corner of our living room of our unfurnished apartment, I held Tim'esa in my arms as she wiped the tears from my cheeks. She looked up into my eyes and said, *"Momma, you know God has boxes with our names on them with everything we need up there." All ya have to do is pray and ask him for it."*

I admit that I wasn't paying much attention to what she said because it wasn't making much sense to me at first. She made sure I was listening though when she came back with "he doesn't have what we want, Momma—just what we need."

Before that day, I'd never actually prayed nor was I sure how to. On that day my four year old told me "just talk to him, Momma, He's listening." I was reminded that He hears us whether we talk or not because when it comes to the Lord, even our thoughts are not private.

As we curled up on the floor in the corner of our living room of our unfurnished apartment, I held Tim'esa in my arms as she wiped the tears from my cheeks. She looked up into my eyes and said "Momma, you know God has boxes with our names on them with everything we need up there." All ya have to do is pray and ask him for it."

I relearned a valuable lesson that day. Somehow over the years I allowed my faith to get away from me. Later in life as my children grew older I began to realize that the Lord had not forgotten about me. It was through my children, His cherubs, that he saved me. I was headed down a very dark and destructive, rebellious path. I allowed rage to overcome my heart, basically giving up.

Becoming a mother restored my faith as well as my strength. I now have my babies who depend on me. Before that day I don't recall how many times or if ever Tim'esa had been to church. To this day I'm still not sure where she learned what she told me that night about prayer, but the sincerity in her voice and the serious look in her eyes is what caused me to always remember that day and to listen when a child has something to say.

As mothers, we tend to be very protective of our children. Once my daughter started junior high I was worried about the friends she would make. Everyone always seemed to adore Tim'esa wherever she went. However, I'd warn her about befriending the "pregnant girl," concerned that such a girl would be bad influence on my baby.

Author (left), with daughter

I hadn't realized or considered that I taught Tim'esa to think for herself. She was not only strong, but she had proven to be a leader and very independent.

One day, Tim'esa told me, *"Momma, my friends don't have to be a bad influence on me. Why can't I be a good influence on them?"* I had never considered that perspective. It was almost as if she'd purposely seek out

the troubled kids, somehow sensing that they were the ones who needed friends. She had never given me a reason not to trust her and once again it was a reminder from my child to exercise my faith—the faith that I'd taught her right from wrong.

Author (right), with daughter

She's the Reason Why?
By Clarence Griffin

To My Mother, Anita

The reason we were never hungry… my mother didn't give in to
it,
Never allowed starvation to take hold of us

She believed in God and his invisible hand that makes everything
out of nothingness

She literally believed that God said, *"let there will be light"*, and
there *was* light
So she cloaked, educated and adorned us in brilliant rays of love

She had the audacity to believe that she was a child of God
And revealed that we were God's children too…

She walked on fire and water in sandals, laced by faith and
prayer…
Her complete attire to protect and empower

With so much love for her little ones, fear dare not visit her heart,
her life, her soul…
One glance from her, and fear is disarmed…
rudderless….destroyed

She is filled with so much amazing light… shadows respectfully
demure at her door
And choose instead to embrace the sun…

Author, Clarence Griffin, on the left,
with mother, Anita McGee Royston

A WOMAN FOR ALL SEASONS

By
Terry L. Williams

Mother, Father, Confidant, Healer

My siblings and I were double-questioned in elementary school when asked to clarify if Earl was the first name of our mother or our father. Indeed, the woman born as Earl Dean Jackson was our beloved mother and we did not grow up with the benefit of a father.

Yes, there was a man present in the household once or twice, but not for long as we journeyed through various rites of passage to adulthood and out into the world. As far as we nine siblings were concerned Mama Earl, as we adoringly called her, was our single mother, father, confidant, healer, taskmaster, disciplinarian, and wonder woman – all in one sacred package.

Born in June of 1920, Mama grew up amid the early 20th Century disparate sharecropping system of the South – West Texas, where segregation, lynching, and inhumane treatment abounded as vestiges of the earlier Reconstruction Era.

Mama was the strongest woman I have ever known. She grew up with her entrepreneurial grandparents. Her grandpa made abundant supplies of syrup and her grandma was an esteemed midwife. Joking about her early life, Mama departed Limestone County Texas in 1938 vowing that she would never pick cotton or eat sorghum molasses again.

So 30 years later, when our young family was literally run out of southern Idaho in 1959, with gunfire at our backs, it was no surprise to her that ignorance and blind hatred can exist in every community. Yet Mother never uttered a word of condemnation to us against the perpetrators. She taught us to accept everyone as God's creation and to honor all people, even when they showed themselves to be dishonorable. She preached forgiveness to us and we have reaped the peaceful benefits of that wise advice.

From our family's humble beginnings in hot, dusty Artesia, New Mexico to growing up in cold, icy Salt Lake City, Utah, Mama ensured that we all attended Sunday school, church, prayer meetings, and choir practice. With nervous stuttering, we duly recited our Easter, Christmas and Mother's Day poems in front of the congregations.

This taught us public poise. She was our constant booster, telling us that we were capable of doing all things well. When one of us made a disparaging remark about someone's looks, Mama would say, *"Honey, there are no ugly people in the world, only ugly attitudes."* When we argued about some silly matter, she would quiet both parties by saying, *"If a wise man and a fool are arguing, which one is the fool?"*

We were always in awe of Mother's sense of grace, hospitality, and acceptance. Mom was the first black woman to be nominated as Mother of Year in the State of Utah.

A spiritual passage in wisdom literature asks, "Who can find a virtuous woman?" We kids already had that answer. We were always in awe of Mother's sense of grace, hospitality, and acceptance. It did not matter what motley friend we brought home (and some were rather ragged and unkempt), Mother would receive them as if they were family.

There was always an instant invitation to stay for dinner and visit again as they were departing. She moved to the top tier of nominees, ultimately losing the honor to a Mormon mother of ten. While we felt disappointed at what we thought was a case of misplaced voting, Mother warmly hugged and congratulated the winning mother.

The Chief Architect of Achievement, Activism and Service

Mama was our inspiration and our biggest fan. We persevered through our various tribulations by the sheer fact of her living example. She had buried her parents, husbands, and babies with stoic gratefulness for their place in her life. Mama served her country as a 'Rosie the Riveter,' working in the West Coast shipyards, departing out of San Francisco, California just shortly before the disastrous 1944 Port Chicago explosion in Suisun Bay.

Mother's four daughters could only be wooed by suitors who could match their fiery spirits. And her five sons were taught to be self-sufficient. Mother also helped to foster church life wherever we lived and served in all official capacities of their service to the community. This taught us all to also invest our energies in civic, social and religious service.

We children viewed our humble achievements through the prism of her encouragement as a single-parent Black woman producing a brood of activists. She displayed photos of her multi-talented firstborn son who became a decorated naval officer and world traveler. And proudly saw her firstborn daughter become the first black employee in a Utah Governor's office.

Mama stood strong as her 9th and youngest child of live birth made history in the summer of 1974 by challenging in court the Boy Scouts of America and LDS (Latter Day Saints) church on racial discrimination against blacks and other minorities by disallowing their attainment of troop leadership positions in Utah. The NAACP suit filed on behalf of this 13-year-old warrior, followed nationally by CBS news, was settled when these organizations summarily ended the indefensible practice.

During the 1970s, she loved to watch the local news after her middle son, a resourceful news journalist, was hired as a reporter by a CBS News affiliate station. In the winter of 1982, she witnessed her second elder son take the oath of office as the first black person to be elected to the Utah State Senate, and again proudly witnessed the Governor signing into law the Martin Luther King Holiday Act, which her son pushed through the recalcitrant legislature in 1996.

Letting Life Speak for Itself

Mama Earl, a devout African Methodist Episcopal Christian, held resolutely to the biblical scripture in Psalms 90, which she believed was God's personal promise that she would live to be at least 70 years old, and perhaps 80. So when we celebrated her 81st birthday she gleefully smiled and quipped that by God's grace she was living on borrowed time.

Though a quiet and ardent worshiper, she often said that she would "not serve a God who she could not feel". Mother was not a saint nor did she claim to be. She had her ominous days of contention and insensitive moments of irritability. After all, it never was easy being alone raising a house full of headstrong energetic kids. Some of her ambitions, such as to be a pianist, singer, or business owner, were never realized. But Mama told us children that we were her whole life.

We were her reason for living and that was her greatest joy. We all knew that she loved us equally and completely. And all of her grandchildren felt the same eternal love from her as we of the 'first generation' did.

In every season, for every reason, when Mama Earl crossed someone's life path, they were never afterwards the same.

In the new millennium, Mama suffered health setbacks, including amputation, heart attacks and strokes, which limited her physical ability – but not her spirit. She continued to travel coast-to-coast to visit her kids and grandchildren scattered far and wide.

At our 2001 family reunion, Mama insisted on everyone in the room, including friends, former spouses, guests and even service personnel, assemble for a 'family picture'. Obedient to her call, we all posed for a final photo because she said that it would be her last reunion. Prophetically, she made her transition to 'that golden strand just beyond the river' four months later. But she did not make

Author's mother and a woman for all seasons

that final journey before she had infused in our hearts the many lessons from her storehouse of wisdom and love.

Her final wishes were not to have a funeral ceremony because, as she put it, she wanted her *"life to speak for itself"*. True to form, her legacy of noble perseverance, quiet faith, endearing hospitality and motherly love is evident in the generations of children who dearly carry her memory. In every season for every reason, when Mama Earl crossed someone's life path, they were never afterwards the same.

My Mother....My Masterpiece
by Clarence E. Griffin

To My Mother, Anita L. Royston —

Mothers are the gate keepers. None come except through you. You are the embodiment of the word bound in flesh. You are the portal that leads to rest. You are past, present and future.

You hold the hope of existence in your cradle. Your words are tidal waves of vibration, dear Momma. Your thoughts... masterpieces: an assemblage of art from Mesopotamia to Mozambique.

The universe is shaped by the movement of your hand through space. With one look, you can erase fear. With one smile, you can give the heart hope infusing it with acknowledged cheer. You, dear Momma, hold the fate of the world in your arms as you comfort your four children, all different, like the coordinates, or the four winds. You know how they blow, and you called them by names that evoke greatness. You named greatness and gave it fuel and structure to be.

I thank you, dear Momma, for naming me with the mark of angels that casts a spell upon the ticking of time and its constituents. I thank you, Miss Anita, for showing your four winds that tyranny of any sort, no matter how small must be challenged at the point of a pen, or staring down the barrel of a 12-gage shot gun.

You, dear Momma, are a hero that many have met, yet few truly know. You are a trail blazer, an organizer, a politician, a dreamer, an artist, a teacher, a motivator, a business woman and most of all a woman of faith the size of a mustard seed found by ants upon a hill, proportionally speaking. You have been blessed to see in the flesh with eyes still open to the joy of life's offerings.

You have traveled the world and tasted the food of our ancestors. You have walked in their shoes, Sista Babe. You have counseled the sick in body and mind. You have housed the homeless and the orphan and have inspired great artist to paint images burgeoning from their hearts.

You, Miss McGee, of legendary book borrowing past, have infected me, your second son with the illness of loving words and loving books as forever friends never to be returned, (Yeah they're gonna get you one day...).

You are the most amazing rose in the garden, one to be admired with care and forewarning. Your thorns are invisible to the careless interloper who cannot see beyond the dazzling eyes and the *"Lord have mercy"* smile or that *"Southern Mississippi hospitality"* into which you were born.

I pray that one day soon you'll get your due, not what you deserve. Grace has covered that, so let it be what you are due for your investment in your four winds (Bruce, Marsha, Benjamin, and me) and the fifth (Kristina), which was a gift.

*Author and his mother,
his masterpiece, Anita*

You have given to us and others, you've touched the opportunity to see why God chose you and all mothers to be the gatekeepers of existence.

Love you, Miss McGee, Griffin, Royston, Napoleon, Sista Babe, Old Yella, MOMMA!

Keeping the Faith
by Ovetta P. Jefferson

Author's mother

Storyteller, strong dedicated woman of God, minister, and sole provider are terms that define my mother, Lillie B. Hall who was born on August 16, 1945 in Montgomery, Alabama. Growing up with her eight siblings in a house made of red imitation bricks presented some challenges.

Perched atop that little house was a thin tin roof that could barely withstand the sometimes unbearable weather conditions. Cold frosty winters with loud howling winds seeped into that tiny house, making it frigid, while in the summers the house was hot, steamy and humid. And when the pitter patter of rain tapped against the roof, it created a tune that the family used to make their own music to.

Born to Elizabeth and John Quincy Adams Bennett my mother was their fifth child. With a smooth iron and washboard to clean and press clothes; and a little red wagon to sell vegetables from her garden door-to-door, my grandmother meted out a living working for white people. And my grandfather worked for the city digging holes for sewers to support their large family.

Courtship to Hardship

As a school girl, my mother recounts how she fell in love with my father. The courtship began when he walked her home from school and carried her books. As the relationship advanced, she would wait for him to come over after he got off work at Maxwell Air Force base as a waiter. Through the mirror of an old dresser, my mother would watch him step up on the porch, as if he were her prince.

In 1963, my mother married her prince. That same year, my older sister was born, then I came the following year, and my little brother was born in 1966. Later my parents divorced, and she remarried, and left her second husband after my other brother was born from that union.

In Chicago, where my mother moved us, we fell on hard times and stayed with my mother's sister for a while until we found a mission that took us in. During our time there, my mother received help getting on her feet, securing a job and finding a place for us to stay.

Through setbacks and tribulations, my mother made sure we attended school every day. More remarkably she always managed to remain in the Word, maintain her faith, keep us together and stay grounded.

Big Mama, the Storyteller and the Undertaker

Since my mother never learned to drive, she did all of her errands and handled her transportation needs by using the bus. Sometimes she worked two or three jobs to take care of our burgeoning family of four girls and three boys.

Known as the Big Mama of Chicago, my mother was a minister at St. James Church in Chicago and a member of Sharing and Caring of Atlanta. On Sundays, with standing room only, she would make and host Sunday dinner for the whole church at her house.

We were in church so much that we did our homework in the backroom. My sisters and I even had this joke where we called ourselves drug babies because our mother always drug us to church every day of the week. My mother kept us laughing by telling us her childhood stories at dinner time, which we loved listening to. A couple of stories in particular were very entertaining.

Author, on right, and mother

When my auntie was younger, my granddaddy told her not to go out. Well she didn't listen and went out anyway. So my grandfather vowed to get her for disobeying his rules by playing a trick on her. Down the street from where they lived was a big brick church that was very spooky and dark at night. Everyone was afraid to walk by it even me and my sister. To teach my auntie a lesson, granddaddy went to the church with a white sheet on and stood on the steps.

Not long afterward, my mother's sister comes by just dancing and singing. Of course she was real happy until she looked up and saw that white sheeted figure and ran home screaming hysterically. My mother said that my auntie never went out again when she was told not to.

The other story that makes us laugh was when my mother's cousin had too much to drink. Apparently, according to my mother, they didn't embalm people when they died back in the day. So when my cousin was found lying on the railroad tracks he was presumed dead and taken to the undertaker. When my grandmother arrived at the morgue to take care of the funeral arrangements, she was placed in the room with all the bodies, including my cousin's. With no warning, my cousin, who was supposed to be dead, woke up, surveyed the room and said, *"What are all of you doing laying here naked! Let's get up and go get a drink!"*

My mother said that my grandmother and the undertaker were so scared that they both were trying to get out of the door at the same time. Now that was funny! I love the stories that my mother told us and all she did for us. She is an amazing mother who I love more than she knows.

The Adventures of Sylvia:
The Free, the Brave, the Spirited!

by
Irene Clark-Brown

Have Car, Will Travel!

Author

The fourth of 11 children, my mother, Sylvia Clark-Horton (Nee Patrick) was born June 16, 1917 to Ottie and Mamie Patrick. Considered the "Goody-2-Shoes" of the brood, she came from the rural south and moved to New York in 1939 when my father found work there. At the time I was two months old, and my brother and sister were toddlers. Differing vastly from her previous surroundings; the city provided new experiences and ways of doing things. So my mother lived, learned and adapted to her new life.

Although mother was uneducated, (receiving a fourth or fifth grade education), she was imbued with "good common sense," which helped her provide a fairly decent life for herself and us when she and my father split up. Family oriented in nature, she was there any time someone had a problem. Mother gave cash, and a place to stay to family when they were struggling to get over the hump. More importantly, she was always there when there was a family event.

With a love for travel, Mother took a lot of drives and was sure to visit family or friends no matter what state they resided in. Her motto was, "Have car will travel!" And she did.

My mother loved having a driving companion, but if no one was available, she went by herself. Quite often I would receive a call at work from my mother who asked, "Guess where I am?" Before I could respond, she'd complete her own sentence. "I'm sitting on your porch!"

Like my mother, I LOVED SPEED! I referred to her as Speedy Gonzalez, which was most apparent when at age 85 she was pulled over by the police for going 85 in a 65 mile zone!

At two or three in the morning, Mother would leave South Boston, Virginia by herself. The last time she did she was 92 years young! In her lifetime, she went on at least six cruises, visited *The Holy Land,* with her church in Brooklyn, New York and took her granddaughter with her. She even took me on a cruise to the Bahamas and we had a fabulous time!

Once, my mother picked up her five grandchildren (aged 3-11) early in the morning for a ride, which she did whenever possible, and they ended up in Canada.

"The kids are fine," she reported.

"But you don't have any clothes for the kids," we said.

"No, but I have a couple of good credit cards." And they stayed for three days...

I don't know when Mother learned to drive but she knew how to go places, even though she never learned to park very well. When she discovered that I possessed those skills, she would

allow me to park the car when I was 15, but she never allowed me to drive without a license.

Like my mother, I LOVED SPEED! I referred to her as *Speedy Gonzalez*, which was most apparent when at age 85 she was pulled over by the police for going 85 in a 65 mile zone! Even though she had admonished me to slow down! I guess the apple doesn't fall far from the tree.

My Mother, the Adventurer

When I was nine, my sister, brother and I decided to teach my mother how to ride a bicycle. So we got her on the bike, gave her a shove downhill which turned into a wild trek covering three blocks. *"Turn right, Mother!"* we screamed following her on our bikes as she neared a cement wall. Then she bounded down a flight of stairs two stories high and ended up on the paved landing next to the Hudson River.

It was amazing that Mother didn't fall until the last step, which had us applauding and rolling in laughter, which my mother didn't find amusing at all. On another

Author's mom at age 94

occasion, we went to the skating rink with Mother. When

somebody bumped into her, she went down and got up with the back of her skirt ripped and hanging down like the train on a bride's dress. Again we laughed, but Mother saw no humor in that either.

Author's mother, traveling abroad

My mother did keep all the windows in her home open, because she liked the cold.

Over the years, there were many funny memories of my mother that time and space precludes me from sharing, but these last few remembrances must be included because they provide a more complete picture of my mother. There was a time when I asked her about one of her jobs, and she replied, "I take care of senior citizens." At the time she was 72!

My mother did keep all the windows in her home open, because she liked the cold. And she never had a hospital stay until a few months before she passed at age 96. She was my *"Pretty Girl,"* one of my pet names for her, and she certainly lived life exuberantly, freely and abundantly!

Author's parents

Author, on left, with parents and siblings

Mother of the Year
by Peter S. Vanderpool

*Author, center, with the Mother of the Year
and daughter, in 1998*

A Relationship and Love like No Other

A true angel, the woman I admire is the one I've been married to for 27 years. A notable person, she is great with people and knows the right things to say and do. She also is a wonderful mother who has a very close bond with our child. When it comes to relating to, and raising our sixteen year old daughter, who has autism, my wife, Joslyn is incredible!

Always positive and passionate about our daughter, my wife never stopped believing in Sydney, nor have I.

Perceptive and giving, my wife understands our daughter Sydney's needs, as well as her wants. They have a very close relationship and often cuddle up together, and hold hands which might seem unusual for a child with a disorder where some children shun closeness.

The only thing Sydney doesn't like about being affectionate is to be kissed (*"too wet,"* she complains). So she and her mom rub their noses together and exchange butterfly kisses (her mom flutters her eye lashes against Sydney's cheek) or my daughter will kiss her mother on the face and provide a bear hug, which she always is up for. I often hear my daughter say to her mother, "I love you so much!" Or when my wife or I say, "We love you!" to Sydney, she responds in a cheery voice, "Love you too!"

From the beginning of our daughter's life, we wanted to do our best for her. Sydney slept on her mother's chest when she was little, unable to rest peacefully on her own. There were also many nights when my wife walked the floor with Sydney and sang lullabies, many that she made up especially for Sydney.

Always positive and passionate about our daughter, my wife never stopped believing in Sydney nor have I. We have rationalized that our daughter had her own way and time table for accomplishments. To enhance Sydney's life, she found ways to help Sydney by getting her as many resources as possible. Even though it has been a difficult struggle, my wife, who I almost lost a few years ago due to illness, has no intention of giving up on our daughter.

Laughter is the Best Cure for any Condition of Heartache

My wife has a way of making Sydney laugh which seems to bring our daughter out of her shell when she is worrying about not knowing how to

Sydney, learning to spell

talk to kids her own age. She also tells Sydney to be herself and often asks her questions about how she feels, and what excites her and makes her happy in order for Sydney to expand her skills of expressing herself, even though social interaction is difficult for many autistic children.

By not using baby talk around her and explaining the definition of words, and advocating for speech therapy for Sydney, she has developed a larger vocabulary. And, the biggest bonus is that Sydney, who is very bright, has been able to share her thoughts and feelings over time. At first, she had very minimal language and found it hard to speak with us without simple one word answers.

There was also a time when Sydney used to cry and complain about reading even a paragraph. Today she proudly reads stories to her 86 year old grandmother and to us. Sydney's other interests include music, humor, games, dancing and road trips. Most exciting is that she wants to be helpful.

By using a calm voice, my wife is often able to soothe Sydney because our daughter has many fears, nightmares and worries. Over time Sydney has gained more confidence, but those concerns still pop up and she reacts violently to them sometimes. When she has good days she thinks she can outsmart everyone—everyone but Mom, who knows most of the time what Sydney is up to and will call her on it.

My wife is there at the forefront finding new ways to work with Sydney and allay her anxiety. She isn't shy about asking others to intervene and searches the internet for resources and doing whatever she can to assist Sydney. Although my wife who has an ultra-busy life, she has found a way to share time with Sydney that is meaningful. She would be the first to admit that this has been a journey unlike any other, but she knows that God gifted us with this amazing child, and our goal, as my wife would say, *"Is to elevate her spirit and bring her joy."* So that is the point where we are now.

Leaving the Nest to Thrive under God's Wings

As Sydney gets older, she is more aware of her autism and continues to struggle with knowing how to fit in, but she wants to, thus we will keep trying to help. Because we know that the time has come to give Sydney more than what we can offer her ourselves, we have had to make the hard decision to send Sydney away to a residential educational facility to assist her with her autism related challenges that could impede her growth. We want for her to get the additional help she needs to function successfully in the home, classroom and community.

It has not been easy getting services for Sydney, which I give my wife all of the credit for trying to locate, but if anyone has been up for the challenge she has been the one because she is the very best mother for our daughter.

Happy family in New Mexico

My wife is the light of my life, and has encouraged me to pursue my own dreams. Always painting a beautiful vision to make my day, she is an example of grace under pressure.

Criticisms, insensitivities, unsolicited opinions and misconceptions from those who do not understand autism, have been constant, but my wife presses on aware that they don't know Sydney as much as we do. Determined to live her best life, she also works to make certain that our lives are good too.

She includes time for friends and family, helps me due to a recent diagnosis of Multiple Sclerosis, and works a demanding full-time job where she gives her time to encourage and listen to students, and those who are in need of resources, motivation and a word of kindness, understanding and compassion.

We are impressed by Sydney's bravery in coping with autism. I am equally impressed that my daughter has a mother who is just as brave in supporting Sydney and loving her enough to let her go. Though we both grieve about Sydney leaving the nest, we believe that our daughter will continue to thrive under God's wings.

My wife is the light of my life, and has encouraged me to pursue my own dreams. Always painting a beautiful vision to make my day, she is an example of grace under pressure. I might add that some of her beautiful traits stem directly from her own mother, who also has been a gift to all of us. So for all my wife does and gives to help not only our daughter, but so many others, she is to me, ***Mother of the Year!***

Author, top center, with family 2014

Section Five

Earth Angels

Grace, the Amazing
For my mother
by **Staajabu**

Thank you mom for the way you and only you
can say my name, Vic-toe-ree-yah
for the hard Foggy Bottom/Centerville
Camden, NJ, Mechanic Street days
The soft cornbread and buttermilk
Marydel, Maryland days
The walks through the cemetery, talks
at the kitchen table, picnics, cookouts, trips
in the trailer, fresh okra and lima beans
fried green tomatoes and eggplant

Thank you for the rides to Sudlersville bank
through the back roads when the leaves were changing colors
 visiting Aunt Sweetie Bell and Uncle Noah in Brotmanville, NJ

Thank you for the fresh tomatoes from your garden
the smell of collard greens on the stove
crocheting, quilting, embroidering, canning

How can I ever thank you enough
for my brother Hubert
Thank you for loving the earth, all its animals and people
for putting up with all the men who promised
to take care of us, but didn't/wouldn't/couldn't.

Thank you mom for being there
without too much fuss when we came home
all tired and beat from
trying to stand on our own two feet

Thank you for loving my child and the grandchildren just as
much… for always being in style
laughing and switching your hips and such
for liking all our silly holiday gifts you didn't need
wearing or using them all the same
as proud and happy as you could be
because we tried so hard to please and thank
you for teaching us to believe in God to
be clean and respect all life
to be truthful, useful, humble and brave
and to let no one or no thing
make us into a slave…

May the Most High Creative Energy
in the Universe bless you forever.

Author's mother, Grace

Mothers Have to Take Care of Their Children
by Anita Vanessa Dawn White

Sometimes we learn invaluable lessons from a child's perspective. As revealed in the following story, this young author clearly loves her mother and has already gained copious amounts of mother wit.

Follow Your Heart and Never Give Up

My mother, Marsha Griffin is supportive and always cheers for me when I'm nervous. She also always tells me to *"be the bigger person, never give up and to try my hardest."* When I lost the kindergarten spelling bee I wanted to give up, but I didn't due to her words of encouragement. *No matter how hard something is never give up! If you give up you can't follow your dreams and if you can't follow your dreams what are you going to do? You have to follow your heart and see if you like what you're doing and if you like it you can do it for the rest of your life. You don't have to be afraid to put your dream in action.*

Since I'm 10 years old, I don't know much about being a mother, but, one thing I do know is that as a mother you always have to take care of your children, which is exactly what my mom does for me.

STRONG ROOTS

My mother is not that scared of anything because she grew up with three brothers. Two were older and one brother was younger. She also has a stepsister who she met at 18.

Both of my mother's grandfathers served in the military. Her grandpa on her mom's side fought in the Korean War and her grandpa on her dad's side was a merchant marine. So she comes from a very strong family.

Since I'm 10 years old, I don't know much about being a mother, but one thing I do know is that as a mother you always have to take care of your children, which is exactly what my mom does for me. I wouldn't want anybody else to be my mom, except Marsha Griffin, because she is the best!

Little Anita and her mom

AN UNQUALIFIED NURSE
by **Sam Kalimba**

Author's mother, Delia

The following is a story by Sam Kalimba who wrote his second contribution for the Brave, Bold and Beautiful Book Series. In a moving tribute to his mother, he enthusiastically reconnects with those who read his previous story about his father.

Welcome back to Africa! A place where there are some who reject family responsibilities due to too much burden. However, I know of a woman from Malawi with a unique and strong character as far as this author is concerned. She braved deaths and carried on with life in the face of countless tragedies. The woman I speak of is none other than my biological mother. Born Delia Nhlabase Tenthani in around 1954, she lived, died and was partly buried in hospital.

Mchinji District is to the West of Lilongwe and borders Zambia to the West. This is where my Delia came from. A member of the Ngoni's, my mother was an unqualified, uneducated and untrained but natural nurse. If all nurses were like my Delia, the world would be a better place to live and life would be meaningful to many a hopeless fraternity.

My Delia was such a good mother. In 2002, she secretly gave me money from which I laid the foundation of this new life I am pursuing. I write what she never would, but told us about in a story that had to be revealed. I always wondered if it was my mother's prayerful life or was it her natural disposition that made my Delia nice to all she came across.

After all, she belonged to a certain Catholic organization whose members were required to live a life of prayer. Addressing various problems in the world with the help of Mary, the mother of Jesus let me know why my Delia conducted herself in a manner that could best be described as pious.

If all nurses were like my Delia, the world would be a better place to live and life would be meaningful to many a hopeless fraternity.

My mother made it to prenatal services ten times but managed to raise four boys. Chances for girl children were there but in vain. Those tragic losses partly demonstrate my mother's strong character. All the times she had given birth to girls were thwarted by their immediate deaths. None of them lived more than three months. Yellow Fever, Malaria and Typhoid brought my mother back to hospital. If not devastating enough, by the end of her life she had seen her sister, cousins, her own husband and many of her other children dying.

In the 1970s my mother lost two boys in a space of seven days. Their untimely deaths came as a result of envy according to her.

"Mum, why have I not seen my home of origin?" I asked in 1990 when I was only ten.

"I do not want to lose you," she replied.

My question led to my mother telling me how my brothers died before I was born. She explained that my dad used to perform *Mganda* (a traditional dance of the Chewa of Central Malawi). Young boys followed him for trainings. Learning by observation the boys knew how each drum beat went.

At one point, the dance group had to perform at a wedding ceremony at Magweru village in Zambia. The children followed and danced beside their dad. Customarily, those who were fascinated by the performance had to offer some cash to the best dancers of their choice.

It just so happened that my late brothers accumulated over half of the total that the real dancers received, which was reason for them to start their journey to where they came from. But the unexpected occurred. It all started with simple fainting for the boys, but upon reaching hospital, my brother Isaac was pronounced dead. In a similar situation, barely one week later, it was his young brother who was stricken and passed away. Two boys remained, Maxwell and Felix who had to be rescued from that calamity that befell my family.

In Lilongwe my mother's hospital life became more salient. She gave birth to two other boys, Godfrey and me. Additionally, she was the guardian and caregiver to her last born sister, Lucia, who suffered from Tuberculosis (TB) and was cured at Bwaila (formerly Bottom Hospital).

My mother also played nurse to my first born brother who was hospitalized for more than twelve months two separate times at Likuni Hospital. He later died in her arms in 2001. As if not enough, her daughter-in-law went to hospital one month after the death of my brother and was in Kamuzu Central Hospital for three weeks being assisted by my Delia, before she too died.

There were many other occasions that Delia happened to be at hospital. The next to last time was for her husband's care in 2004. After his death, it would be her turn to return for good to her place of pleasure in 2008. This time it was at Bwaila where she was diagnosed with TB.

After six months she was discharged. However, she lost weight, and had to walk with the support of crutches, as her legs were swollen. She did more than seven HIV tests from different centers but all proved negative. Frequent TB check-ups were done which indicated that she was cured but when the swelling of her legs persisted other doctors suggested it was an effect of the TB treatment.

Still while at home she could not be nursed back to health until another expatriate doctor diagnosed her with Diabetes in 2010. All the symptoms and signs described above clearly indicated that it was Diabetes. Unfortunately, it was too late for her treatment. Her left leg had to be amputated.

"I am dying slowly son," she whispered to me, not by design but because she was too weak. *"I don't know where they have buried my leg,"* she continued, leaving all those who overheard our conversation, laughing because her face showed that she was joking.

Luckily enough she was alive by 25 December of 2010 when I shared her hospital life the whole day since it was a holiday. We prayed and joked later. This thing I want to mention is what inspired me the most and I reached the utmost of my happiness and ecstasy of life that I will live to remember. This was when I told her that I was returning to Blantyre that night.

"Don't go Hamilton," she gently pleaded, calling me by my childhood name. *"You make me happy."*

Oh! I did not know what to do—to cry or jump and hug her? But she was sickly for vigorous hugs! When all others left since the hospital attendants had to work in that room, I still went back, held her hand and bowed in kissing her palms. The attendant advised me to leave and come to see her again the following day.

On 6th January, Friday afternoon, she started gulping the little liquid she had in her digestive system and minutes later my beautiful Delia, the unqualified, untrained nurse returned home for eternity.

Mama

by **Terry Moore**

I could feel you praying for me
Asking God to help me along the way
Asking God to be there for me
To give me strength to pay the dues of life
I have to pay

I could see you watching me
Knowing that I was in good hands
As the years went by I began to
understand
There was a lot that you just couldn't do   *Author and his mom*
So you just trusted that your prayers would get through

I could feel you holding back your tears
I could feel you praying through your fears
But looking strong whenever I came around
Just smiling at me without making a sound
Because you knew all along
That the Lord would guide and make me strong
There is no one else like you
And mama all of your prayers made it through
Thank you and don't think that I didn't know
I knew it Mama even when you didn't let it show

Now I'm praying for you just like you did for me
I pray that dreams come true are what you'll see
Because you deserve it, blessings you will surely get
Thanks for all the prayers and all the love Mama
Because of you, all of my needs have been met.

Memories of My Strong, Determined, Loving Mother
by
De'Lone Waddell King

The author's family, mother on the left

"Finally, my brethren, be strong in the Lord, and in the power of his might." Ephesians 6:10

Planting corn, peanuts and cotton in the spring and canning during breezy winters are a few of the precious memories that come to mind when I think of my early childhood growing up on a tobacco farm. In those days I assisted my mother as her jar washer and got as wet as the jars I was scrubbing.

Born on April 1, 1914 on a middle class farm in Caswell County, North Carolina, my mother was the second daughter of Walter Warren Brown and Annie Caroline Faucette Brown. Ada Matilda "Marie" Brown Neal was the strong, determined and loving woman who created much of the happiness that would enrich our lives and sustain us for years to come. In October of 1933 she was united in Holy Matrimony with John Selmar Neal Sr. The Lord blessed them with three children: John Selmar Neal Jr., De'Lone Waddell Neal, and R.J Neal.

As children we watched Mother work late into the night doing all she could to keep the family household in good condition. At breakfast we all had to say a Bible verse and morning prayers before our meal. Despite all of our mother's hard work, we still had fun with her on winter nights because she knew how to keep my brothers and I occupied during the evenings.

Since the Bible was the most important book, she read it to us religiously, but she also shared stories like *"Peter Pan"* and read with so much enthusiasm in her voice that I could picture the characters in my mind –Captain Hook, Wendy, pirates and Peter Pan! Other activities that were as joyful included, seeding cotton, roasting peanuts and popping popcorn near the fireplace with a three-foot handle and a square-shaped wire container which was customary in the 1930s.

As children, we watched our mother work late into the night doing all she could to keep the family household in good condition.

When my dad made my mother a quilting frame that hung from the ceiling, I remember coming home from school and watching as my mother placed flattened cotton between the quilt and stitched it together. Quite the seamstress, Mother made pillowcases which she embroidered with great artistry and cozy flannel pajamas which made all of us children feel as *snug as a bug in a rug*.

Mother also made me a beautiful silky white dress more than 70 years ago. Always thoughtful, my mother even used some of the money that my father gave her to purchase our winter clothes and took me to Strader's Shoe Store and bought me a pair of brown alligator shoes! All of my mother's efforts and particularly that lovely dress she made me are warm remembrances of her.

Love, Sweets and Forgiveness Too!

"Who did it?" my mother asked, when my brother beat the blooms off of her beautiful prized red roses in her garden.

"R.J." we all replied without hesitation.

"Everything I do you blame on me!" R.J. cried.

When it came to my mother's baking skills, she could make all kinds of cakes, like caramel, chocolate, pineapple and coconut.

Like R.J., I was spared too one afternoon when my curiosity got the best of me. While watching my mother prepare cookies for us, I tried to get a better look at what she was doing so I stood on the lard can and my foot slipped inside of it. My mother stopped what she was doing, cleaned my foot off and continued working, but she never told my dad about it.

When it came to my mother's baking skills, she could make all kinds of cakes, like caramel, chocolate, pineapple and coconut. She also made wine and peach brandy, and at Christmas and only Christmas, my mother gave us two ounces of peach brandy with our cake.

One afternoon, in an effort to emulate my mother's culinary abilities, my brother, John and I agreed that I would bake a cake and he would do my job of cleaning the house when mother was away with her family who helped take care of her. Just as my Uncle Charlie pulled up in the driveway with the family, my brother finished mopping the floor, as I was putting the finishing touches on the first chocolate cake I had ever made. It was delicious!

Undoubtedly, my mother taught us very well because her major concern was always for the betterment of her family, and the progress of her church and community. In all three she was accomplished. Musically inclined my mother learned tunes and had the ability to play the banjo which was passed down from her dad at a young age. Due to my mother's special interest in music, she became the first pianist of Browns Chapel Missionary Baptist Church. She accompanied the choir and played for all services and activities.

My cousin said my mother taught her how to play the piano and encouraged her by telling her that she could achieve success in becoming anything that she wanted to be. As for my mother's other burgeoning interest, she delighted in teaching Sunday school and rearing children in the Christian way. If the sun was shining and the weather was warm we would walk the 1 ½ miles to Sunday school. Afterward on Sunday afternoons many of our friends and cousins around the neighborhood came to my mother's house for delightful and joyful times.

On Angel's Wings and a Song She Flew Away

One morning as my mother was getting ready to go to the doctor, she told me, *"When I get back, I'm going to get you something."* So I waited, and waited for her to come back, but she never did. When my father arrived home without Mother, he said that the doctor sent her to the Baptist Hospital in Winston-Salem. Seeing the condition she was in at the hospital was disheartening.

During that time, the only way we received messages about Mother's medical progress was through my cousin who had a phone and had to inform us that she had gotten worse. My dad told me to tell my grandparents. So on the way down to their place I prayed, making one solemn request, *"God, please don't take my mother away."* Unfortunately, later that evening we went to bed only to be told by our cousin that my mother had died. It was Mother's Day 1950 and I was 11 years old.

My dad told me to tell my grandparents. So on the way down to their place I prayed, making one solemn request, "God, please don't take my mother away."

Deeply saddened by my mother's death, I recall when my aunt fretted that Mother was too sick to be in the choir stand. Mother sang *I'll Fly Away* with such divine grace before she too, flew away to join the angels in Heaven. Writing about her brings both good and sad memories. I still remember my mother saying that she wanted her children to take care of themselves when she died. And I truly learned so much at my mother's side.

Today, my mother's youngest sister, Teressa Graves, is still alive in her nineties. She would always say, "I must teach De'Lone to cook before I die." Of course she taught me to the best of her ability and to this day I cook like mother and hold memories of my mother who was always strong, loving, determined and beautiful to me.

The Bringer of Light
by
Erica D. Smith

The name "Cindy" means "bringer of light." However, to me the term "light" goes beyond being an illuminating source, but refers to guidance and the light of the world—Jesus Christ

For someone to bring light means they themselves are not the light, but a means of showing and offering you the true light. That is the most accurate description I can provide of my mother, Cindy, who is always giving of herself. Without God, and my mother bringing the light, my life would be drastically different.

My mother always has called me her Buddy and referred to all of us as her "loves."

The earliest memory I have of my parents, sister and me is at a doctor's office, a scene that would play over and over due to my diagnosis of Sickle Cell. I remember the countless doctors and hospital visits, the medications, and missing school, but when I look back at my childhood I don't see all those images. What I see is a full life!

My mother kept me around positive talk and enveloped me with love, joy, and hope. She never treated me as a sick child. Instead she elevated me with words like, *"God is your healer. Therefore, you do not have to live with the mentality of "having" an illness, because it doesn't have you."*

My bringer of light gave everything, so that I may have life -- but not just life on Earth, eternal life with the Lord. By taking time to read the Bible with me daily she demonstrated her dedication. Even when I was inside my mother's womb, she and my sister read the Bible to me, not knowing what was going on inside my body. Sharing the Bible is still a part of the force and fabric of our relationship.

In Sickness and in Health

Wherever I was, my mother was there bringing, love, light and nurturance. On two occasions she left work to stay with me when I was very ill. One of my hospital stays occurred when I was seven and I had to be admitted for double pneumonia. At the time, I didn't fully grasp the seriousness of my condition because my mom was present, diligently praying, playing games, coloring and reading with me.

She carefully watched and listened to everything the doctors, nurses, and visitors did and said to me. Above all she imbued me with the Word. I knew intrinsically that, *with God all things are possible* and I remember saying, *"God is the real doctor."* The doctors, who said there was nothing else they could do for me, were now taking out IVs and shortly thereafter, sending me home.

Though she may not be world-famous, to this starfish (me) she made a difference. And not because she set out to gain a name for herself, but because she just lives her life as a truly godly woman.

In school, my mom told me to do my best because *"I can do all things through Christ that strengthens me,"* and because I am smarter and brighter than the children of the world (those statements are from a book of prayers we read from). Not because I was any better, but because I belonged to and trusted in God. She always helped me with homework, studying, and most memorable—my lunch.

Although packing a lunch may not be glamorous to most kids and their parents, to my mom and me it was a labor of love. In elementary school, my typical lunch consisted of a peanut butter sandwich, grilled cheese sandwich, applesauce, Goldfish crackers; bottles of water, juice boxes, and a Rice Krispy treat.

When asked why she packed me so much food, my mom said, *"It's not that my daughter can eat it all. I'm just hoping she will eat something,"* (I may have been a picky eater). This wasn't over the top to me, just my mom ensuring I had a good lunch and a healthy body. It's a memory we still laugh about.

The Legacy of My Buddy

My mother always has called me her *Buddy* and referred to all of us as her "loves." Whether it was our car chats, or giving money and gifts to others, chauffeuring family and friends to wherever we needed to go, or planting seeds of Biblical truth she made me feel loved through word and deed. I have never witnessed her being malicious or gossiping about anyone.

Some may have given up on being a light in the darkness because it seems like such a daunting task in a dark world. This is not true of my mother who not only radiates light but illuminates the light within us. Her life of leading by example, reminds me of a story I heard about a little girl who was throwing a starfish into the sea after thousands of them had been washed up on the shore after a storm on the coast. A man walking by asked her the following: *"Why are you even bothering when there is no way that you could save them all by yourself? What difference could you make?"*

The little girl held up a starfish and said, *"To this one I made a difference."* I feel my mom is like that little girl. No matter what life brings or how difficult the situation seems, she continues to trust in the Lord and be a bringer of His light. Though she may not be world-famous, to this one starfish (me) she made a difference. And not because she set out to gain a name for herself, but because she just lives her life as a truly godly woman.

My mother understands that she will be held accountable for the part she plays in preparing her children and generations to come thereafter.

Author (foreground) and her mother, the Bringer of Light

My mother's lasting legacy will be that she gave of her time to get deeply into God's Word for herself and then bring it to her family. She knows how important it is to sanctify yourself first before you can even try to teach someone else. My mother understands that she will be held accountable for the part she plays in preparing her children and generations to come thereafter.

Therefore, because our actions never only affect our individual selves, my mother always talks about making the "turn" in the family towards God and how my sister and I need to keep it going so we don't lose any ground that was gained by the ones that went before us.

Now that I am older, my relationship with my mother is still the same. We read the Bible together every morning before we do anything else. Then we spend a lot of time laughing, talking, and enjoying one another's company. Sometimes she even still offers to pack my lunch for work!

Through every trial, illness, crisis, and friendship, my mother puts God first and then care for her loved ones. I am so thankful that I had a chance to form a strong relationship with her early in life so we can share many happy years and memories. She continues to be my mother and buddy, Cindy, but most critically she is the bringer of light that clearly and assuredly radiates within all of us. And I thank God, for allowing her to be my mother.

She Is

by **Arianne Adams**

Dedicated to Tanja Stanton

Author's mother

She is beautiful
through the battles
that left her scarred

She is wonderful
through the mistakes
that showed her
flawed

She is amazing
through the darkest
pit that showed her
light

She is fully living
through the dullest
moments of life

She holds the key to
her own eternal
happiness

She is faithful though the future promises nothing to us

She has so much passion and love for what she does its
unbelievable

Her soul is uniquely unlike any other... truly incredible!

She is intelligent, sincere and keen

She envelopes herself in the arms of God so that she isn't seen; to allow God's radiance to beam

She stumbles and falls every hour, yet she refuses to remain on the floor...

She is love in every form

She is what every female desires to be

She is the daughter of our Lord, and simply mother to me

"My Guardian Angel"

by **Angelique Peters**

Ministering to Wounded Women

Author's mother

My grandmother told me, *"Your mom was a peculiar child. She was already blessed from my womb."* My mother entered womanhood a beautiful, bold, brave, blessed woman of God! Lillie Carol Adams, was humble and never thought she was above others. I am so blessed that she was my mother, and best friend. When in the presence of family she was a light and respect was given her.

I often thought to myself and said, "If I just could be like Mom..." Then the voice of God and the words of my mother would echo, "Don't just be like me. Be better."

My mother was not just a mother to me and my siblings, she touched others' lives too. In her lifetime she had many roles: mother, wife, and daughter; elect lady of a church, friend, missionary; and so much more. She led with authority and dignity. I often thought to myself and said, "If I just could be like Mom..." Then the voice of God and the words of my mother would echo, *"Don't just be like me. Be better."*

Since I had traveled on a personal journey that had not been easy, one which was filled with great heartache and pain along the way, God spoke to me and revealed my life's purpose. I was called on not only to share my testimony by ministering to teen girls and women who have endured great pain in their lives, but to intercede so that they would be delivered. So in 2006 White Doves Women Ministry was born, which is now known as White Doves Outreach Women's Ministry.

When 70 Percent Won't Do

There is nothing like a strong woman. Today I can be the wife and mother God would have me to be because I was raised by a GOD fearing woman that knew how to take a stand. I'm glad that I also have a strong relationship with my daughter. We can talk about anything like I did as a child with my mom, who gave me true love.

I strive for perfection every day for God, not man; I recall my grandmother saying, *"Seventy you can't make it, eighty God won't take it, ninety that's close, ninety-nine in a half is almost, but you got to make a hundred. God wants a hundred percent from us spiritually and whatever we set to do in life!"*

I thank God for removing the junk from within and filling me because the greatest feeling of God's love is to humble oneself and serve others. So I have no doubt that if God told me to *do it* then I know he will see me through it.

I strive for perfection every day for God, not man. I recall my grandmother saying, "Seventy you can't make it, eighty God won't take it, ninety that's close, ninety-nine in a half is almost, but you got to make a hundred.

Although I will be with my mother in heaven one day, at this time I have work to do on earth. My father would often tell me, *"As long as you're here on this earth Lillie Adams will live."* And she does! My mother has inspired me more than life itself. I'm proud to be a black, bold, brave, and beautiful woman of God! And I know my mother is all around me in spirit, helping me to go on in life because she's *my guardian angel.*

She
by Noah Hayes

*A gift opens doors for the one who gives it and brings him into the
presence of great people. Proverbs 18:16*

She taught me how to love The Lord
She is the igniter that sparked my creative inferno
Soul of Nat Turner that liberated possibility by any means
necessary
She is the beginning that showed me how to exist with no end
She said be...
She lives vicariously through me
She is hope
She is light
She is she because he said "Let there be..."
She moves forward in the manner of Sankofa
Hope... Faith... and Love
The greatest of these is She
Given name is happy, lucky
I'm fortunate because She is
Mom

*Author's mother and inspiration,
Felecia*

The early years, author with his mother

My Bold, Black and Beautiful Mothers!

by Michael Cleveland

I can look back now and see how truly God has blessed me because my mothers are BOLD, BLACK, and BEAUTIFUL! But I don't have just a mother. I have a momma, a ma and a mother and other mothers. And each has molded my heart.

Steps Don't Exist When Love Is Enough

My BOLD, BLACK and BEAUTIFUL mother or some would say, step-mother, Meddy is my dad's wife and much more. However, I don't like the term "step" anything, including brother, sister or whatever. Although she didn't birth me, Meddy was at the birth of each of my daughters.

But she wasn't just there; she took an active role in each of their births. I appreciate what she did, but what I really love about Meddy is her straight forwardness. She always tells it as it is. If I wanted the truth about anything I could go to Meddy. I have become a part of her large, extended family.

Being that I left most of my family down south when we moved to Cali from Mobile, Alabama, my new extended family filled a lonely void, especially my cousin Lil Rob, Meddy's nephew. Even though I wasn't that much younger than Meddy, she exhibited the wisdom, love, and kindness of a much older woman. So thank you, Meddy for being my mother and showing care and concern for me and my girls. I also thank you for my twin siblings Rashad and Kenisha and brother, Micky.

In retrospect, Ma could have had an abortion or given me up for adoption. I know she was ridiculed for being such a young mother back then.

When Your Mother is a Child — The Value of Perspective

The BOLD, BLACK, and BEAUTIFUL woman that gave birth to me is Ma. I lived with her when I was very young in the front bedroom of her Aunt Woneda's house. I remember getting up at night and going to the bathroom in the bedpan instead of walking to the outhouse.

I did not see Ma from the age of 8 until 19. I got one letter from her and talked to her on the phone once. I used to wonder why I didn't live with her like my siblings Patrice, Jonathan, Tyrone, Joe, and Jason did. This bothered me when I was a child. I wasn't thinking about my mother being a child herself when she had me. I didn't have all the facts, but that was common within black families.

Sometimes everything didn't come out until you were an adult, and at times, not always then. I asked my mother, *"Why didn't you raise me? Why didn't I see you? Why didn't you come to visit me or send for me during those years?"*

Unsatisfied with Ma's answers, I replied, *"There's no way I wouldn't fight to play an active role in the lives of my children and they would know that!"* but I don't mean to speak negatively about her.

When I was about to get married it was Ma and my father, who came to the rescue and gave me the money for the wedding to move forward. In retrospect, Ma could have had an abortion or given me up for adoption. I know she was ridiculed for being such a young mother back then. Ma has shown me how to not only be a survivor, but a victor through the process. From her I have learned some people aren't initiators but that doesn't mean they don't love you. *Ma, I know you love me, and I love you too!*

I'll Always Love My Mama

My BOLD, BLACK, and BEAUTIFUL Momma was there for every significant moment in my life. When I lost her, and Momma went on to glory, I was happy for her. But man was I hurting inside. As a minister I have dealt with death in comforting others many times. I know that earthly death is not the end. I knew I would see her again. So I put on a good face. Thought I was fine. I really was too.

Then one day almost a year after Momma's passing I was in the car on my way home from work. The song *I'll Always Love My Mama* by the Intruders came on the radio. I lost it. Had to pull off the highway. Could barely see because of the big crocodile tears running down my face. Daisy Lee Cleveland was the best cook, seamstress, comforter and supporter that God could have blessed me with.

Momma, thank you for loving me so much I forgot all about the hurt and abandonment I felt as a child without my birth mother.

Momma made me want to be the best football player I could be. One day I was at home, when she and daddy came in from a booster club meeting at the school. When Momma came in she was crying. I asked daddy, *"What's wrong?"*

He said, *"She is proud of you. At the booster club meeting, Coach Sullivan said some things about you that made both of us very proud to have you as our son. That's why she is crying. She is proud of you."*

That was it. After that it didn't matter what it took, I was going to be the best football player to come out of Highlands High School. I may not have succeeded in achieving that goal but it wasn't because I didn't try. I think that was the beginning of me becoming a minister.

You see the word minister means servant. Because of Momma I realized my mission in life was to be a servant leader. That's the passion God gave me, a passion to serve others. I started with Momma, Daddy, my brothers, sisters, then later my wife and daughters, before extending out to all God's children.

Jesus said, *"For even the Son of Man did not come to be served, but to serve, and give His life a ransom for many."* —Mark 10:45.

Thank you Momma for giving me the love that opened my eyes to God's mission for my life of SERVITUDE! True servitude is like true love, UNCONDITIONAL. I learned that from the love of Daisy Lee Cleveland, my MOMMA!

By the way Momma was technically my grandmother, my dad's *Ma'dear. Most of my friends did not know this until years after we were grown because the love Momma exhibited to me was not the love of a grandmother but the love between a mother and son no less! Because Momma embraced me as her son my Aunt Vera and Uncles James and David have accepted me as their brother, which I am.

As I said in the beginning, Daisy Lee Cleveland was there for many of those significant moments in my life like the time when my friend, Steve Hawthrone and I got kicked out of school in Junior High for fighting with the opposing basketball team after our school beat them. We went undefeated that year.

The next day, our mothers took us up to the school, faced down the vice principal and got us back in school. They were no joke! *Momma, thank you for loving me so much. I forgot all about the hurt and abandonment I felt as a child without my birth mother. Daisy Lee Cleveland is a real mother for ya!*

Sometimes It Takes a Village of Women to Raise a Man

These women were part of my village and in some way partook in me being the man I am.

There have been other BOLD, BLACK and BEAUTIFUL women in my life that have played integral roles who are primarily mothers of my friends. Women like Mrs. Turner, Gary's mom. *Man, Mrs. Turner could cook!*

There was also Mrs. Anderson, Glen & Tyrone's mom who was very protective of her family. And Mrs. Hawthrone, Mrs. Murphey, Mrs. Rogers, Mrs. Pickett, Mrs. Estrada, and Glen's mom whose last name I never knew. So to me she was known as just Mom.

Eve Young and Georgia Stevenson, my mother-in-law, also were there and welcomed me and my daughter, Lovette, into her family and made us feel like we belonged. Ms. Sewell trusted me not only with her daughter, but with her car, which was big to me back then. These women were part of my village and in some way partook in me being the man I am. I love and appreciate them all.

P.S. One benefit of all these mothers playing such an integral part of my life is they have been instrumental in forming the father that I am. I have three daughters by blood, two by marriage, and one by relationship. All six are my daughters. That's it. No step, just daughters. Then I have many more daughters, who are friends of my daughters, just as I was son to my friends' mothers.

I was a single father for many years. Loved it! Never felt the need to have a son like some of my friends. And I think I did a good job because of the relationships and learning provided to me by all of my mothers. *Told you I have been blessed!* One last thing about being blessed; when you truly are others close to you can't help but to be blessed with you!

Author's Family

Grandma Mable and Me: A Love Story

by Francene G. Weatherspoon

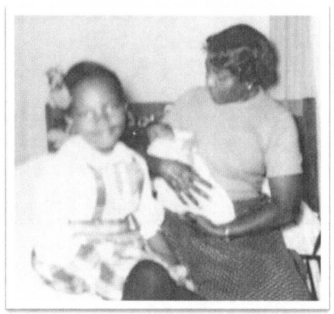

Author, far left with Grandmother Mable, and baby sister

Sweet Perfection

She (my Grandma Mable) has left me a lasting legacy of love and acceptance and exemplified what a grandmother should be.

Have you ever known anyone who was absolutely perfect? I have. That person was none other than my dear Grandma Mable. Born on June 29, 1911, Mable Hayes Jones could do no wrong. She could cook, clean, shell peas, hang wash, help me with my homework, sing, entertain, garden, and boy could she pitch a wicked fast ball!

In the early 1950s, when my father was deployed in Korea during the war, Grandma, my mom and I lived in a small duplex commonly known as a "shot-gun house" on Mercer Avenue in Albany, Georgia. A shotgun house had a straight path from the front door to the back door. In other words if you shot a gun through the front door, the bullet would travel straight out the back door. Nevertheless, we had nice furnishings, and a nice kitchen, with indoor plumbing! *Aaaah, such memories!*

Grandma's home was very neat and well-organized. When the savory aroma of stews, fried chicken, collard greens, yeast rolls, or lemon pound cake wasn't wafting through the house; the smell of lemon pledge was present. Covered by crisp white doilies (courtesy of my mom's crocheting skills), the tables and piano were polished to a high gloss.

As a "day worker," Grandma made a living working for "white" families for decades...

Grandma had a round metal music box on her bedroom dresser that was a light blue color with a tiny ballerina inside. If I stood on my tippy toes I could reach it. By simply removing the lid and turning the knob underneath, the little ballerina would dance, round and round to "The Anniversary Waltz." I could watch that ballerina and listen to that music for hours on end.

Summer days and nights in Albany were sweltering. Those were the days before ceiling and boxed window fans, and air conditioners when the weather was unbearable. Grandma and I would go out on the front porch with a bowl of peas and shell them. I think that it was barely sunup as we sat together on the (metal) porch swing in the cool morning air.

The breeze was refreshing as we dutifully pulled one string of beans after another. We weren't the only ones up at that early hour, however. Our neighbors were sitting on their respective porches doing the very same thing. I remember it as if it were yesterday the gentle exchange of pleasantries across the way.

"Hey Mae. How are you and Francene doing?"

With a Song in Her Heart

As a "day worker," Grandma made a living working for "white" families for decades. Her uniform from head to toe was completely clean and white, including her apron, dress and orthopedic nurse's shoes. She cooked, ironed, cleaned and took care of her employer's children. Of course when she came home at the end of a very long day, she had to perform those very same tasks at her own home.

Even though Grandma worked hard, she always had a song in her heart. Her voice was a beautiful melodious high soprano that I loved to hear. I remember her singing songs like: *Without a Song*, which was recorded by gospel artist, Mahalia Jackson. So touching…it still brings tears to my eyes when I hear it. Since Grandma sang in the church choir, naturally we had to attend choir rehearsal (along with Bible study, Sunday school, mission meetings and church services) once a week. I enjoyed going.

In those days we didn't own a car and there were no paved sidewalks or grass on our side of town. So we walked to the grocery store, church, and the doctor's office, as well as to visit neighbors on the dirt roads that dotted our community. By the time we arrived at our destination our shoes were pretty dusty.

My Grandma the Nurturer and Straight Shooter

I don't recall going to the doctor's office very often. On those occasions when I didn't feel well Grandma would give me aspirin or a seltzer drink. It seemed to cure whatever it was that was ailing me! She was also "young at heart." On occasion, the two of us would play hide and seek. Grandma was a good "hider." I will never forget that there was a small area behind the refrigerator that was not flush against the wall. When I came into the kitchen to "find" her she would jump out of that space and scare the living daylights out of me!

Grandma always kept a pistol in the night-stand beside the bed. I remember that it was short and had a white pearl handle.

Before turning in for bed, I had to get my bath and my grandma always saw to it that I had strawberry bath salts which came in a little red and white paper pouch with pictures of strawberries on the package.

If you really sniffed them you could tell that they smelled sort-of-like strawberries. I would get lathered, lotioned and powdered in scents of lavender. Despite taking my bath, the humidity of the hot night air made my skin sticky. Even clothes were unbearable. So it was hard to put on my pajamas!

In order to keep me from having to go far to the bathroom during the night; my grandma provided me with a chamber pot (it was really a red bucket). Now mind you, the toilet was less than 50 feet from the bed but my grandma was looking out for me.

During the hot summer days Grandma would make a pallet of homemade quilts and pillows for us in front of the back screen door where we hoped to catch a breeze while napping. At night we shared her bed which seemed huge. When she got in she warmed up the entire bed. Years later, I would take notice that the bed really wasn't that large. It was only a double bed, but to a little girl, it was huge!

Grandma always kept a pistol in the night-stand beside the bed. I remember that it was short and had a white pearl handle. She only had to tell me once not to touch it. Needless to say, I did open the drawer on occasion, but only looked at it.

In regard to Grandma's gardening skill, she had an amazing "green thumb." She was known to have plenty of flowers and vegetables in her garden and took pride in tending it and sharing it with our friends and neighbors. Sometimes the neighborhood kids' ball would fly over her white picket fence, landing in her beloved garden. Grandma was kind enough to toss the ball back a few times; what an arm! However, when the ball came back in the garden a third time; she kept it.

My Grandma Mable has gone on to be with our LORD and I know that someday I will join her in a sweet reunion. She has left me a lasting legacy of love and acceptance and exemplified what a grandmother should be. Now that I'm a grandma I only hope and pray that I will be the grandma (to my grandsons) that my grandma was to me.

Picture of author that beloved
Grandmother kept on her nightstand

Incredible Spirit, Incredible Mother!

by
Terry Moore

Winning Isn't Everything

My mother raised four successful children and is simply an incredible woman because of her spirit, and how she cares for the well-being of others. While some mothers might drive their children to get theirs in life, my mother taught me to give to others, be considerate, humble and aware of consuming more than my share of blessings.

A prime example of how my mother held true to her teachings is when she noticed I had won a few 'Best Poet" awards in a row and encouraged me to step away and remove myself from the category so that somebody else could have a chance to win. I thought that was incredible! She told me, *"You have nothing to prove. You're already a winner with me and I would love you the same either way."*

While some mothers might drive their children to get theirs in life, my mother taught me to give to others, be considerate, humble and aware of consuming more than my share of blessings.

I appreciated that. Even though I'm 47, my mother is still teaching me a thing or two about life. I took her advice and asked the community not to vote for me. In fact, I was not even nominated.

My mother and I went to the awards show, as I was to receive an Image Award which is greater than a "Best Poet" award and watched a gentleman win the award that I had garnered consistently for the past 12 years. He was so excited and my mom's face beamed with happiness for him. It was a beautiful moment for her and for me as well. It's something I will always remember about her.

Yes, it was a little challenging to watch my award being handed to someone else at first, but I envisioned the new recipient of the award and his family celebrating at home after the ceremony and it made me feel so good inside. I remember the first time I won that award and how good it felt. And it was my mom who helped me to appreciate someone else receiving a blessing.

In return for my obedience, God gave me a greater Image award. But at the end of the event, I looked into my mom's eyes and at her smile. It was then that I realized that there is not an award on earth that matches the value of her presence in my life. I am truly humbled and I am truly content.

Author's mother and inspiration

The Book of Ruth

by

Joslyn Gaines Vanderpool

My Mom overheard me smugly telling a friend that I knew her like a book when I was a teenager. *"Oh you do, now?"* my mother said, with her hands on her hips, looking a bit perturbed. Yes, I did know she was strong, smart and beautiful, and from then on learned that she could not be so easily rolled over as I had assumed.

She was named after Ruth in the Bible, but because of my mother's unique take on life, and how she speaks her mind, in often humorous ways, I tease her about never having heard some of her viewpoints in the Bible, although she has always been a woman of immense faith. In those instances I tell her that she must be quoting from The Book of Ruth, which is her own book of philosophies.

Author, bonding with her Mother (1959)

Funny, Fearless and Faithful

"Child, where did you come from?" my mother asked, as if she had no clue. I lay part of who I am on my mother for teaching my sister and me to be independent. I took it a bit further and was a non-conformist, happiest when following my own unique path, which didn't always mesh with my mother's desires for me.

My mother who was born July 17, 1928, is smart, sassy, and progressive and disdains cruelty, gossip and bigotry. Her heart is large enough to include people from every stratum of life. Ruth Jones Gaines, is love, and deeply loved. Giving selflessly without expectation, Mom often left gifts on the edge of our beds for us for no particular occasion when we were children. She prays for, and gives cards, money, words of wisdom and hope to our friends in need and has scores of admirers.

She calls me her brown-eyed girl, and tells me how proud she is of my sister and me for the women we are. She listens attentively to every story I write, and has encouraged me to *"Go for it!"* And she has grown to believe that an individual's dreams should not be compromised.

With no appreciation for idleness, Mom was forever sweeping and cleaning. When busy she impatiently pushed us aside, and said, "Move out of my way child! I've got work to do!"

I admire my mother's fearlessness. In 1996, when she was 68, she discovered a cancerous lump that an earlier Mammogram failed to detect. Our family was already immersed with sorrows (I lost my firstborn that year and my father began his descent into dementia). It was a frightening diagnosis, but not for *"Ruthie J."* which my late father affectionately called her. She merely referred to it as a condition and that was enough to keep us from worrying.

Masterful at putting aside pain, my mother relied on an unyielding faith in God, which is the most tremendous gift she has imparted. When her stunning silver hair fell out during her chemotherapy sessions, Mom simply put on a lovely African inspired hat and went on about her business, taking her prescribed treatments and caring for our father. To date, she has been cancer-free for nearly 20 years!

Without trying my mother is very funny. When I took her to see the film *Ghandi*, Mom was so busy eating her popcorn that she missed part of the movie. *"What happened to his wife?"* she asked after there were but a few kernels left in her popcorn box. *"She died thirty moments ago,"* I whispered.

When I complained about having leftovers again, my mother, would sharply reply, *"Well this is not a cafeteria!"* With no appreciation for idleness, Mom was forever sweeping and cleaning. When busy she impatiently pushed us aside, and said, *"Move out of my way child! I've got work to do!"* Then she'd realize she was being rude, and self-corrected. *"I mean excuse me. Now move!"*

Until recently, Mom kept herself entertained by reading the Bible, watching the Waltons, Bonanza and Gunsmoke and doing crossword puzzles. Before she was slowed by arthritis, she knitted amazing quilts and played the piano. I've never known her to complain about being lonely or bored. Even now at 87, she loves to go!

Also without a doubt, she's the strongest person I've known. For the past 13 years, she's lived alone after my father died, in their large dream home she and my father purchased after years of living in military housing. Being the last survivor of her core of friends that she had known since the 1930s, she visited the cemetery, left flowers and swept their gravesites, all the while calling those who died and left her, *party-poopers!* In later years, her home was frequented by new generations of friends who adored Mama Ruth because that's how they thought of her, as a mother figure.

A Woman Ahead of Her Time

In the '50s and '60s, some women stayed home and managed the household while their husbands went to work to provide for the family. My mother did most of those things too, but she insisted on working full-time because she wanted to use her abilities and knowledge and give us a better future. Yes, she also maintained a beautiful home, and served delicious meals on our finest china on Sundays. And our house was filled with music from the hi-fi (that's a stereo for those born after the seventies) or classical piano music.

My mom and dad set a high bar, so my sister and I knew that we were expected to excel in school and in the world, without my mother having to say too much to us. She was our example of success, living what she wanted us to learn.

In 1949, at the age of 21, Mom bought a plot of land, and she purchased a home for her mother years later. When we purchased our home, my mother gave us an unsolicited sizeable down payment that we are forever grateful for. My mother, whose father was killed when she was young, lived with her grandmother, Frances, and her mother Mable, amazing women who worked to assure my mother's future on domestic workers' salaries.

Mom pitched in by working as a dental and nursing assistant and by picking peanuts under the hot, unforgiving Georgia sun as a child. She still bears a faint scar on her soft brown face from falling off the work truck. In 1950 Mom graduated from Albany State with a degree in Education. That same year she married my father, Morris Lee Gaines.

My parents' relationship was full of humorous banter, and quiet sessions of reminiscing about the past and sharing their faith. My mother did what she wanted, and my father accepted it, but made comments ever so often, particularly when Mom shopped. As if defeated, he would say in a sorrowful voice, *"She's got those credit cards again."*

When she promised that she was just going to the Mall to pay a bill, I went with her to keep her on track, but she broke free and went through racks of clothes store-after-store. My attempts to stop her were futile. My father shook his head and sighed, *"She can't help herself. Just let her go."*

She showed me that being an African American is a beautiful thing, when I had heard nothing but negativity about it, and that being a woman mattered...

In regard to men, my mother had no father, but she married a good man. She always dispensed wise but funny theories concerning the male gender. One of my friends decided to find a male companion through an online website, and my mother bluntly stated, *"Tell your friend, not to get a man through the mail!"* I once joked that I wanted a Sugar Daddy to which my mother said, *"You don't need a Sugar Daddy, get you some Sugar Money!"*

Her responses were all about independence and not settling. My mother definitely has lived her life her way. If she is so moved, she will act on what she feels. One Sunday she stood up in a predominately white church and began singing by herself. Now that would be cool in a black church, but not so much in that church, because I was a pre-teen, and some of my friends where

Author, on far right, with sister, center, and mother, on the left

in the congregation. The next day at school one of my classmates asked me, *"Hey, did you see that lady who stood up in church? Do you know her?"* Embarrassed, I replied, *"I've never seen her in my life."*

Now, I am grateful for my mother's ability to stand up for what she believes, and for her powerful perspectives. She showed me that being an African American is a beautiful thing when I had heard nothing but negativity about it; and that being a woman mattered, and living fully and using my God given gifts, including my mind and my heart are critical, particularly if they are utilized to do good deeds.

A History Lesson in Living Color: Keeping It Real

Knowing and connecting to our history was important to my Mom. We spent several summers in Georgia to see where my parents grew up. When Mom spoke of her past, it was like a documentary I'd seen on film reels. A storyteller, Mom's recollections are the fuel that ignited my interest in writing, history, digging into the past, and desiring a chance to slip into yesteryear.

While living in the south during the Great Depression and World War II, my mother's community experienced night marauders who terrified black neighborhoods with lit crosses and hateful rhetoric. Mom was poor in regard to means, but rich in love and belief in God's provisions. She resided in an immaculate tiny two room house with no indoor plumbing. She experienced meatless Tuesdays, which seemed to be nearly every day.

During Christmas, people splurged by baking delicious homemade cakes to give as presents. Children received oranges, nuts and chocolate coins. My mom owned one doll made out of a soup can and socks. Life was simple in concept, but hard in regard to survival, but they made the most of it by pulling together.

Once, Mom asked how I was doing, and I said I was trying to hang on. "Then take hold!" she boldly proclaimed.

For my mom, days were spent walking arm-in-arm down the dusty roads with her friends, singing songs by Sinatra, Nat King Cole and Glen Miller. I still hear my Mom's perfect phrasing of *"Did you see Jackie Robinson hit that ball!"*

She listened with neighbors to a floor to ceiling radio, and cheered exuberantly when the *Brown Bomber*, aka, Joe Louis, knocked out Max Schmeling, which signaled a sense of racial pride, and symbolically represented a victory for democracy over fascism, as Schelming was German and Adolph Hitler had boasted of Aryan supremacy.

My mother proudly spoke of her classmate, Alice Coachman, who was the first black woman to win an Olympic gold medal in track and field in the 1948 London Games. Although Alice wasn't allowed to use the track at the local college, due to segregation, she won anyway!

In the war years, she remembers black-outs in preparation for potential air raids, and the speeches of President Franklin D. Roosevelt who was a champion of many black Americans and others. Mom even worked at the military base cafeteria where German prisoners of war received better treatment than black folks in general, according to Mom.

Mom revealed how black people were denied the right to vote if they didn't know the Constitution, and sometimes even when they did. So her college Civics professor took the entire class to the courthouse to vote in the 1948 elections after she had prepped them on all nuisances of the doctrine.

When Dr. Martin Luther King, Jr. came to my parents' hometown of Albany, the place where Freedom Songs originated during the Civil Rights movement, we were living miles away in Japan. However, once stateside, I was introduced to racism. Barely four, I recounted the spit running down my face, when three boys expressed their anger by spitting on me and calling me *"nigger!"* — a word I had never heard until then.

My mother was my comfort who bought dolls that looked like us to build our confidence, dressed us like princesses, and searched valiantly for books about our heritage. Then most critically, continued to provide examples of valor regarding our people, to counter the sting of racism that always managed to filter through, but could not suppress our dreams.

Throughout my mother's formative years, she had dedicated teachers and elders who built the esteem of black children, who were admonished to hold their heads up high. Thus my parents didn't tolerate mediocrity, but spoke with positivity, and used wisdom when they spoke to us. Our voices were important, as were our thoughts. Nothing could deter us from our promise because my parents let us know that we were somebody in a world that was clearly not in our favor.

Mama, Me and Flip Wilson: A Life of Endangerment, Entanglement and Excitement

Recently I lamented to my mother, that she and Dad had embarrassed me sometimes. Without hesitation she said, *"Did it ever occur to you that you embarrassed us?* Then I remembered those gigantic lopsided afro puffs I used to wear in the early '70s, and the psychedelic mini-skirt ensembles, as well as laughing too loud in public and forgetting the notes at a music recital.

Smart aleck kids were no match for Mom; even though I was willing to challenge her. We went to church every Sunday, much to my disdain, shopped almost every Saturday, which I disliked and I took piano lessons, which I hated! Still my mother tried to define a path that I refused to follow. *"Get a good government job!"* she'd say. *Nope.* I didn't want to. How I dressed and who I dated were all matters scrutinized by my mother, who has finally learned (I think) to keep her opinions to herself.

Dissension between us has turned to respect, but it wasn't always that way. I was always pretending to run away because I wanted to hear my mom admit she had wronged me. So I hid in the closet and waited for her to come looking for me, imagining that she would discover me missing and launch into a panic attack replete with tears. However, that scenario never came to fruition.

"Come out, Joslyn. You have chores to do!" Damn, what was wrong *with that woman?* Not to be deterred I simply played dead. Sure that this would be a great scheme to get my mother to repent. I envisioned her dropping to her knees near my lifeless body and apologizing for being too hard on me. I continued to wait with one eye slightly open, so I could see her approaching. *Here she comes. And there she goes.* The woman stepped right over me and sat down to watch television. *All of that work for nothing!*

After the Revival, my sister, who had just attained her Learner's Permit, was at the wheel, with my Dad beside her, and my mom and I were in the backseat.

There would be many more occurrences when I tried my mother's patience. I recall giving my sister's favorite doll a Mohawk haircut, which led to a couple of spankings in a 20-minute span; the first one was for the initial act, the second for hitting my sister for telling on me.

Then I got in so much trouble that my mother removed all my dolls. Lonely without them, I went to the kitchen and got a near empty bottle of dishwashing liquid and took it to bed with me for comfort. After seeing me clinging to that bottle, Mom wiped the spilled liquid from my neck and returned all my dolls.

Then there was the evening that I went to choir practice with a hanger still in my coat because my mother forced it on me when I refused to put it on myself. I was clutching the window sill, yelling, *"I don't want to go!"* as my sister watched the spectacle unable to contain her laughter.

Yet that paled in comparison to what happened in 1971 on a Thursday night when I was 12, and my mother stood between me and the Flip Wilson show. Back in the day everyone liked Flip! So I was shocked when Mom told me that we were going to a church Revival. *She'd lost her mind! This could not be happening!*

"But Mama, Flip Wilson comes on tonight." Despite my pleas, my mother was unmoved. After Revival, my sister who had just attained her Learner's Permit was at the wheel with my Dad beside her and my mom and I were in the backseat.

Still reeling, I turned to my mother and said, *"We missed Flip Wilson for that?"* Oh, you better believe there was a volcano that erupted and her name was Ruth! She swung at me, as my sister ducked. *"Just drive, Fran,"* Dad implored. Still annoyed, I raised the stakes. *"Well, we still missed Flip Wilson."* And another fisticuff ensued, but mercifully I'm ALIVE to tell about it!

Despite all of our disagreements and lively entanglements, my mother has learned to couch her words a bit. While visiting me in my apartment in Washington D.C., she sat on one of my little chairs and asked, *"Do you like your furniture?"" Yes,"* I replied. *"You do???"* my mother asked incredulously.

On another occasion, my Mom attempted to be tactful by saying, *"Perhaps we can go and get our split ends trimmed,"* which really was hilarious because she clearly meant that I should get my split ends trimmed. We've had our fair share of hair fights. I had a massive head of thick, coarse hair, and my mother was bound to tame it no matter how much it hurt me.

So I often feigned sleep. Thank God I had an ally in my father. *"Let her sleep, Ruth."* And he'd cart me off to bed. Once he left the room I pulled the sheets over my head and giggled because I escaped from another tortuous hair session with Mama.

There is extraordinary love between my Mom and I, a bond beginning from birth. My mom and I can talk about anything and she always listens with compassion, and interest. What she has taught me will last a lifetime and she has given me wings to fly.

Most recently, Mom begrudgingly conceded that it was time to come to California to reside after a nearly 40 year absence, so she could be with her immediate family. She loves her independence and dreaded having caregivers, who she called, at least to us, *"babysitters,"* in her home. She is with us now; and we are so BLESSED that she is here to enjoy her two great grandsons, and for all of us to enjoy her. Life couldn't be sweeter than it is with Ruthie J., my mentor, mother, spiritual guide and forever friend!

Ms. Ruth, at the funeral of her beloved husband

Ms. Ruthie J.

*Author's mother receiving a
performance award*

Section Six

Mamma to the Rescue

The Personification of a Mother's Love
by Jacqueline Webb

*Author on left,
with granddaughter*

My Mother, Nora Lee McGee is BOLD, BLACK and BEAUTIFUL! From my earliest memory of her, she personified those three powerful adjectives. We grew up hearing her say, *"Don't mess with my man or my kids; and we can get along just fine."*

Because I was born with some health issues, my mother would go easy on me when my siblings were getting in trouble. In our home, my father was the provider, the prankster and the preacher. And Momma was always stern, strong and sympathetic. Since we have a rather large family, (we had ten biological children and three additional children my parents loved, raised and cared for to this day), everyone has their favorite Momma story to share when we get together.

With my mother jumping in the driver's seat, my Dad in the passenger seat, and I in the back, my mother drove as if she was on the racetrack of the Indy 500. My father asked, "What's going on?"

My favorite story of my mother was when I was in the sixth grade and the principal at my elementary school was coming into the hallway as I was exiting. He asked if that was my class as he pointed to the classroom which was in fact mine. I answered, "Yep." He asked what I just said, and I answered, "Yep," for a second time.

Before I knew what happened, that grown man grabbed me and told me that I deserved to be paddled. I was in the hallway on the ground getting spanked by this grown man. After he finished, he stood me up, marched me into his office, locked the door and left. I didn't cry but I was mad, scared and amazed about what had just happened.

At 3:30 pm, the bell rang, and I kept waiting for the door to open. When it finally did, the principal walked in and told me that I was lucky that he was a nice man, because he wasn't going to tell my parents how disrespectful I had been. I walked home and kept playing the scene over and over in my head.

Now, my parents had taught me that I should respect my elders. And at home we had to answer with *Yes Ma'am* or *Yes Sir* and I was disrespectful to that grown man. I thought maybe I shouldn't say anything to my parents.

My Mother to the Rescue

When I got home, the world seemed to be moving in slow-motion. My father wasn't home from work yet, and my siblings were there, but I could not really focus. I was scared of what was going to happen to me. My mother asked, *"What happened at school today?"*

"Nothing," I responded.

"I got a call from someone at the school. What happened today?" she repeated.

Then it all came out. I told my mother everything, not leaving anything out. I heard the van pull into the driveway and stop. As my father was walking into the house, my mother grabbed my hand and the keys from my dad in one swift movement. My father turned and followed us. With my mother jumping in the driver's seat, my dad in the passenger seat, and I in the back, my mother drove as if she was on the racetrack of the Indy 500.

I know that I am the kind of mother that I am today because I was blessed to have this BOLD, BLACK, BEAUTIFUL woman as my mother.

My father asked, "What's going on?" And my mother, the little soft spoken, genteel lady that made our house a home, told my father in a soft voice, "That man hit my baby." I remember roaring into the school parking lot.

My parents jumped out of the van and rushed into the school. Still lost in slow-motion, I lagged behind. When I got into the office, my mother was telling the secretary that the principal better be in his office in the morning, or she would be back with the Black Panthers.

Making a long story short, Nora McGee lived up to her mantra of "No one messing with her kids." By the end of the week, my principal was no longer the principal of that school. He was out.

I know that I am the kind of mother that I am today because I was blessed to have this BOLD, BLACK, BEAUTIFUL woman as my mother. Thank you, God, for giving me to her and her to me! I love her dearly.

Author on right, with mother

Author's mother, second from left, first row.
Author far right, wearing head band

Virtuous Momma

by Vanessa Coleman

She seeks wool and willingly works with her hands...

Dearest Momma,

My entire life, you've said just *one* rose would do. This is my rose, my thank you/love letter to you:

Thank you, for always being loving and consistent in your faith, and in your walk with the Lord. You laid a foundation that consisted of loving, giving, being patient and living in peace, whether people are looking to embrace and accept those principles of humanity or not. I am able to build on that foundation with my own family.

Thank you, for never giving up on me. Your encouragement makes all the difference in the world. *It always has!*

Momma, thank you, for showing me how to love the unlovable and to give when I am running on empty, when I have nothing left to give. You were with me through so many highs and lows in my life. You were there for me, and you held my hand when I buried my son. I thought my life was over; but you weren't having it. I love you. Thank you!

When Jacqui was born in April instead of June, and I said I wanted my Mommy, you made your way to San Francisco. I love you. Thank You!

During the big earthquake on October 17, 1989, you were right there with me. I love you. Thank You! *Who knows what would have happened if you weren't there?*

For you taking me to the hospital the day Joshie was born; and for all you've done and continue to do for Bricey—I love you. Thank You!

I know we didn't always see eye-to-eye about things, and that was mostly my fault, and for that, I am truly sorry. As we age, our dynamics seem to change. I seem to do a lot of things like you with my children, because I want what's best for them.

Momma, we've shared many wonderful memories—Alberta coming home from the hospital and you letting me peep at her in the basinet, Jerome playing with matches, racing Don on crutches and getting in trouble, me, spending the night with Cheryl.

The memory that stands out the most is you waking me early Sunday mornings to press my hair with the electric hot comb. Not only will I cherish our alone time forever, but I love you and I rise and call you blessed…

Your Butterfly,
Vanessa

Author (left) and mother

Black Fictive Kinship[1]
by Tammy "Goody" Ballard

Never would I claim to know everything; however, I do believe it is my responsibility to nurture, educate, and share what I do know. Life's experiences are necessary so that we may grasp knowledge to teach others along the way. They say "it takes a village to raise a child", or that "two heads are better than one." Perhaps it took me a little longer than most to receive and fully comprehend that message. — T. Ballard

Author with grandson

A Neighborhood Away from Reality, but So Close to Heart and Home

Drastic change occurred in my life when I moved into a new community far removed from my reality, four years ago. After being laid off from a position I held for quite a few years with an income that had been steady and enough for my children and I to live comfortably, our lives were definitively altered. No longer could I afford our apartment in what was considered to be a moderately classed neighborhood. So we were forced to move into a low-income housing complex that was very different than what my children and I were used to.

My days were marked by sitting at my kitchen table staring out the window as I wrote in my journal. As a mother I was concerned about what I witnessed and was overcome with a range

---

[1] Black Fictive Kinship: The bonding of people who demonstrate concern, affection, and responsibility for one another; although they are not related biologically or through marriage.

of emotions from sadness, anger, and confusion. Guys standing around with their pants sagging, smoking marijuana, and wasting precious time was a constant and pervasive event. Overwhelmed with tears, I knew the Lord was present and would ask, *"Why did you do this to us?"* Day in and day out like clockwork, it was the same pattern from usually the same group of young men. Every now and again a new one would come along and join the pack.

After a year or so of unsuccessfully searching for employment and watching a landscape of deprivation, I decided to go back to school...

For nearly the first year of living there, I rarely spoke to anyone, choosing to remain unconscious to the issues surrounding my family and myself on a daily basis. Like most, I turned up my nose trying to convince myself that it wasn't my problem.

I constantly witnessed young children no more than three to five years old playing with no parent in sight. Often I'd watch them for hours, waiting to see if someone, anyone, perhaps a mother or father or maybe an aunt would come looking for them, which almost never happened.

Usually, it would be a sibling who came to the rescue who was not very much older than the child who was left unattended. After a year or so of unsuccessfully searching for employment and watching a landscape of deprivation, I decided to go back to school because I was tired of just sitting around as the scenery grew more depressing.

Maternal Mentality

It wasn't until I became part of the Umoja Saku Learning Community at American River College, in Sacramento, California, that I began to think differently about what I'd been witness to. Being involved with Umoja was more than learning typical subjects like math, science and college success. I learned about interdependence and how so much more can be accomplished by working together. I learned what it means to care about someone else and receive that same love in return.

The most valuable lesson is that being an African American woman during these times means that I cannot continue to ignore the events taking place around me. As a mother I am not only responsible for the children "I" gave birth to, but also for my community as a whole. Everyone has a voice. We all need encouragement and to be uplifted. My Umoja family did that for me, how dare I not do the same for another. Everyone, regardless of color just wants to be loved and know that they matter.

The Umoja experience motivated me to reevaluate my maternal mentality. After all, I am a mother raising a teenage son in this environment and doing my best to keep him on track. I can no longer ignore my surroundings.

A good mother, a responsible mother cannot simply ignore the circumstances that are devastating and destroying those around her. So I decided to face them head on. It wasn't long before I realized how much of a positive influence I'd become within the community. Not only is there respect, many also depended on me for words of advice and encouragement. It's an amazing feeling to come from being angry and somewhat frightened at not knowing what to expect, to being called "Ms. Tammy" or "Mommy Tammy" knowing that people appreciate you.

The most valuable lesson is that being an African American woman during these times means that I cannot continue to ignore the events taking place around me...

Regardless of our circumstances and surroundings, it is the responsibility of black women to take advantage of every opportunity to motivate and uplift our *brothas* and *sistas*. Often times all it takes are a few kind words of encouragement or to just let a *sista* know she's beautiful. Say a prayer with someone and let your brother know that he does matter. There are times when all that's required is to listen. Feed a child when it is clear that they are hungry. Take the initiative to change the soiled diaper of the two year old running around even though his mother doesn't seem to notice.

It may not seem so initially, but kindness does have an impact that goes a long way. Caring gestures also makes a huge difference and has a way of spreading to others. Mothers are commonly the thread that holds families together. Somehow along the way, the ties of unity began to unravel. It is of the utmost importance that we make the effort to strengthen that bond even if it means doing so one sista or brotha at a time.

The Unschooled Scholar
by Rodney Snell

We are told that in order to teach, one must hold a degree, which is untrue. I've studied under celebrated scholars at fine institutions. Yet the greatest, most practical lessons came to me just beyond my back door. — Rodney Snell

Money Management 101

Author's Aunt Sarah

My great-aunt, Sarah, slipped into death on October 13, 2008, gracefully and quietly, just as she had lived. To a passive observer, her life probably seemed simple or mundane. Her routine was certainly not that of a mover and shaker. However, those blessed to know her, even the most casual acquaintance, realized this quiet, unassuming woman was extraordinary. Her eighty-five year journey was nothing short of remarkable.

She exuded energy that pronounced her presence in a crowd and magnetism and warmth that compelled people to seek her friendship. With matchless generosity and a spirit of loving kindness, she fiercely protected her people. In moments of distress, emotional or financial, Aunt Sarah had a solution. For our entire family she was a well of inspiration, supporting endeavors, championing causes and cheering from the sidelines.

Access to education was limited not only by the inequality of racially segregated schools, but also the reality that all hands, young and old, had to work the fields...

On March 30, 1923, in Mount Vernon, Georgia, Sarah Lee Robinson entered a world plagued by poverty, oppression and racial terrorism. She was the ninth of eleven children born to sharecroppers. Any semblance of a traditional childhood ended at age four when her mother's death left older siblings to care for the younger children.

Access to education was limited not only by the inequality of racially segregated schools, but also the reality that all hands, young and old, had to work the fields, and Sarah worked hard. In stolen moments, under the tutelage of an older cousin she learned to write her name. By age 19 she was a single mother, uneducated but endowed with the desire to create a better life. Entrusting her infant son's care to her younger sister, she joined the Great Migration to accomplish goals and realize dreams.

We are told that in order to teach, one must hold a degree, which is untrue. I've studied under celebrated scholars at fine institutions. Yet the greatest, most practical lessons came to me just beyond my back door.

I clearly recall the day Aunt Sarah entered my life. I was three years old, in my grandparent's kitchen. She was 47, newly married and planning a move to the garage apartment behind our house.

"Come hug my neck," she said, smiling.

I looked to my grandmother, who nodded approval of the lady whose features she shared. She scooped me up into loving arms and for the rest of that day, I was her shadow. I toddled along as she walked her contractor through each room, pointing as he made notes. She was clearly in charge.

At the end, she reached into an envelope and gave him cash. He wrote a receipt, which she placed in the same envelope and used his pencil to mark the front. That was my first, though not last lesson in accounting.

Aunt Sarah was extremely meticulous with her finances and could account for each dollar. With a formal education she might have been one of the great financial minds of her time. She possessed an entrepreneurial spirit and an innate ability to make money grow.

"How much will I make if I put ten thousand dollars in this money market account?" she asked, holding a letter from a local bank. "Use that thing I bought you," referring to my very first calculator. In addition to four savings accounts at two banks, she kept three lines of cash: two for employment earnings and another from investments.

During quarterly bank runs to gather the accrued interest on her accounts, I learned percentages. I would also make deposits. She would call me over after having counted an amount and completing the deposit slip. Before leaving, I would check the amount. Sometimes it was off, which I attributed to errors in calculation. I soon came to see those errors as intended tests.

Indirectly, the bank runs introduced the concept of emergency management. One day I went over to find $1,500 in a neat stack with a deposit slip on top, but there was another stack of crisp bills that amounted to nearly $8,500. I asked about depositing the larger sum.

"I need to keep something in the house, just in case," she replied.

Aunt Sarah to the Rescue

I understood and appreciated Aunt Sarah's need to be prepared, especially after our three-car caravan was detained on a Georgia-bound road trip in the early 1970s. During the wee hours of the morning near South Hill, Virginia, our lead car was clocked speeding.

The other drivers noticed and pulled over just ahead. Perhaps the officer saw earning potential in three new carloads of Negroes from up north. Without cause, the other vehicles were also cited and escorted to a small municipal building deep in the country. While my grandfather attempted to reason with the magistrate, Aunt Sarah was counting out cash for the fine.

Though the bulk of Aunt Sarah's leisure time was spent at the track, contrary to what the pious and judgmental believed, Aunt Sarah did not gamble...

Most of Aunt Sarah's investment capital was acquired through a local "broker," the New Jersey Sports and Exposition Authority. Aunt Sarah loved horses and the sport of racing. We lived less than a mile from Monmouth Park Race Track. For many years she traveled and worked for Harry M. Stevens, operator of concessions at tracks along the east coast.

During that time, by observation, she learned the practice of handicapping; a method by which spectators, through the collection and analysis of data, predict and qualify the results of the race.

Though the bulk of Aunt Sarah's leisure time was spent at the track, contrary to what the pious and judgmental believed, Aunt Sarah did not gamble. Gambling has a specific economic definition, referring to wagering money or something of material value on an event of uncertain outcome. She didn't deal in uncertainties, especially where her money was concerned. Instead, before placing a wager, she crunched numbers and values to determine the outcome. Her explanation of the process when I was twelve helped me pass graduate statistics two decades later.

Even before that, the process of greasing her scalp prepared me for basic arithmetic. She taught me to work in sections, dividing hair first in half, then quarters, subsequently dividing each quarter to result in the equal application of Ultra Sheen to the whole scalp. In other words, fractions made simple.

The Proverbial Professor of Life Lessons

In addition to the Applied Sciences, she also offered Social Sciences, and Humanities. History lessons began with the period immediately prior to the United States joining World War II. Through engaging lectures she painted a vivid picture of the depression-era south, recounting the story of her migration north, first to Pittsburg and then Long Island, New York, where she roomed with, and was mentored by the Horowitz family.

"I was so country," she'd laugh, *"I'd say Mr. Fred"* and he would say, *"No, Sarah. It's Mr. Horowitz."*

Having taken lessons with Arthur Murray, (she danced rumba to the sounds of Xavier Kugat) music appreciation was lively! She introduced the vocal styling's of Nat King Cole, Sam Cooke, Dinah Washington, Clarence Carter and the Isley Brothers.

On cherished Saturdays, with records spinning late into the evening, she cultivated my sweet tooth on vanilla ice cream cones and slices of pound cake by *Sara Lee*, a company I believed she owned until I was old enough to know better.

Unbeknown to us both, Aunt Sarah offered college level instruction without benefit of a degree or letters.

At Emerson College, I began advanced coursework in Speech Communication. To my surprise, I discovered Aunt Sarah had already taught me a linguistics concept of code switching, the use of more than one language or variety in conversation. By noting the difference in how she spoke with family and addressed her employers, I learned professional speech.

She ran a writing lab, where I practiced penmanship and grammar, composing and addressing holiday greetings. She took great pride in praise from her employers on my penmanship. Eventually, she allowed others to address holiday cards, except those for her employers. Each year, regardless of my location, I sent them without fail. Sometimes, before I'd had a chance to let her know, she would find out when thanked for the lovely card.

Perhaps the greatest lessons taught were with examples of faith, benevolence, trust and unconditional love that she showed upon those closest to her. I received an extra measure. She believed I could do absolutely anything and little wrong, even when I messed up. The feeling was entirely mutual. Perhaps more than my parents, she provided a consistent source of security and comfort.

"You always have a home," she would say, and I trusted her.

Despite everything we shared, I always believed she knew more than she cared to reveal, especially after receiving my formal ed ucation.

Treasured photo of Aunt Sarah,
taken by the author

Unbeknown to us both, Aunt Sarah offered college level instruction without benefit of a degree or letters. Throughout a remarkable life, she observed, learned and shared practical knowledge gained from experience. For this, she deserves an honorary doctorate.

My Mother...My Advocate

by Joslyn Gaines Vanderpool, Francene G. Weather spoon, Ruth Gaines

If you're happy so am I.
If you're hurting, so am I.
If you need me, I'll be there.
— j gaines vanderpool

A Fierce Threesome

Author, in the arms of her advocate and mother

Since the death of my beloved father in 2002, my mother, sister and I have become a fierce threesome of faith. When I try to go it alone on occasion, my mother reminds me that, *"We may be a small family, but we are all you got!"* And that is absolutely true because my sister and mom have always been there for me.

So it began in the spring of 1996 when my first born daughter, Kiara died. The loss was one that the entire Gaines and Vanderpool families suffered. I personally was acquainted with the death of one's own child which leaves a chasm of pain often too difficult to bridge or bear. My mother also knows that pain, losing her only son a few weeks after his birth in August 1960 when we were stationed in Japan.

There were no relatives or family to help my mother through that tragedy because we were so far way, but when my child passed away, without hesitation, my sister rushed to my side where I was residing in New Mexico because my mother was taking care of my father who was very ill at the time.

When I try to go it alone on occasion, my mother reminds me that, "We may be a small family, but we are all you got!"

Despite my mother's physical absence I knew she wanted to be there for me, and she was present on a number of levels. In those dark days, it was my mother and sister offering me comfort when I thought I could handle no more grief.

Then, if things couldn't get any worse, my mother was diagnosed with breast cancer the same year the baby died. Before my knees buckled, my mom and sister were there to catch me. My mother, as a matter of fact, had so much faith that she believed her healing had already taken place. And so she prevailed and has been a nearly 20 year breast cancer survivor and is 87 now.

In 1998 when I had *"our"* Sydney (because she belongs to all of those who love her), my mom and sister were completely overjoyed. Again it was my sister who flew out with my youngest nephew to welcome the new baby. She brought the cutest music box with a little piano playing mouse happily pecking out, "Yellow Bird!" to celebrate this momentous event.

Although there were a few touch and go issues with Sydney during her first year of birth, she seemed to be a healthy, thriving baby until she was slow to speak. Crying inexplicably for hours was also a cause for concern.

When she was four or five, Sydney was diagnosed with autism. For the most part, while challenging and stressful, her case was manageable, but as puberty approached everything changed. Prayers became more intense as did attempts to find a way to give her a quality of life.

My husband and I are still seeking our own form of peace from a storm that keeps approaching in the form of a difficult to cope with disorder. I did try as much as I could do to afford to help her, but so little is known about autism, even to this day.

I also was under tremendous pressure that caused me to ignore my own health and happiness. Yet, I was not truly alone, as outlined in the abbreviated letter my sister and mom penned to First Lady Michelle Obama to save, "Our Sydney!"

*Author (left) with her advocacy team: sister, Fran
(center) and mom (far left)*

*Author, center, with mother and father to the left,
and groom and his family on right*

The Case for Saving Sydney

May 1, 2013

Mrs. Michelle Obama
The White House
1600 Pennsylvania Avenue, N.W.
Washington, DC 20500

Dear Mrs. Obama,

I am writing to you on behalf of my 14-year-old granddaughter, Sydney Vanderpool. I live in Georgia, and Sydney and her parents live in California.

Sydney has been diagnosed with autism. Although my daughter has health insurance for Sydney, it is not enough, nor does it adequately provide coverage for the many autism services and treatments Sydney requires. Sydney has been prescribed all types of medications and has even been "hospitalized" because of her recent violent behavior.

Despite this, Sydney is regressing, and no one seems to know why, and neither can anyone offer my daughter an effective and long-term solution. Medical professionals give her conflicting advice and offer her fragmented and expensive approaches for treating Sydney.

In her ongoing attempt to get help for Sydney, my daughter has paid large sums of money, out-of-pocket money that she can ill-afford to pay, as she is the only person working in her three-person household.

I am quite distressed when my 54-year-old daughter tells me of her numerous letters, visits and appointments with health care providers, medical doctors, psychologists, psychiatrists, the school district, Autism organizations, advocacy groups and even California legislators. I am grieved because my daughter has had a heart attack and subsequent surgery.

I am sure that it occurred, in part, because of her ongoing crusade and diligence in trying to get aid for Sydney. Compounding this problem is my son-in-law's illness. He has been diagnosed with Multiple Sclerosis, which has caused him medical challenges of his own. While he does what he can, the support that he is able to provide to my daughter (and to Sydney) is very limited.

God willing, I will celebrate my 85th birthday in July. I am a widow, and although I send them money from my pension check, whenever I can, it is not nearly enough to pay for the treatments and ongoing medical expenses needed for Sydney. I would rest easier, knowing that my daughter and her family get the assistance that they need.

We need help now, Mrs. Obama. I know you to be a woman of faith, compassion and a strong supporter of children. I also know that you are extremely busy and that you tirelessly promote numerous and worthy causes. However, we are at our wit's end and can see no other way to get the help we need for our Sydney.

I am hoping that your staff will give you this letter. Whatever help and/or assistance that you can grant to my struggling daughter and her family would be most appreciated.

Thank you in advance for your time, and I eagerly look forward to your response.

Sincerely,

Ruth Gaines

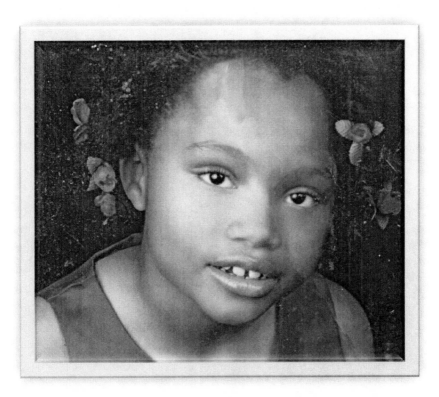

Our Sydney

Queen...Saint...Mama the Great!

By Tony Gunter Jr.

Mama Knows Everything

The question often crosses my mind, Why is my Mama so great? And I then realize it is because God made her that way.

Author, with his Queen and mother

My mother, Michelle K. Gunter, along with my father raised my younger sister and me, and I must say that they both did a wonderful job. My mother always made sure my sister and I knew God and formed a bond with Him.

A devout Christian, Mama modeled her commitment to God through prayers, words and deeds. When she prays she knows without a doubt that she is going to hear from God. So while she waits she lets her faith work and she gives God the glory. By her example of trust, she's taught me that same principle.

Born and raised in Chatham, Virginia, my mom gave her life to Christ and joined the Shockoe Missionary Baptist Church under the leadership of the Late Reverend George Pass. She is the daughter of the late Leroy Kelly and Maynell L. Kelly and is married to Tony G. Gunter Sr. Besides being employed by Pittsylvania County, my awesome mother is an entrepreneur who refers to herself as, "Queen", and owns Michelle's House of Beauty.

Mama knew everything about us. She could tell when we were sick by the way our eyes looked. She also knew when we had something up our sleeves; or when something wasn't right. My mom fervently believes and has faith. When we were living in our old home, she had a recurring dream of the Lord showing her a new house. Being a woman of curiosity, she began to pray about what it was that God was trying to tell her. Later my mom was driving through the neighborhood of my aunt Doris and there it was! The house the Lord had shown my mom or at least we thought it was.

My mother got in touch with our cousin, Alfreda Bennett who is a real estate agent and they began to work and bombard Heaven together. Well while this was going on we went and looked at the house which I didn't like for some reason. Anyway, it just so happened that someone had outbid us.

My mom still knew that God surely hadn't let her down. My cousin called my mom to inform her that the house the Lord had shown her was actually three houses down and was exactly like the other one but was in foreclosure. My mom and cousin were still praying as my parents placed their bids. God moved in such a way that we knew that the house was ours. The favor of God is real, as my mom often says.

Watching my mom work hard faithfully to the Lord showed me just how good He is—which is a lesson that I will use for all my days of living.

Radical Mom... Strident Supporter

My mama has taught me so much in life. As a child she taught my sister and I how to be kind and helpful at all times. Everything we wanted to do as far as being active in church, school, sports, hunting and fishing or whatever it was, Mama was in our corner pushing us along.

I honestly would have to say my mom is my biggest supporter! As a sixth grader I had an agriculture teacher who also helped mold me into the young man I am today. Ms. Jessica Jones encouraged me and introduced me to the Future Farmers of America club. When I told my mom that I wanted to join, she was supportive.

Every award I won and certificate I received from FFA, my mom made a binder and laminated each one!

After my FFA meetings, Mama would pick me up and ask how it was and if I liked it. She took a lot of interest in FFA through me. My mother was one of the radical moms when it came to her children achieving something! My mom would submit news articles and pictures just to say how proud she was of her children.

Every award I won and certificate I received from FFA, my mom made a binder and laminated each one! Soon after I joined FFA my mom became an active parent in the organization earning an Honorary Member award plaque, certificate, and pin. Mom you are awesome! The more and more I got involved with things so did my mom.

When I was selling fruit for FAA, my mom wanted to participate, so she got it cleared with her boss and she was working harder than I was. With my mom and dad's help, but mostly mom's, I was able to sell 90 boxes of fruit; and I was awarded the *Top Fruit Salesman from the Florida Farm Bureau.*

By the eighth grade, I took an interest in showing livestock animals. I started off with hogs, and as always, my mom was involved, taking pictures of my animals, giving them names and buying feed for them. There was also the time I had a show the week my family went on vacation and my mom told me that if I wanted to stay back and show, *"Stay,"* because it was my last heifer show. Although others didn't agree, my mom still supported me. She even left me money and fueled up both of my vehicles.

A Calling to Preach

As I became older, I started doing more in school and church. The biggest thing that my mom stood behind me on was when the Lord called me into the ministry to preach. At night I would have dreams of the Lord talking to me, and I told my mom about it. *"Keep praying and stay before the Lord,"* she would say. I then asked my mom if I could I talk to my pastor.

At that time, I felt that I really needed to tell him and my mom said, *"Pray."* So I prayed the prayer of faith that God showed her. The pastor preached and the word of the Lord came forth and it said, *"If you feel as though God is calling you come on up."*

At night, I would have dreams of the Lord talking to me, and I told my mom about it. "Keep praying and stay before the Lord," she would say.

I went to my mom after church and said, *"I have to go."*

"Then go on," she replied. So I talked to the pastor who told me the Lord had been shown him.

As I started my journey people would talk about me, and say, *"Your mom put you up to this,"* or *"God didn't call you."* Still my mom stood beside me encouraging me to run on. I thank God for my mom because nobody understands me like she does.

There will only be one Michelle Elaine Kelly Gunter! So, Mom, if you are reading this, I love you and I bless God for you, your strength, your faith, and your prayer life.

Thank you, for God's love surrounds you and touches others' hearts. You are just one amazing woman of God. You have instilled so much into my life and so many lifelong lessons I will never forget.

Because of you, I will be able to show and teach my children, just like you taught us. So for that, Mom, thank you! If I could give you the world, I would, but I know Jesus has so much more to offer. You deserve it all. Keep being the saint you are!

Lady Day

by

Naa Harper

Home is a Mother's Embrace

As a ten-year-old hearing the words, *"Good morning Lady Day,"* was music to my ears because they were spoken by my mother who had the sweetest sounding voice in the world: low and delicate. Knowing that she loved me meant everything. If you weren't listening close enough you would miss hearing it. But she also could yell and fuss when my brother and I failed to listen or do what she asked. Or she would exhibit a certain look that effectively indicated that she meant business.

One thing I can say about my mother is that she loved to show me affection. She often gave me great big hugs even when I became an adult. I can remember one time in particular when I drove home by myself from Virginia to Pennsylvania. It would be a short vacation for me— a small amount of time away from work.

As I set foot on the front porch of my parent's home I struggled to ring the doorbell. As soon as my mother opened the door I collapsed because I had been suffering from the flu and wanted to go home so badly that I drove for six straight hours at night to make it into my mother's arms. Even though I was grown it felt so good to be wrapped in her warm embrace while she kissed and welcomed me home.

When my mother met my father, she knew God had truly blessed her. He was a man who stuck with her when she was and wasn't feeling good.

There was no other place that I loved to spend time than with my mother cuddled up on her bed watching a good movie, or catching up on the latest family gossip. The most important things to my mother were family, good food, music and living life. She liked to travel but was not able to go very far except to places like Philadelphia. Although she did go on a cruise once and she loved it.

My mother was the best cook out of everyone in my family and could throw down in the kitchen! She enjoyed it because it helped her relax and took her mind off of her illness and the subsequent pain it caused. Homemade pot pies, macaroni and cheese and peach cobbler were just a few of the foods that she lovingly made from scratch.

With her favorite radio station on, playing oldies music, it always amazed me how she knew every song. She even remembered the words to songs by the Temptations, Nancy Wilson, and Angela Bofill.

Model Mother: Longing to Live Life to the Fullest

My mother, Margie E. Younger was born in 1948 in Pittsburgh, Pennsylvania. The second oldest of eleven children, she was ten when she began to get ill from a genetic disease called Sickle Cell Anemia, which can be devastating and is quite prevalent in the African American community. During the forties not much was known about the disease or its impact. So unfortunately, my mother's parents didn't believe her, and she was often punished and made to sit on the front steps of her parents' home.

Since my mother's father was an alcoholic who caused the family a lot of turmoil, she went to live with her grandparents, who were ministers in the Christian church, at the age of fifteen. Her grandfather became her father figure. Although my mother never graduated from high school, dropping out when she was fourteen because of her illness, she tried to make up for lost time by hanging out with her sister and friends when she wasn't sick.

During the forties, not much was known about the disease (Sickle Cell Anemia) or its impact.

Despite my mother always being in some sort of pain, she loved to laugh and live life to the fullest. With a natural taste for expensive things, she harbored a dream to one day become a model. Tall, skinny, and light skinned, my mother was beautiful! Then in 1989 her dream came true when she was crowned Ms. Sickle Cell Anemia which involved participation in a local parade and being a special guest on television.

Rest in Peace, Mommy

When my mother met my father, she knew God had truly blessed her. He was a man who stuck with her when she was and wasn't feeling good. He never left her but did everything he could to make her laugh and watch out for her, my brother and me when she was in the hospital for weeks at a time.

It was a normal way of life to us. I had my first door key at the age of five and I was taught at an early age how to be independent. Whenever my mother was ill my brother and I would get dropped off at Aunt Fran's house where we would stay until my mother was released from the hospital. I guess you could say they had a special bond.

The last time I was physically in the presence of my mother I watched as my father pushed her wheel chair up the cracked sidewalk in front of my childhood home. From his car all the way up the walkway I silently watched as this grown woman, my mother could no longer care for herself. The closer she got to me on that walkway the more I could see her eyes light up as she set eyes on me, her Lady Day.

My mother, who was one of a kind, spoke very few words. She made head turns because of her external beauty, but what I was amazed by is how she brought love and light to my life.

In September 2010, my mother passed away with my father at her side in a hospital room. The week before her passing I sent her a bouquet of flowers. She called me and in a raspy voice and told me how much she loved them. But deep down past those words I could hear her longing to see me one more time before she left Earth.

I told her I loved her and I would see her soon. Soon never came. The damaging effects of the disease caused her to live her final days on dialysis, enduring multiple blood transfusions; and experiencing much pain. I was told by my father that she also suffered from an early onset of dementia.

The presence of God was so strong on my mother that day I will never forget. It was in that moment that I knew He was with her. I never made it to my mother's bedside while she was dying because my own family and I were in a place of financial strain. We had just relocated from the East Coast to the West Coast and with a new baby and me not working, money was tight.

I beat myself up for years for not being able to make it there to be with her. In my mind I had let her down. Even though my mother passed away five years ago, I remember it like it was yesterday. We buried her in the same cemetery as her parents, brothers, and cousins.

There are days when I still talk with her and I know she is watching over me. My mother, who was one of a kind, spoke very few words. She made head turns because of her external beauty, but what I was amazed by is how she brought love and light to my life. With her I knew love, felt love and am loved because I know my mother is still with me in spirit. Rest in peace, Mommy...

Author (right), with her mother

The Limitless Bounds of a Mother's Love

by
Jerome Mc Gee

I never knew the pain or pleasure children bring to their parents until I became a father. I never understood how fear and faith can coexist in the heart of a believer until I had someone who called me Dad. I consider myself an intelligent person, and many say that I am wise and seek my council. I am university educated and seminary trained, but there is one thing I have concluded that I will never figure out nor do I seek to understand, and that is, a mother's love.

What I have learned from the relationship I have with the woman who gave me life (Nora Lee McGee); and the woman who made me a Dad, my wife and mother of all my children, Donna Y. McGee, is that a mother's love has no boundaries and doesn't know the words impossible or quit.

Something takes place during the 40 weeks the child grows inside the womb. It's more than a physical connection between the mother, child and umbilical cord. During prenatal development, the umbilical cord is physiologically and genetically part of the baby and normally contains two arteries (the umbilical arteries) and one vein (the umbilical vein).

The umbilical vein supplies the baby with oxygenated, nutrient-rich blood from the placenta. Conversely, the developing child's heart pumps deoxygenated, nutrient-depleted blood through the umbilical arteries back to the placenta.

I consider myself an intelligent person and many say that I am wise and seek my council. I am university educated and seminary trained, but there is one thing I have concluded that I will never figure out nor do I seek to understand, and that is a mother's love.

I believe there's a permanent connection that can't be explained or thoroughly understood. These connections neither transcend time nor does geography sever its spiritual flow. That said, it seems to me to be the only way I can begin to understand how my mother knows when I'm well or challenged. She still calls me *baby* and has never failed to express her love for me and my family.

Special Above All

After completing my third tour to the Middle East, while in the United States Air Force, it was determined that I sustained a line of duty injury that resulted in the deterioration of my joints, disc's and nerves; and damage to my muscular skeletal system.

I had always provided for my wife and children and now for the first time in 14 years I was unable to work. My wife, who at the time was in her senior year at the University of South Alabama, had no choice but to drop out of school and work two jobs. Now 2000 miles from home, she had to care for a disabled husband and our four school-aged children, one who was terminally ill.

I had always provided for my wife and children and now, for the first time in 14 years, I was unable to work.

Although Donna's life, at times has been inundated with overwhelming challenges, she still managed to finish college and become a tri-credentialed administrator in one of California's largest school districts.

Over the years, our relationship has endured; despite tests to our commitment. And my love and admiration for her has been evidenced in word and deed. I greatly respect and honor her. I believe God has brought into my life two incredibly loving women to shape me into the man I am. The two He chose for me shall always remain special, above all.

Pastor Jerome McGee

Author with mother

EBONY QUEEN

by
Frank Withrow

Whether I am right or whether I am wrong
I am an Ebony Lady and I will always be strong

You may not like me or love me in the least,
But treat me like an Ebony Lady and not your beast

An Ebony Queen is what I am
I am not a nigger or a low down woman

Everything you have and everything you do
Is because an Ebony Lady gave her contributions, too

I am amazing and will do well
Because ladies of Ebony are born to excel

I am an Ebony Lady with a strong, rich past,
A lady of Wisdom, Beauty and Class

I am Doctor, Lawyer, Educator and Mother
And truly in life, I am the Black Man's lover

My cultural awareness keeps me wise,
I can read your mind by looking in your eyes

I am a role model for the young and the old,
I have been proclaimed pure Ebony Gold

I am Outstanding, Intelligent and Very Kind
I am an Ebony Lady with a super mind

I will never give up, I will reach my dreams
And wear my crown proudly as an Ebony Queen

Section Seven

Transformation

FORTITUDE OVER FEAR:
A SURVIVOR'S TALE

Author's mother and friend

Dedicated to My Mother, My Friend
by **Marsha Washington**

The Day We Ran for Our Lives

The first day that I knew that I loved my mom and that she was my friend was the first day we struggled to survive. I was running with my brother on the left side and my mom in front of me.

At first, I didn't know why I was running so hard and so fast except I was scared and wanted to save my mom. When I looked behind me I saw my Dad, standing there, with a wooden stick, and at the end of it was a large fork, which I remember seeing at my uncle's farm. They used it to pick up piles of hay.

Totally out of breath and exhausted, I heard a voice call out with urgency from the window: "Marsha, Bruce—get in here now!"

The day we ran for our lives left me overwhelmed with emotion. "Move out of the way!" my mom screamed while pushing me to the side, as my father threatened that he would kill her. My heart started racing faster and faster before I hit the side wall of our garage and fell in slow motion.

The stick with the fork at the end of it went flying in the air. When I turned to see where it was flying toward, it was soaring in the direction of my mom, who kept running until she was thwarted by a locked gate.

My mind told me to close my eyes, as I didn't want to face what seemed inevitable. So I did and when I opened them, the gate was knocked down and my mom went through the gate with everything she had to survive. The massive pitch fork that was hurled at her landed in the middle of the white gate and fell with a thud to the ground. But the nightmare was not over, I heard my dad hollering out to us, *"Shut up. I'll kill her!"*

Totally out of breath and exhausted, I heard a voice call out with urgency from the window. "Marsha, Bruce get in here now!" With tremendous and unrelenting fear, my brother and I ran inside only to see my Dad load up his gun and shoot my mom.

At that time all I knew was that I was alive! Despite all that we went through with that experience, my Mom went on to conquer her fear. She proved that she was going to work; and she was going to assist others whether she lived or died trying.

After that awful afternoon of terror, my mother completely adopted the mantra that no human would stop her from surviving for her family. And so she lived.

Back to Basics: The Re-modification of the Family
Finding Love Where Love Is

My Mom went back to school and received her teachers' credential and taught at the Correction Youth Authorities for Boys in Stockton, California. I realized that through my mother's strength and fears, she was determined to survive for my brother and me to exist.

There is no trial or tribulation that I can't overcome due to my mother's example of bravery. I learned that I had to believe in me.

My mom let it be known that with any bad situation you can turn it around. Without the bad how would you know what is good? A frown is only a smile that is turned upside down and with any obstacles in my way, it is up to me to choose what to jump over.

> *Fear and not the one that kills our body,*
> *will destroy our soul,*
> *if it isn't extinguished.*

The path my mother blazed was not only for her, it was for my four sisters, four brothers and me to share with our children and our grandchildren. My mother and heroine, Jacie Lee Hendrix Washington, demonstrated that we must teach future generations the tools to succeed by embracing their fears and learning how to gain their own direction. Fear and not the one that kills our body, will destroy our soul, if it isn't extinguished. Dr. Derek Gier says *"No one can ride your back unless you bend over."* So I must now return the favor in memory of my Mom.

As the ninth child, I came from a family that has endured many challenges to attain success. My dad with a third grade education and his own will to survive for his family as the head of household, overcame his own challenges to become the first black bus driver for the Metro Stockton Public Transit.

My uncle became the first black police officer. My aunt became the first black surgical registered nurse. Following their lead of achievement, my goal is to operate a transitional housing facility for foster children that have been through the system only to return to the streets. In order to address that problem, I want to continue to provide a service to give emancipated foster youth the strength to survive.

I also have a desire to work with senior citizens. By assisting them, I want to honor them and learn about our ancestors and their contributions to society. This is a part of my dream to remodify our family structure. Back2Basics is the name of the foundation I continue to build. I firmly believe that it's not always the family that I'm born to that will be there. It's also the family that I meet along my way to survive that will be there to the end.

Despite that terrifying day in 1957 when we ran for our lives, our family and my parent's marriage endured until their respective deaths because Mom was a loving, and forgiving mother. We all wanted to hate dad, but because Mom always believed in God, she made us love him and not speak a harsh word against him. She always said, *"You must honor and love your parents, no matter what they did."*

Thus through Mom's faith, determination and strength, we all moved forward as she brought balance to our world. With that said, I have put aside fear because I have too much living to do, goals to reach and dreams to realize.

Author's mother

Beauty isn't a Size

Beauty is Fearfully and Wonderfully Made!

by

Denise Rochelle Allen

Author and concerned Aunt

A letter of support from an aunt to a young niece who grew tired of living after being body shamed and bullied... By the way, the niece is doing well now.

It takes a lot of courage to stand and deliver as you just did! I am proud of you! I think you are very articulate in speech! And as for all of that long pretty hair you have, it's so great, particularly when auntie is buying hers! Ha ha! It's ok because I make this look good!

Beauty my doll, has always been in the eye of the beholder! Your first beholder was God and He created his master piece and said you were fearfully and wonderfully made!

All of the women in our family are healthy honeys! A guy will just have to deal with it! Ha ha! Well that's another talk for another day! Beauty my doll, has always been in the eye of the beholder! Your first beholder was God and He created his master piece and said you were fearfully and wonderfully made! God doesn't lie! You are too young for all of this drama! Unless you're on the movie screen or on the radio getting paid for it like Auntie! My point is you have time to figure it out!

Don't let the lies and tricks of the enemy cause you to do something stupid like not believe in what God says! Don't believe the lies! It is hard to get harsh words out of your head! But not impossible! Can't nobody beat you being you!

If you don't like your look, can't nobody put the proper fruit and veggies in your mouth, but you! Your body only does what you tell it! If you tell it pizza and cake it will say yes! But if you tell it fruit and baked fish it will say yes! And you will look like the results of it if you make a lifestyle change! It's not according to others! The Bible says be it done unto you according to your faith!

And my goodness that huge mansion you live in if you walk the property line 3 times a week you will see a change! If You want to! If you are happy with you, buy the cute thick girl clothes, get your manicures and pedicures and keep it moving! Love the people who love you and bless those that curse you and pray for those that use or abuse you! God's got your back! If those people pay your bills or do some great thing for you then maybe you should listen! If not? Fill in the blanks!

Auntie love!!! Besos Mami!

'It's All Mother's Fault'
by Theresa J. Gonsalves

It's all Mother's fault that I am incapable of allowing someone to love me because she never loved me herself. When she looks at me, I am a reflection of my father. For the nine months she carried me in her womb, father was jailed for rape. She blamed me; for if not pregnant with me, she would have been able to make love to her husband. I am that constant reminder. I am the memories that brought on the beatings, the neglect and the lack of love.

While it is truly mother's fault that I have not the capacity in my heart to allow love to be a constant, it is also mother's fault that I am a strong black woman.

In surviving, I tried to give, therefore, learning how to give but not to accept. For eighteen years, I lived with this woman called my mother and endured this treatment, wondering *'why?'*, only to find the answer during one of mother's drunken rages.

In knowing me, one wonders how I am capable of loving with so much commitment, yet unable to accept love in return. While it is truly mother's fault that I have not the capacity in my heart to allow love to be a constant, it is also mother's fault that I am a strong black woman.

Author at book signing

Rue: The Story of My Beautiful Butterfly

By **Cindy Smith**

A Struggle to Soar

I've often heard different people tell the butterfly story. *A man sees a butterfly struggling to get out of its cocoon and decides to help, but discovers that only through the struggle can the butterfly truly soar. Unknowingly, in an effort to free and help the creature, he clips its wings, crippling and stopping the butterfly from gaining its vibrancy and color, and impeding it from growing properly and reaching its full maturity.*

Author's mother and beautiful butterfly

Thus begins the story of my mom, Rue, and my butterfly story. Although I wanted to protect her throughout my life, it was only after her death that I fully understood the true meaning of the butterfly story, and learned how to grieve and hold on to memories.

A man sees a butterfly struggling to get out of its cocoon and decides to help, but discovers that only through the struggle can the butterfly truly soar.

Unfortunately, there are no pleasant memories of my mother and father's married life. I remember the fights and the cold-heartedness of my dad toward her. Although a preacher's son, there was no evidence of a Godly life when I think about him. I see immaturity and domination on his part and no responsibility in leading his house.

I think about the struggle of the butterfly in the cocoon and see the struggle my mom had. One moment in time there would be fighting with the children witnessing it. With snow on the ground he pushes her out the door in her bare feet and throws a bucket of cold water on her. Not a pretty picture at such a young age for us to see. It played a part in me going into a protective mode over my mother who had nine children with my dad.

Despite back-to- back pregnancies, my father shirked his responsibilities as a husband and dad by leaving my mom a few months after giving birth to her ninth child, and moving on to start the same cycle with another woman miles away. He would never help my mom support and raise us.

So to sum up her married life, she had babies from 1950-1963, with only three years of being pregnancy-free. She never married again, but had one more child in the middle of her life out of wedlock, making me fifteen years older than my baby sister. We didn't know our father and neither did this last child. No matter what, however, I loved my mom.

More importantly, my mom raised ten children on welfare, and she ensured each finished high school. None went to jail, and some of us even went on to college.

Even though my mother faced many challenges, there was still something wonderful in her – a special skill she possessed. She could style hair very well. She cut men's hair and pressed, cut, and curled women's hair.

However, when it came to doing my hair, which I hated, I really thought my mom didn't like me because I was tender-headed with long, thick, nappy, coarse hair. When combed, it hurt! I remember being smacked more when getting my hair done than any other time in my life, but my mom would make my hair so beautiful.

Besides styling hair, my mom helped neighborhood families by cleaning and cutting up fish brought to her from the river behind our house and cooking any kind of wild game they captured, including deer, turtle, rabbit, squirrel, etc. I even saw her kill a chicken by wringing its neck on the clothesline.

She also planted gardens, did carpentry work, and painted our house. More importantly, my mom raised ten children on welfare, and ensured each finished high school. None went to jail, and some of us even went on to college.

Transformation in the Making -- A Butterfly Emerges

I loved my life with God, and shared that love of Him with my mother and children. My mother's latter days were blessed. When she was in her sixties, she gave her life to God, no longer wanting to party and hang out. My desire was for her to have holiness and not ignorance in her life; and I wanted her to have the best—Jesus.

Since I wanted to share my life with my mom, I strived to do for her what my dad didn't. There were trips to the zoo, church, her favorite flea market and eating out with her grandchildren. She continued housework on and off in her life and we found her a house in town near us that she loved. My mom observed every holiday, and each child's birthday was celebrated with a cake.

In her seventies, my mom was still beautiful, but at age 72, she was diagnosed with liver cancer. Within a few months of her diagnosis and with many hospitalizations in between, she died. During her illness I remember leaving my family to stay with my mom in the hospital. In those nine days, I read the Bible to my mother day and night at her request. We were preparing her soul to meet Jesus and grow in the Spirit. Through it all God gave us time together, which is something that money could not buy.

While growing up, we were the only blacks in our small town, but my mom was loved by many. When she died, she had befriended people like doctors, lawyers and others that she worked for, who traveled from all around to be at her funeral in North Carolina. Their presence really touched our hearts.

My mom, the butterfly, shows up at times that only God could coordinate.

At my mom's funeral, there were butterflies flying around and landing on us. Even now when one flies into my yard, we all call it "Rue." My mom, the butterfly, shows up at times that only God could coordinate. Even though there was struggle for my mom, it did not stop her from emerging from her cocoon.

Afterwards, it was ingrained in my mind to take all of the ribbons from my mom's memorial flowers and craft them into butterflies. A pastor from my church had received an e-mail telling the butterfly story and was thoughtful enough to bring it to me, not knowing I had been making butterflies for weeks and weeks after my mom's death.

Even though my mother and I did have misunderstandings sometimes in life, I always respected her. Through making butterflies my grief eventually turned to peace, quiet and solace. I now know that my beautiful butterfly is finally free! And I thank God to this day for the honor and special time I had with her. God is good!

Strong Towers[1]
by Camille Stone Younger

Dedicated to my Mother, Katie J. Stone and Grandmother Geneva W. Jefferies — My Strong Towers

As a young woman, I was an angry, volatile person, due to events in my life. When certain situations arose, I went into fits of rage, cursing, and slamming doors, but when I observed my mother and grandmother, they seemed to handle crises and frustrations differently.

Perplexed, I would often sit quietly and watch them. Nothing caused them to lose their composure. There was a tear here and there, but they displayed no emotional outbursts and exhibited no ill will toward others. I couldn't understand why they didn't react the same way I did when encountering difficult challenges.

I used to believe that if someone hurt you, you should get them back.

When I became older, God revealed to me that my mother and grandmother were strong towers and not the doormats that I had assumed they were. I would ask, *"Aren't you upset, because you say or do nothing?"*

I used to believe that if someone hurt you, you should get them back. Then God showed me that I had to become a strong tower and emulate the strength and fortitude of my foremothers. I thank God for revealing to me the error in my ways and putting two awesome women in my life as role models.

I now understand that my mother and grandmother's silence was their strength. Instead of allowing anger to prevail in their

---

[1] Taken from the *Holy Bible King James Version*, "Hebrews 4:16."

hearts they sought wise counsel and relied heavily on prayer. Mighty strong towers, beautiful, gracious, meek, loving, and longsuffering are words of admiration that define the two women whom I dedicate this story to because they truly have built the foundation on which I stand.

Author (right) with her Strong Towers, grandmother left and mother, center

"Eighty and Fourteen"[2]

by **Steven A. Royston**

My mother was strong. She had to be or she would not have been with us for 86 turbulent years. She was a force for good and a force for whatever the circumstances called for at the time. She was a beautiful, smart black woman in America at a time when strong black women were killed with impunity by their white male and female oppressors and treated as second class people by black men. And she was outspoken at a time when women, like children, were supposed to be seen and not heard. She passed away on Wednesday April 17, 2013.

Was She?

Alice Ruth Royston

So *who* was Alice Ruth Royston? Was she the chocolate brown *girl* who grew up poor in black St. Louis in the depression where life was cheap, prejudice real and black on black violence, physical and mental, everywhere?

Was she the *daughter* of a deep brown-skinned Baptist Shreveport woman and a New Orleans light skinned alcoholic who despised his dark skinned daughters ("splits", he called them) and admired his light skinned ones? Was she the *"fast girl"* whose own Mother feared she would 'shame the family' and therefore banished her at 14 to live with her sister in Vallejo, California to work at the Mare Island Naval Shipyard where, ironically,

---

[2] *"Eighty and Fourteen"* is a reference to being chronologically 80 years old, but being stuck in the past and unable to move beyond events that occurred at the age of 14.

numerous black sailors took to her like bees to honey? [She quipped that doing so was like *'throwing Br'er Rabbit into the briar patch!'*] Was she the *Lindy Hop queen,* who danced to local notoriety and success with husband, Seaman James Thurmond, winning jitterbug and hop contests from San Jose to Sacramento?

The most significant thing that happened to her that she would cussedly admit, as if a sign of weakness itself (which she could not stand) was she actually had children.

Was she the *mother* of five children with her second husband who experienced all of the highs and lows of a materially comfortable life she provided for them by hard work-plus?

Was she the *wife* of Benjamin Henry Royston, an Arkansas country boy who tried to tame the St. Louis woman with Jesus and a homey life, yet retain her urban charms in the most unequally yoked marriage of all-time?

Was she an *authority on jazz music and movies* who owned more VCR movies, LP records, CDs and books than she did shoes and clothes—which was monstrous in its quantity?

Was she a union *janitor* for eighteen years in San Francisco who bought her home at age 45 and eventually owned it by the sweat of her own labor as a twice divorced woman who retired to a comfortable life?

Reluctant Motherhood

To use a trite-wrap around expression, she was all of these things and more. She was strong and she was weak, especially when it came to us, her children. The most significant thing that happened to her that she would cussedly admit, as if a sign of weakness itself (which she could not stand) was she *actually had* children.

She did not want them; she said so. From 1953 to 1959 she had five. But she also said *"something happened to me when I looked at each one of y'all...Goddamn it! I just melted because y'all were so cute and helpless..."*

She loved us as just about as much as she loved herself. When I found myself in trouble once at 14 with a school bully I had tried to kill with a small kitchen knife, with her approval (to the everlasting anger of my Daddy, who I didn't tell my plan), she told the bully at a school meeting *"Oh, you don't have to worry about Stevie anymore because if you mess with him again, I'll kill you myself."*

That fellow went on to become a friend perhaps because he thought my mother was serious. She was. She was more resolved about stuff than he was. [Note: that would-be leather coat *"jacker"* bully ended up stabbed to death as a San Quentin inmate about 20 years later. He went there as a convicted robber.] And so, we were exposed to her very tough, no hugging love all of our lives.

I came to understand that my mother, like everyone, was trying to do what she could under the crushing burdens this life deals out.

Do well, well, that was expected. Underperform due to laziness or inattention would get your behind torn up and a tongue lashing that hurt even worse. We were extensions of her and our bad performances reflected poorly on her; we were mere pawns on her chessboard.

She was the queen of cutting one liners most of which I will spare you because they were very off color. One mild one I will share is about trust. She was not trusting of strangers or family members because she would say *"I don't trust the ass I sit on 'cause if I don't wash it, it will stink!"* When told a person could not lie, she would say *"which way is his mouth cut? If it's not cut straight up and down, he will lie."*

She was funny in a rough, honest way that was very sharp if you did not develop a thick skin, like she did throughout her life. She expected you to get over it, if there was anything to get over, because the one liners were just words, after all…air released to the air.

The idea that words can hurt was foreign to her because that's the way people communicated in her world, bluntly. If a movie prompted a little child to tears, her comfort was, *"C'mon, it's just a movie,"* meaning something that was not real or worth any emotion other than entertainment, period. *Control yourself.*

I could tell a million stories but I won't because space will not permit and I'd have to change too many names to protect the non-innocent. But I will tell one that sums up, I think, how she would have shaped life if she had the power, and had not instead pragmatically resigned herself to, as the James Brown song, *Think,* goes, 'use what [I] got to get what [I] want', as singer Marva Collins belted out in 1970.

The Happiest Day of Her Life

Dancing Queen

Born in 1927,
Ms. Alice Ruth Royston moves like heaven
Lord how that girl could dance!
No one else on the floor had a chance!
Oh she jitterbugged and lindy-hopped,
her insatiable rhythm has never stopped!
Independent, feisty and so alive!
Ms. Alice Ruth has enhanced our lives!
A golden soul she is indeed,
her spirit remains beautiful and free!
For eighty years she's graced this earth,
displaying her beauty, wisdom, worth.
We love the woman for who she is…

our mama, sister, lifelong friend!

So lace up those shoes for me and you
and sashay like you did in 42! – *J. Gaines Vanderpool*

(Dedicated to my Mother, on the occasion of her 80th birthday)

Once, she said an event was *"the happiest day of my life."* On or about August 23, 2007, her 80th birthday, my former wife gave a party for her at the Old Spaghetti Factory in mid-town Sacramento. More of my wife's family members attended the event than mine, because her family epitomizes family love more than any family I've ever met.

Salty as my mother was, at first she didn't want to come up from her Richmond home because she didn't like (or so she said) fuss and fawning, which she always to me regarded as insincere and manipulative. But I harassed her into coming and her longtime caretaker, my older brother Philip, drove her up.

We both hoped she would not lose her temper or say something nasty and ruin the thing, which she was known to do, with all of these churchy preacher types and otherwise nice people there. Little did I know that my wife's people were not ivory tower saints themselves, having experienced some of the seamier sides of life, growing up in depression era Greenwood, Mississippi, and later in Oak Park, Sacramento, before many of them found Jesus and decided to follow Him.

Anything Mother may have said or done would not have phased them in the slightest, because *they knew all about the rankest sin, grace, forgiveness and restoration within God's great diverse family.*

Queen Alice holding court with aplomb and dignity! I was seeing a side of her at my 53rd year of life, that I had never seen before,

non — Mother Alice.

The party was great! Four generations of families were there! The food was delicious and affordable. The conversations were heartfelt and the smiles real. Philip and I watched her like a hawk for signs of fake graciousness or acting skills because she could front people off with the best of them, and the McGee family was no exception.

To our amazement (and some degree of sadness because she never showed us those feelings!), she thoroughly enjoyed the party and took the praises to heart with surprise, humility and acceptance.

She was the life of the party, unabashed star of the show, and she didn't have to do anything to buy it. Queen Alice holding court with aplomb and dignity! I was seeing a side of her at my 53rd year of life, that I had never seen before, non — Mother Alice.

She was trusted Alice again 67 years later, at a time before the serpent entered the Garden.

Eighty and Fourteen

Mother proclaimed with naked sincerity *"This is the happiest day of my life! Thank you, Anita!"*

Philip and I were stunned, and I was a bit mad. *'What? What about so-in-so, wasn't that the happiest day of your life?'* I thought to myself. I was so jealous! However, I got over it to learn something important. Mother had been deeply hurt at not being trusted by her mother to 'keep her dress down and her pants up' when she was exiled to Vallejo in around 1943.

She developed, if not before then, at that moment, a traumatic trust disorder and an emotional arrest at age 14 or so that lasted the rest of her life which was understandable because people then and now do not trust black women to be the best people they can. In other words, they assume the worst from them.

When people are not trusted, they learn not to trust anyone, including themselves, and some strangely twisted people develop. I learned all this from Anita and she was, for once, absolutely correct. Understanding such people is one thing, but you can never get over and love away the hurt they inflict on you with their distrust unless Jesus' grace, love and forgiveness enters you and empowers you to understand, forgive and walk with them and their messy stuff.

I came to understand that my mother was and is *everyone* trying to do what they can under the crushing burdens this life deals out. She would have changed the world to make it loving like her party demonstrated, but she could not do that; someone else who she came to know did that.

I will love her forever and love Jesus too, because He first loved messy Alice, messy Steven and messy everyone else. He's the only one to do that unconditionally. I am trying to do that myself each and every day.

Author's mother, the Dancing Queen

Epilogue

Our Black Mothers, Brave, Bold and Beautiful!

by Anita McGee Royston

Black mothers are special to us not only because *we are* proud members of that unique sorority but because as *insiders* we can intimately relate to their struggle and objectively chronicle their triumphs and tragedies. This is an important perspective to bring to this book for the following reasons:

Legends make for great sagas, tomes, ballads, movies, poems and other popular culture entertainment. But they are notoriously unreliable as their persona is sometimes built on a combination of facts and fiction that glamorizes them. However, most people (ourselves included), would likely guiltily admit that they prefer legends because they are bigger than life and near perfect which are unattainable traits for all of us, but so fun to imagine!

The *real* story of black motherhood needs a *historical* recitation that includes all facets of what it means to be a black mother and the truth of what she has endured. Whether positive or negative, the point is that these true stories will live on to inform, instruct and may even inspire and enlighten. It is not a simple chronology, but it is as complex as the lives of black matriarchs highlighted in this anthology -- the revelation of in some instances, *hard truths.* Our goal was to reveal the rock solid foundation on which the pillars of our brave bold beautiful mothers' love is established as they themselves or their reliable biographers tell their impactful stories.

Collecting biographical histories and completing this anthology has been an uphill trek and a labor of love for us. Since the publication of our first book, *Our Black Father's Brave, Bold and Beautiful!*, we have gathered materials from and about extraordinary women from Africa to America, who have lived and died for the benefit of their families, and in some cases led revolutions for freedom and fought for their countries. As black mothers we know the enormity of fulfilling the expectations of our roles, which have never been easy.

From the moment we began this book, major upheavals have occurred in our own lives, but as black mother's, matriarchs and storytellers, we knew we were on a mission that could not be denied or deterred. No, this cause was destined. My friend and co-collaborator, Joslyn Gaines Vanderpool, has survived life threatening maladies of her own while caring for her husband who was diagnosed with Multiple Sclerosis during the writing of this book and raising an autistic child who is now a teenager on her way to success.

Although these circumstances may have caused a few setbacks, they have not detracted her from continuing this important history project. As you read over her submissions, you will see that many trials and tribulations have been sent to test her faith; however patience and perseverance have strengthened her resolve and processed her faith into a diamond-strong power.

Our layout designer, Fabiola Figueroa, also was critically tested. Unexpectedly, she lost one her closest friends to cancer at the young age of 45 during this project. Maria Alvarado was a dedicated mother, who left two small children behind.

Though wracked with grief, Fabiola managed to work twelve-hour days, raise her three younger children, and lay out the book on weekends, during the wee hours of the morning, while her children slept. She persevered and gave us her best effort during most challenging times.

I, too, have suffered health-related difficulties. Moreover, I moved from the west to the east coast in 2011 and what a culture shock I experienced coming from California to stolid southern Virginia! Suffice it to say that Virginia is a state whose American slavery roots go back to 1607 and its Old Dominion traditions over the past 408 years run deeper than those in the dot com obsessed, technology driven, fast-changing Golden State.

Additionally, my almost 20-year marriage ended in divorce, and I began a new career in radio after nearly thirty years as a public education/ parent-community policymaker in Sacramento, California. Times are indeed "a 'changin,'" as septuagenarian Bob Dylan reminds us.

As we lovingly collected these biographies and our own personal travails beset us, we learned much from our fellow yoke bearers doing their best against the odds to make things better for their families and communities. We discovered by their actions, not words, that the essence of black motherhood is to persevere in love when others have given up, to save those in distress. We gained from their strengths and became better mothers because they had plenty of strength to spare for us, and were willing to pass it on.

We stand on the pillars of their strength today, salute them and try to pass that strength along as they would expect us to. Thus, we never discussed or even fathomed abandoning this anthology. True, progress was slowed, but we kept that old song rolling on in our hearts and minds, *"Ain't going let nobody, turn me round."*

Strangely, by doing *this* anthology, I believe the universe *required us* to endure our own obstacle courses that were perhaps not as dangerous as those of Pauline Zawawdi's mum, who fought in the Mau Mau rebellion in Kenya or Frank Withrow's aunt, Dr. Allie Harshaw, *"PFC to PHD"* who traversed many roadblocks in times past. However, our own trials contained enough personal trepidation to remind us as in Langston Hughes famous poem *Mother To Son* that *"life ain't no crystal stair, emphasis added)."*

Indeed, the 'crystal stair life' remains the antithesis of the lives *all* black mothers experience today as in yesteryears. We could not do justice to the subject by being mere [bourgeois] scriveners, compilers, historians or talking heads. We, like Bessie Royster asserted when talking about her life to her daughter, Macia, in *A Feast for Life, "hate the elitist attitudes, which exclude others."* We had to pay some dues. We *needed reminding* to put a reality stamp of sisterly approval on our book!

As a result of our personal trials, if we know anything, we know better now that the path of human life is rough and only made smooth if we faithfully pass through it with God ever present.

It is in this spirit that we proudly present to you our readers, the transcendent historical biographies of the heroines of *Our Black Mothers, Brave, Bold and Beautiful!* The writers and/ their subjects are magnificent examples of the triumphant of human spirit over unspeakable travails all made good by a force that we hope emerged in you as you read each story.

And yet, ironically, *if truth is indeed stranger than fiction,* Joslyn and I may have stumbled from another wonderful history book to a more wonderful hybrid book in this our second anthology: an *historical anthology* more educational, and commemorative, honoring of the honorable and *fun to read* than the usual *schlock* (as Sister Moma would say, "look it up":-). We hope you enjoyed reading this collection of historically sound biographies and autobiographies.

Email us at *anitaroystonca@gmail.com* and tell us what you think of the stories we were blessed to include in this great book.

Live Bravely, Boldly and Beautifully!

Anita & Joslyn

In Memoriam

Honoring Those who Healed Hate

Sadly, as we were putting the final touches on *Our Black Mothers, Brave Bold and Beautiful!*, a racially-motivated hate crime was committed in Charleston, South Carolina, on Wednesday, June 17, 2015. During an evening bible study class at the historic Emanuel African Methodist Episcopal Church, nine brave, bold and beautiful souls were killed by a lone gunman because of the color of their skin.

Despite the massacre, hate unequivocally failed and love resoundingly prevailed, as the lives and ultimate deaths of Cynthia Hurd, Susie Jackson, Ethel Lance, DePayne Middleton, South Carolina Senator Clementa Pinckney, Tywanza Sanders, Daniel L. Simmons, Sharonda Singleton and Myra Thompson began the process of unifying a nation scarred by symbols and vestiges of pain that had hurt so many for so long.

Shortly thereafter, the Confederate flag was lowered from the grounds of South Carolina's capital, and the wide, turbulent river of dissension relented and started to merge. As creators of the anthologies, *Our Black Fathers, Brave, Bold and Beautiful!* and *Our Black Mothers, Brave, Bold and Beautiful!* and other books to come, our philosophy is to share stories that record history, inspire, enlighten, and most significantly, heal.

As we commit our collected biographies and autobiographies for your sustenance, it is fitting that we honor the traditions of our ancestral African tribes and cultures in offering libations for those who have transitioned by remembering and calling their names, so they will never perish.

Thus our beloveds' spirits will forever reverberate and our memories of them will never fade as we celebrate their lives and the legacies they leave behind. Also in this section we remember two mothers who recently passed away and whose lives will never be forgotten.

A Farewell to Mommy

by
Charlotte Cooper Williams

In honor of my mother... Ida Mae Spann Cooper
June 22, 1936 - February 5, 2014

Hey Mommy,

I know that all is well with you and the rest of the family. We are all well here, just anticipating the day we see you again. We made the difficult decision to let you go with our only consolation being the fact that you never wanted to be on a ventilator and that you were ready to go. It has been very hard to face days without you but we rest in the knowledge that you were a God loving woman who walked in your faith daily and that your absence here on earth denotes your presence with your Lord.

We wanted to be with you when you made your transition but you wouldn't allow it. You were always a woman of quiet strength and great courage...whenever you had your mind set on something no one could change it. We told you we were going for coffee and that we would be right back but you waited until we got to our cars and you asked God, *if we were out of the building.* Then you made your departure. I've often wondered why you waited for us to leave but I trust your decision.

You loved us so much and I know that you wouldn't return if you could. Many would trade a lifetime for one moment in Paradise...you're there honey... Enjoy!

Love you Mommy,

Charlotte

Ida Spann Cooper was born June 22, 1936 in Winnsboro, Louisiana and raised in Sunflower County, Mississippi. A god-fearing woman, she was the mother of four whose biggest passion was sewing. Everyone she met was touched with love and a smile as she always had a kind word and counseled in love.

Remembering Ms. Bettie

Bettie Ann Hope was born January 30 1944 and died on January 24, 2013, less than a week before her 69th birthday. She was a loving mother, grandmother and nurse.

About the Authors

Permissions and Acknowledgements

Every effort has been made to secure proper permission/acknowledgement for each story in this work. If an error or omission has been made, please accept our apologies and contact Five Sister Publishing, PO Box 217, Gretna, Virginia, so that corrections can be made in future editions.

Permission to reprint any of the stories from this book must be obtained from the original source. Heartfelt thanks to all of the contributors who allowed their work to be included in this collection of stories.

She Is

Arianne Adams is an ambitious, energetic young lady who aspires in the future to become a well-known author, distinguished gospel artist and motivational speaker. She has one published poem and has performed original pieces on numerous occasions throughout her local community. She is a member of the group Poetic Unity.

Though she is known for poetry, her passion is music. In her spare time, she enjoys reading and listening to all genres of music. She currently resides in Virginia where she is a manager at a local restaurant. *She Is,* Copyright © 2015, Arianne Adams. Used by permission. All Rights Reserved.

Beauty is Not a Size—Beauty is Fearfully and Wonderfully Made!

Denise Rochelle Allen is a 30 plus year radio announcer with a BS in Communications. *Nisey* as she is known on the radio started in Broadcasting at the age of 14. After becoming a Christian in 1982, she turned her focus to Gospel music as a means to reach others.

Born in New Haven, Connecticut she attended the University of New Haven. Today you can find her on the mic, announcing or in the production studio cutting a commercial! She is the proud mom of one son, Richard Joel Allen 27. *Beauty is not a Size— Beauty is Fearfully and Wonderfully Made!,* Copyright © 2015, Denise Rochelle Allen. Used by permission. All Rights Reserved.

My Black

Mahalia Barrow is the second of three daughters born to Eduardo and Alberta Barrow. She wrote "My Black" when Mrs. Tama Brisbane, founder of With Our Words (W.O.W) asked her to write a piece for a Juneteenth celebration held in her hometown of Stockton, California.

Throughout her poem, Ms. Barrow pays homage to her grandparents whose wealth of experiences planted the seeds for her to blossom into the young lady she is today. Ms. Barrow is currently a first year business student in the CEO Academy at the illustrious Clark Atlanta University. *My Black,* Copyright © 2015, Mahalia Barrow. Used by permission. All Rights Reserved.

5th Generation Girl; Black Fictive Kinship; The Blind, Beautiful Faith of a Child

5th Generation Girl; Black Fictive Kinship; The Blind, Beautiful Faith of a Child

Tammy "Goody" Ballard is a happily married mother of two and a "G-Ma" (grandma). Born in Warren, Arkansas, she currently resides in California and is pursuing an AA degree in English at American River College, with plans to transfer to Sacramento State University. An active leader and role model in her community, she works with teens sharing and teaching poetry, as well as providing insight for young parents to prosper.

The author notes that she uses the acronym "T.O.Y.A.," which means *Thinking of You Always* and has a design that is captured within a heart that she will use in future writings. Its meaning is significant because it symbolizes the courtship with her husband. They wrote one another as a way of getting to know the heart and soul of the other. T.O.Y.A. inspires her work which is about the struggles and triumphs of others in the world who have shared similar experiences. Her prayers go out to all, "God Bless!" *5th Generation Girl; Black Fictive Kinship; the Blind, Beautiful faith of a Child,* Copyright © 2015, Tammy "Goody" Ballard. Used by permission. All Rights Reserved.

True Grace

Kimberly Biggs-Jordan decided at the age of 12 that she wanted to make a difference in the lives of young women someday. She began living her childhood dream at the age of 48 after a long illness, when she founded a non-profit youth organization. She mentors youth and provides motivational

inspiration to women of all ages. The thing she loves to do the most is being of service to others, by doing whatever she can to help make their world a better place.

As a writer she enjoys writing and performing spoken word pieces with a voice that captures an audience. Kimberly is a married mother of four and has six grandchildren that affectionately call her Gma. She will often tell people that her mother's love, guidance and inspiration are the reasons she is the woman she is today. *True Grace,* Copyright © 2015, Kimberly Biggs-Jordan. Used by permission. All Rights Reserved.

The Adventures of Sylvia: The Free, the Brave, the Spirited!

Irene Brown loves people and living an adventurous life! She has a love for speed, doing things at the spur of the moment, traveling extensively, being up in a hot air balloon, riding mopeds and motorcycles, salsa dancing and listening to jazz. Irene also enjoys reading books and working jigsaw puzzles! She always has been in the field of nursing or doing telephone work.

At 72 she is retired and living in South Boston, Virginia by way of Clifton Heights, Pennsylvania. A courageous person, who was born in October 1939, she loves telling her age and looks forward to skydiving! *The Adventures of Sylvia: The Free, the Brave, the Spirited!*, Copyright © 2015. Used by permission. All Rights Reserved.

Born Free

Dr. Melissa Cadet is the Chief Executive Officer of Lifepath Works, Inc., a non-profit research, strategic evaluation, and fund development firm. Dr. Cadet is an expert grant writer and has written over 400 million dollars' worth of funded grants and proposals. She also was the former Assistant Superintendent of the Sacramento City Unified School District and executive director of the California Small School Districts' Association and chief executive director of the Sacramento YWCA.

Ms. Cadet established the State of California's Surplus Food Program which has distributed billions of dollars of food products to needy families in the state; and expanded the Sacramento

Parent Teacher Home Visit Program to 18 states with funding from the U.S. Department of Education. She was featured in the national best-selling book, *A Few Good Women* with 10 other Fortune 500 female executives. She holds a B. A. degree from Stanford University, Master's Degree from California State University, and Ph. D. degree from the University of California, Davis. *Born Free*, Copyright © 2015, Melissa Cadet. Used by permission. All Rights Reserved.

Homemaker Extraordinaire

NO PHOTO

Fannie Callands. *Homemaker Extraordinaire,* Copyright © 2015 Fannie Callands. Used by permission. All Rights Reserved.

And Still I Watch and Pray

Gloria Campbell is the first lady and co-founder of The Bible Way Cathedral in Danville, Virginia. She and her husband, Apostle Lawrence Campbell established the church in 1953. They preached where they could including, street corners, alleys, houses, and wherever they could witness for Jesus Christ.

In 1961, Mother Campbell fought for the integration of the Danville Public Library and for public accommodations. In 1963, she was beaten severely for protesting against segregation, and her husband was arrested several times for civil disobedience. Both walked and worked with the late Dr. Martin Luther King for civil and human rights.

Ms. Campbell is the mother of three very successful children, Larry Jr., Phillip and Althea, who participated in integrating Danville's schools in the early to mid'60s. *And Still I Watch and*

Matrilineal Reminiscing

Dr. V.S. Chochezi recently graduated from Drexel University with a doctorate in educational leadership and management. She has a Master's degree in communication studies from Sacramento State and a Bachelor's degree from Delaware State College. She is a part-time professor, a leadership development trainer and a certified MBTI practitioner.

She has guest lectured for many institutions. Additionally, she is a widely published poet and an accomplished spoken word artist. She and her mother, Staajabu perform spoken word as the dynamic poetry duo *Straight Out Scribes*. Dr. Chochezi is a long-time member of ZICA creative arts and literary guild. She is a pescatarian, a free spirit, a dreamer, an idealist, a creative soul, and a matriarch in training. *Matrilineal Reminiscing*, Copyright © 2015 V.S. Chochezi. Used by permission. All Rights Reserved.

My Multi-Dimensinoal, Most Sensational Mama!

April Clark was born and raised in Sacramento, California. She graduated from Cal State East Bay with a degree in Business. April currently lives and works in the Bay Area for a nonprofit that helps the homeless. *My Multi-Dimensional, Most Sensational Mama!*, Copyright © 2015, April Clark. Used by permission. All Rights Reserved.

My Bold, Black and Beautiful Mothers!

Michael Cleveland has lived a multi-faceted life that includes playing football, working for the Sacramento Kings basketball organization, rising to prominence in the music producing industry and being called to the Ministry. *"As an ordained minister of the Gospel of Jesus Christ, First and foremost I love the Lord Jesus Christ and am dedicated to being obedient to His will for my life."*

Other than his relationship with Jesus Christ, he cherishes and is most proud of his daughters, Aisha, Jill, Kara, Ashley, Olivia and his youngest, Lovette who he refers to as exceptional young women. Mike produces a community radio show, titled: *"The Show with Mike and Dave."* He is also establishing a podcast to assist anyone interested in a career in the music business, *"whether as an artist, writer, producer, manager, agent or whatever your desire, I hope to be able to help you make it happen."*

His blog and web address can be found on *Make It Happen with Mike Cleveland,* which is also the name of his Facebook page. Mike can also be followed on twitter at MichaelCleveland@cleverock1. *My Bold, Black and Beautiful Mothers!* Copyright © 2015 Michael Cleveland. Used by permission. All Rights Reserved.

Virtuous Momma

Vanessa Coleman is from Sacramento, California and is number nine of ten children born to Drs. Josephus and Nora McGee. She currently resides in Virginia where she is an educator in a public school district.

Vanessa inherited her love of learning from both of her parents and her love of books from her mother. She can inhale a book in one evening. Vanessa has four gifted and talented children and one beautiful granddaughter who has captured her heart beyond belief. *Virtuous Momma* Copyright © 2015, Vanessa Coleman. Used by permission. All Rights Reserved.

A Farewell to Mommy

Charlotte Cooper Williams was born and raised in Jackson Mississippi and currently resides in Las Vegas, Nevada. The married mother of three adult sons and one teenaged daughter is also the proud Mimi to two little people who, "bring me so much joy!" She works as a cosmetology instructor and enjoys reading and sharing the good news of Jesus Christ. *A Farewell to Mommy* Copyright © 2015, Charlotte Cooper Williams. Used by permission. All Rights Reserved.

A Feast for Life

Macia Fuller is the proud, firstborn daughter of Bessie and Jimmie Royster. She also is the wife of Paul Fuller and mother of Aaron, Rachel, Jeremy and David and the grandmother of Hannah, Hope, Kayla and Benjamin who are the four great joys of her life.

Like her mother, she is a beloved Auntie and has several acquired children. Macia lectures, teaches the Bible, and designs & curates exhibits on African and African American contributions to the world. She conducts workshops within Sacramento area schools and developed a series of art projects to teach students the value of faith, family, hard work, education and artistic expression.

Macia was trained in catering skills by her mother, Bessie and carries on the tradition of hosting family events under the eagle eye of her mom. This is Macia's first contribution to a literary publication. *A Feast for Life* Copyright © 2015, Macia Fuller. Used by permission. All Rights Reserved

Breaking the Classroom Color Line

Johnnie M. Fullerwinder is a retired administrator and supervisor of the Danville Public Schools. She was coordinator of Math and Science K-12, assistant principal at George Washington High School, first female administrator at E.A. Gibson Middle School, a science teacher and the first African American teacher at George Washington High School (1966).

During her career, she was honored as assistant principal of the Year for the State of Virginia by The Virginia Association of Secondary School Principals in 1992. A native of Spartanburg, South Carolina; she has a B.S. Degree in Biology and General Science from Livingstone College, and a Master's Degree in Administration from Lynchburg College. She has also done post graduate studies in mathematics at the University of Virginia.

The former elementary principal is married, and the mother of two children, Arthur and Tonya Fullerwinder-Mayo (both educators). She also has five grandchildren. *Breaking the Classroom Color Line* Copyright © 2015, Johnnie M. Fullwinder. Used by permission. All Rights Reserved.

It's All Mother's Fault

Theresa Gonsalves was born in Boston, MA, the only girl in the middle of four brothers. Her life was transformed at age 12 when a young Michael Jackson looked into her eyes, and said, "Will you please sit down so I can get on with the show?" while performing at the Boston Gardens.

Theresa fell back into the seat behind her and an instantaneous connection occurred. The moment led to Theresa sending a barrage of letters to Michael, who upon reading them recognized the talent in her writing as he read her letters astutely for years before they met. Michael knew she was destined to write, but it wasn't until the age of 45 that she actually pursued her writing career.

For 30 years she worked in the accounting industry, and opened her own business which entailed a variety of software training and accounting services. Theresa always loved to teach, and share knowledge of whatever it was she herself learned along the way. Her books about Michael Jackson, *Obsessions* and *Remember the Time*, garnered great interest, and *The Man in the Woods*, won three literary awards and received attention from the Oprah Winfrey Show. *It's All Mother's Fault* Copyright © 2015, Theresa Gonsalves. Used by permission. All Rights Reserved.

She's the Reason Why; My Mother... My Masterpiece

Clarence Griffin is the Director of Partnerships and Educational Policy Relations for Loyola Marymount University's School of Education, and lectures in the university's Executive M.B.A. program.

He earned his M.B.A. from LMU and B.A. from Pitzer College, and has worked with the Sacramento County Office of Education, the California Assembly and the University of Zimbabwe. Clarence is married to BeNeca Griffin and they have three children: Aaliyah, Alani, and Tiyanane. *She's the Reason Why; My Mother...My Masterpiece* Copyright © 2015, Clarence Griffin. Used by permission. All Rights Reserved.

Queen...Saint...Mama the Great!

Tony Gunter Jr. is a freshman at Virginia Polytechnic Institute and State University, who is majoring in animal science with a minor in agriculture education. Tony is very active on campus with social clubs, where he serves on several committees.

The son of Tony and Michelle Gunter, he has one sibling, Kellie Gunter. His grandparents are Ms. Maynell Kelly and the late Leroy Kelly and Freddy & Irma Walker. He is a proud member of Little Mt. Zion Pentecostal Faith Church where the honorable Pastor is Bishop Mandora B. Hayes.

Tony loves to play the organ, drums, and sing; and he is also an ordained minister. *"In my spare time I farm, I show cattle and hogs. I also create and decorate cakes, and I cater with the help of family. Cooking is also a huge hobby of mine that I thoroughly enjoy."* **Queen...Saint...Mama the Great!** Copyright © 2015, Tony Gunter Jr. Used by permission. All Rights Reserved.

Tenacious! A Mother's Story of Tragedy, Trials and Triumph!

Aisha Rene Hall currently lives in Cedar Hill, Texas with her husband, Jerry. She is the recent author of *Write Your Obituary Now* and is on a current book tour. She is the mother of five children, retired as a biologist after working for the Department of Agriculture for eighteen years and currently works as a substitute teacher for the Cedar Hill School District. *Tenacious! A Mother's Story of Tragedy, Trials and Triumph!* Copyright © 2015, Aisha Rene Hall. Used by permission. All Rights Reserved.

Gretna's Gold

Sadie Haley told her story to Anita Royston, co-creator of *Brave, Bold and Beautiful* Book series, shortly before she died in 2014. She was a business woman, mother, wife and friend. Through her eyes you could sense she had a playful and engaging spirit. She clearly enjoyed her 92 years on that mountain and on this earth.

Although her work is done, she has left an amazing legacy of strength, faith and mother wit. Because she lived and shared her beautiful life with us, others will surely be inspired to thrive. *Gretna's Gold* Copyright © 2015, Sadie Haley. Used by permission. All Rights Reserved.

Lady Day

Naa Harper is a Christian speaker, author, and Bible teacher who has written two books: *After*; and *Living Your Dreams: A Woman's Guide to Fulfilling Destiny*. Being a wife, and mother is one of her first loves.

She also loves sharing messages of hope, faith, and overcoming through the Word of God. A graduate of Liberty University Theological Seminary, Naa has a Master's degree in Religious Education and enjoys teaching and serving believers from every denomination and culture.

Naa, who is has been married for six years, lives with her husband and daughter in California. *Lady Day* Copyright © 2015, Naa Harper. Used by permission. All Rights Reserved.

She!

Noah L. Hayes is a multifaceted entertainer from the Sacramento area that blends his love of musical storytelling and social consciousness to spread an uplifting message.

Over the past 10 years, he has performed in the British Isles, México, Canada, and Hawai'i. He was a member of the Sacramento Slam Team 2005-07 representing the Capital City in Albuquerque, NM and the following year in Austin, TX. Over the years, he's toured the nation performing at some of the premiere venues.

In 2008 he earned his BA in Theater from Sacramento State. As an actor, he's performed with the Sacramento Opera, the Sacramento Theater Company, Sons/Ancestors Players, Sacramento Music Circus, and B Street Theater.

In regard to his musical side, he has performed with Frank Dupree and the Midday Moon, Milt Hinton, Ray Naciemento, Carl Anderson, and Tricia Yearwood. *She!* Copyright © 2015, Noah Hayes. Used by permission. All Rights Reserved.

My Mother, My Rose

Sandy Holman is the founder of The Culture C.O.-O.P., an organization that assists people and organizations working with equity/diversity in education, business and the community. She has served as a consultant to countless organizations, locally and nationally, to help meet the needs of diverse populations.

Committed to advocacy for children and education, Sandy's experiences as an educator, program coordinator, counselor, outreach consultant, prevention coordinator, diversity specialist and author have given her a practitioner's insight into the challenges communities and organizations are facing.

Sandy received her B.A in Psychology from the University of California at Davis and her M.S. in School Counseling with a focus on Education, from California State University, Sacramento. She has served on the Board of Directors of numerous agencies serving youth and adults, including the Youth Services Task Force and The National Dropout prevention network.

She was recognized by Governor Wilson's office with a Golden Rule award in the state of California for her implementation of a model parent involvement program at an "at risk" school. Sandy has also received several awards and acknowledgments for her

presentations and books. *My Mother, My Rose* Copyright © 2015, Sandy Holman.Used by permission. All Rights Reserved.

Keeping the Faith

Ovetta P. Jefferson was delivered at the home of her grandmother by a midwife on August 9, 1964. The second eldest of seven children, she grew up in her birthplace of Montgomery, Alabama and in Chicago, Illinois. She is the mother of eight children, which includes six boys, two girls, and nineteen grandchildren, soon to be twenty!

She returned to school and graduated high school in 2006. A few years later she attended Sacramento City College from 2011 to 2014. Ms. Jefferson has been a certified nursing assistant (CNA) for 18 years. "I am a woman who loves family, and I love trying new things. I have just recently remarried and I am now entering a new chapter in my life." *Keeping the Faith* Copyright © 2015, Ovetta P. Jefferson. Used by permission. All Rights Reserved.

Unqualified Nurse

Samson Kalimba is a family man, who is married to Scholastica. They have two children, Theophister and Yankho Sam Kalimba Jr. He has also brought up one Mada Delia Kalimba who took after his Mum, the only child and daughter of his late brother Maxwell.

He attained a Certificate in Journalism in 2001. Later from 2009 to 2011 he obtained a Diploma in Education from Domasi College of Education. For few months he taught at one of the secondary schools in Blantyre before he joined the Tobacco Association of Malawi (TAMA) as a communications officer (CO) in March 2013.

As a CO, Sam has produced a lot of writings through newsletters and aided the organisation in publishing the first ever annual magazine. Apart from that he personally contributes to Malawi's newspapers on different topics.

He is currently compiling some of his works in a form of a book, which will be a collection of poems, short stories and topical subjects. *Unqualified Nurse*, Copyright © 2015, Sam Kalimba. Used by permission. All Rights Reserved.

Memories of my Strong, Determined, Loving Mother

De'Lone Waddell King is a resident of Reidsville NC. Married to Rev. Robert King Sr. she has served as first lady for a number of years in two different churches. She and her husband raised a grandson who is the joy of their life.

In addition to being a professional homemaker, she is an activity coordinator working in several residence facilities, as well as a seamstress, and bakes and sews when she has time. Delone believes that people should have a healthy diet and she always tries to lend an encouraging word. *Memories of my Strong, Determined, Loving Mother* Copyright © 2015, De'Lone Waddell King. Used by permission. All Rights Reserved.

Bygone Era, Lifelong Memories

Doris Lovelace is a retired administrative assistant for the Pittsylvania County School System. She was employed at Mount Airy Elementary School in Gretna, Virginia for 40 years; and has been retired nine years.

Besides being the mother of two daughters and one son, she is involved with outreach ministry which consists of volunteering at the Lynchburg General Hospital, where she has amassed over 1,000 hours of volunteer work.

Additionally, she volunteers twice a month at the Gretna Rehabilitation Home assisting residents with playing bingo. Doris is a member of the Mount Airy Baptist Church, in Gretna, VA and serves in many capacities of the church.

She has been married to her second husband, Dallas J. Lovelace, for 9 years. Her first husband, Latane Miller, the father of her children, passed away in 2003. *Bygone Era, Lifelong Memories* Copyright © 2015, Doris Lovelace. Used by permission. All Rights Reserved.

Trailblazer: From Military to Motherhood-A Life of Service

Jeri Marshall is an educator, published author, and a motivational speaker who *"elevates consciousness by engaging in holistic thought."* Jeri holds a Bachelor's degree from Sonoma State University and Master's degrees from the University of La Verne and Oklahoma State University.

As an adjunct professor and outreach specialist at American River College, in Sacramento, CA, he teaches college success courses with a specific emphasis on the Afro-centric experience.

A gifted athlete, Jeri played college basketball, and later shared his love and knowledge of the *game by* coaching. He directs summer youth camps, continues his work as a violence prevention consultant and is widely sought out in the community due to his expertise.

Jeri has a deep compassion for humanity and has a sincere desire to nurture the wounded with hope. *Trailblazer: From Military to Motherhood—A Life of Service* Copyright © 2015, *Jeri Marshall.* Used by permission. All Rights Reserved.

The Limitless Bounds of a Mother's Love

Dr. Jerome McGee, Sr. served in the United States Air Force where he sustained a line of duty spinal cord injury and was medically retired. A 4th generation pastor/ministry leader through his father and 3rd through his mother he attended

Southern University, Mt. Zion Triune and Sacramento Theological Seminary and Bible College and has been active in ministry since 1978.

Dr. McGee holds a Bachelor's degree in Theology, a Master's Degree of Theology and is a Doctor of Divinity. He is married to Donna Romby, and together they have four children, Jerome Jr., Tiffany, India, Jared, and, courtesy of Mr. & Mrs. Jerome Jr., two grandchildren, Jada and Jerome III (Trey). And Jared has given them a granddaughter, Taren.

He's the founder and director of Jubilee Training Center in Sacramento California, is the author of a book entitled *The Power of Our Daily Confession* and a contributing author of *Our Black Fathers, Brave Bold and Beautiful!* The CEO of JM Technologies and Services LLC, The McGee Foundation, The International Network of Ministry Leaders and serves on the board of directors for The Fellowship Covenant Ministries International. ***The Limitless Bounds of a Mother's Love*** Copyright © 2015, Dr. Jerome McGee. Used by permission. All Rights Reserved.

Living by God's Plan

Dr. Nora Jefferson McGee is an author, trained Christian counselor and former seminary English professor. She also is the mother of 10 children, and has 34 grandchildren, 45 great grandchildren and 1 great-great grandson.

Widowed after being married to the love of her life for 53 years, the late Reverend Josephus McGee, she is the author of *Family Reunion*, which can be found on Amazon.com. In addition to her own story in *Our Black Mothers, Brave, Bold and Beautiful!*, which is dedicated to Dr. Nora Jefferson McGee and Mrs. Ruth Jones Gaines, several stories have been written about her for this anthology that have been penned by several of her offspring from their point of view.

Currently, Dr. McGee lives in Gretna, Virginia. *Living by God's Plan* Copyright © 2015, Nora Jefferson McGee. Used by permission. All Rights Reserved.

A Mother of Two Sons, the Farmer's Wife and One Smartass Grandma

Sunda Meyers is married and the proud mother of two sons and a lovely granddaughter. Happily retired, she loves to travel with her husband. Both continue to devote time to volunteering in their community. *A Mother of Two Sons, the Farmer's Wife and One Smartass Grandma* Copyright © 2015, Sunda Meyers. Used by permission. All Rights Reserved.

Five Feet of Courage

Ruth Mitchell was born in a small town in Arkansas. If you blink you'll miss it. The seventh child of a family of ten she learned to share at an early age, as well as self-persevere. *"Our mother taught us the value of life and how to respect and appreciate it. We learned that God is our keeper and that we are able to do all that HE has created us to be. We are in control of our destiny, but first we must know what that is."*

She is the mother of three, two are college graduates and all three have the desire to be financially self-sufficient. *"I see their drive and appreciate those things that my mother instilled in me, which I see in them. And for that I say to "God be the Glory! My mother's works lives on." Five Feet of Courage* Copyright © 2015 Ruth Mitchell. Used by permission. All Rights Reserved.

The Original Multi-tasking Mother

NO PHOTO

Linda Monroe is dedicated to helping previously incarcerated individuals successfully return to society. She often spends time in the library working on projects. *The Original Multi-tasking Mother* Copyright © 2015, Linda Monroe. Used by permission. All Rights Reserved.

Mama; Incredible Spirit, Incredible Mother!

Terry Moore has featured with and opened for some of the world's top entertainers! He has won seven "Best Spoken Word Poet" Awards, on "Best Live Performer" Award.

He has also appeared on the world famous Showtime at the Apollo and BET, won multiple competitions, hosted numerous events, been in documentaries and coordinated workshops for men, women and children of all ages and races. Terry is a household name in the spoken word community. *Mama; Incredible Spirit, Incredible Mother!* Copyright © 2015 Terry Moore. Used by permission. All Rights Reserved.

Guardian Angel

Angelique Peters resides in Chatham, Virginia. A wife and mother of two children, she enjoys her family life. She is the founder of the White Doves Outreach Women's Ministry (non-profit organization).

"Our purpose is to help all women and teens, for those who are going through emotionally, physically, spiritually, and everyday life problems. Our Fundraisers help to support cancer and diabetes victims and also women shelters and other programs. I know that the road to success is not straight. There is a curve called Failure, a loop called Confusion, speed bumps called Friends, red lights called Enemies, and caution lights called Family.

You will have flat jobs but if you have a spare called determination, an engine called Perseverance, insurance called Faith, and a driver called Jesus, you will make it to a place called Success." *Guardian Angel* Copyright © 2015, Angelique Peters. Used by permission. All Rights Reserved.

A Faithful & Fearless Mother

Ruby H. Robinson has a college degree and worked in Aerospace for 20 years. She was widowed after 46 years of marriage to a wonderful man. She is a mother of three beautiful children, and the grandmother of five which includes four handsome grandsons and one adorable granddaughter. She is proud of her two oldest grandsons who are at UCLA. *A Faithful and Fearless Mother* Copyright © 2015, Ruby H. Robinson. Used by permission. All Rights Reserved.

Eighty and Fourteen

Steven A. Royston is a resident of Inglewood, CA. He is a Christian, writer, and deacon-in-training at True Vine Baptist Church. He teaches Sunday school and sings in the inspirational choir. He taught law school for ten years and practiced law for 29 years before determining that it is a corrupt, hopeless, predatory and hypercritical profession. He is an avid cyclist, photographer and peacemaker. *Eighty and Fourteen* Copyright © 2015 Steven A. Royston. Used by permission. All Rights Reserved.

Rue: My Beautiful Butterfly

Cindy Smith loves being a mother of two girls who are now grown up. Her oldest has three children, whom she also got to "mother" until they were school-age while their parents were at work. She enjoys bringing music with her family, to the community.

She has been married for 35 years to her husband and attributes everything to God. Cindy also loves art, crafts, reading, being with her family, and enjoying life with Jesus. *Rue: My Beautiful Butterfly* Copyright © 2015, Cindy Smith. Used by permission. All Rights Reserved.

Bringer of Light

Erica Smith holds a Bachelor's of Science in biology with minors in chemistry and humanities. She also went on to gain her Associates degree in

Applied Science in Medical Laboratory Technology and is a nationally registered MLT with the American Society of Clinical Pathologists. She works in a hospital clinical lab in Virginia. Erica also enjoys painting and music, with her primary instrument being the flute. She also plays piccolo, piano, melodica, and the ukulele.

She enjoys bringing music with her family and friends to local nursing homes, schools, churches, and other community groups. Erica loves spending time with her family, friends, and her Australian Shepherd, Toby, and thanks God for the life He has given her. *Bringer of Light* Copyright © 2015, Erica Smith. Used by permission. All Rights Reserved.

I'm Here

Sha Vonn Smith states, "I am a big girl in a small world, ready to experience all the world has to offer. By the grace of God one day I will be a psychologist, a motivational speaker, and an author. I am healer to all wanting to be healed." Ecclesiastics 3:1— To everything there is a season, and a time to every purpose under the heaven. *I'm Here* Copyright © 2015, Sha Vonn Smith. Used by permission. All Rights Reserved.

The Unschooled Scholar

Rodney Snell is a New Jersey shore native with ties to Georgia's Magnolia Midlands. He holds a B.A. in Creative Writing from Emerson College in Boston and is completing credits toward a M.A. in Speech Communication. He began writing in elementary school and has never stopped. In addition to blogging, his work has been featured in Gangsters in Concrete; Velocity Magazine; and *Our Black Fathers, Brave Bold and Beautiful!* Rodney is a dynamic speaker, skilled moderator and creator of several engaging workshop series.

He is also an accomplished vocalist. Currently, he is working on *SHINE*, a book of motivational essays and completing the collection, *If I Tell You, I Have to Kill You: Whispered Stories and Recipes,* inspired by adult conversations overheard as a child. He lives in Brooklyn, NY. *The Unschooled Scholar* Copyright © 2015, Rodney Snell. Used by permission. All Rights Reserved.

A Beautiful Line; Grace, the Amazing!

Staajabu means "full of wonder" in Swahili, a name she has been called since the late 1960s. Born in New Jersey, she cherishes her role as a mother and grandmother.

Staajabu and her daughter, V.S. Chochezi, are known as the *Straight Out Scribes* who have written poetry books and produced a spoken word CD. They are a powerful team who often perform together.

Stajaabu earned a journalism certificate while serving in the United States Air Force, and she is an advocate for civil rights and supports the better treatment of people who are incarcerated. *A Beautiful Line; Grace, the Amazing!* Copyright © 2015, Stajaabu. Used by permission. All Rights Reserved.

A Sacred Inheritance

NO
PHOTO

Claire P. Taylor is one of Clara's grandbabies and also a New Hampshire resident, vocalist, voiceover artist and writer. *A Sacred Inheritance* Copyright © 2015 Claire P. Taylor. Used by permission. All Rights Reserved.

PJ, Mama and the Case for a New Pair of Shoes

Percy Taylor was born in Oakland California in 1948 and is the youngest of Lillian and Baniester Taylor's five children. He was educated in Oakland California's public school system during a time when teenagers could freely walk the streets on a weekend night in search of open house parties.

He received a degree in Political Science from San Francisco State University and a M.A. Public Administration from California State University Hayward. He is a retired systems analyst who enjoys writing stories about his childhood so his grandchildren and future great grandchildren can laugh at and learn from his experiences. *PJ, Mama and the Case for a New Pair of Shoes* Copyright © 2015, Percy Taylor. Used by permission. All Rights Reserved.

Remarkable Woman with an Uncommon Name; Mother of the Year

Peter Vanderpool is a father of a very special daughter and has been married for 28 years. He has an interest in architecture, travel and art and attended the University of New Mexico and the University of the District of Columbia.

He has served as a co-host of a gospel radio program in Davis, California and enjoys spending time with his family. *Remarkable Woman with an Uncommon Name; Mother of the Year* Copyright © 2015, Peter Vanderpool. Used by permission. All Rights Reserved.

Fortitude over Fear

Marsha Washington was born to Clarence Wilbur Washington Jr. and Ja'say Lee Hendrix-Washington on October 6, 1954. The youngest of nine children (five girls and four boys) she graduated from Edison Sr. High School in Stockton, California where she grew up. She is the divorced mother of two beautiful children; a son and a daughter.

After 12 years of working for the state of California and in several different positions, she is currently retired and enjoys being a Nonnie (grandmother). The Village by Back2Basics is her non-profit business venture. Marsha loves to bowl, travel along the coast, bike ride and read.

However, making others feel good about who they are is also important to Marsha who asks God to help her help someone that is in a bad place; and believes that it is not their fault. She advises, "If you just hold on, God would see you through by faith." *Fortitude over Fear* Copyright © 2015, Marsha Washington. Used by permission. All Rights Reserved.

Grandma Mable and Me: A Love Story; Enraptured Melody

Francene Weatherspoon serves as the first lady of the New Hearts Baptist Church in Rancho Cordova, California and is actively involved in the music ministry and various church outreach ministries throughout the Sacramento region.

In 2012, Mrs. Weatherspoon was honored as one of several recipients of the EMG (Music Group Alliance) Trailblazer Award. She has been married to Reverend MacArthur Weatherspoon for 35 years, and is a proud mother to two adult sons: Rev. Mac Arthur Weatherspoon II and Mr. Adrian J. Weatherspoon. She is grandmother to beloved grandsons: Adrian Jr. and Desmond.

A graduate of California State University, she received a B.A. and Teaching Credential in Elementary Education and a M.A. in Education with a focus on educational administration.

After 32 years of service as a proud civil servant, Mrs. Weatherspoon retired from her (Information Technology) management position with the State of California. *Grandma Mable and Me: A Love Story; Enraptured Melody* Copyright © 2015, Francene Weatherspoon. Used by permission. All Rights Reserved.

Personification of Motherhood

Jacqueline Webb was born and raised in Sacramento California. She is an educator and currently teaches in the penal system where she is dedicated to helping women realize their potential through education. Jacqueline is the proud mother of three sons, grandmother of four and the mother-in-law to two amazing women. She is the fifth of ten children born to Josephus and Nora McGee. Her parents taught her to value family; and cherishing and loving her family is what she does best. According to Jackie, it is critical to "cherish the little everyday family nuances, because one day you will look back and realize they were really the big things that brought you closer." *Personification of Motherhood* Copyright © 2015, Jacqueline Webb. Used by permission. All Rights Reserved.

Mothers Have to Take Care of Their Children

Anita Vanessa Dawn White is 10 years old and a 5th grade student at Ceasar Chavez Intermediate School, she also is an aspiring guitarist who loves to read and be the best at everything she tackles. Today she has a new baby brother who was not yet born at the time she wrote and submitted her story. She enjoys helping her mother to take care of baby Marshall. She lives in Sacramento and is looking forward to upcoming book signings. *Mothers Have to Take Care of Their Children* Copyright © 2015, Anita Vanessa Dawn White. Used by permission. All Rights Reserved.

Of Tea and Quilts

Dera R. Williams lives, works and plays in the Oakland Bay Area. A recent retiree of a community college, this California girl with southern roots is a contributor to anthologies, journals, and academic encyclopedias.

Dera believes in the power of stories and is the family historian and genealogist. She is the co-author of Mother Wit: Stories of Mothers and Daughters. She is currently finishing up her collection of stories about growing up in Oakland. Dera dotes on her granddaughter who is always willing to listen to her stories. Of Tea and Quilts Copyright © 2015, Dera Williams. Used by permission. All Rights Reserved.

A Woman for All Seasons

Terry Williams holds a B.A. in Political Science from Weber University, a M.S. in Economics from the University of Utah, and Doctor of Ministry degree from Wisdom University. He is a retired health sciences administrator with the University of California Office of the President.

As the first black State Senator in the state of Utah, he sponsored social justice legislation including the bill creating the Martin Luther King State Holiday. Mr. Williams has also served as an ordained elder and pastor in the AME tradition and was appointed as bishop adjunct in the Calvary Methodist Episcopal Church based in Ghana, Africa.

His interest in fostering ecumenical spiritual practices from various faith traditions has included spiritual journeys in various countries. A founding member of the OneLife Institute in Oakland, CA, Mr. Williams also serves on non-profit boards, and volunteers and tutors with local schools and museums. *A Woman for All Seasons* Copyright © 2015 Terry Williams. Used by permission. All Rights Reserved.

From PFC to PHD: A Tribute to Dr. Allie G. Harshaw, USAF; Ebony Queen

Franklin Withrow was born and educated in Washington DC, for three-plus decades he was a teacher and administrator in the Sacramento City Unified School District. As the chairperson of the United Black Student Unions California Advisory Board, Frank works with more than one thousand African-American high school students and one hundred schools.

Student conferees learn about relationships, responsibility, the political process, jobs and how to get into the college or technical school of their choice. Besides being a noted poet, who is affectionately called the "The Middle Aged Rapper" and "The Kappa Rapper" by friends, Mr. Withrow is a prolific writer and entrepreneur.

He also has been inducted into the International Educational Hall of Fame. He holds a B.S. degree in Business Education from Fayetteville State Teacher's College and a M.S. degree in Educational Administration from California State University, Sacramento. *From PFC to PHD: A Tribute to Dr. Allie G. Harshaw, USAF; Ebony Queen* Copyright © 2015, Frank Withrow. Used by permission. All Rights Reserved.

A Mother's Prayer; Strong Towers

Camille Stone Younger is the daughter of Katie Stone and the late Bernard Stone. She is married to Pastor Chadrick Younger of Franklin Grove Missionary Baptist Church and is the mother of Jared and Joel Lovelace and a stepson, Isaiah Younger.

Camille was called by God and licensed under the leadership of Pastor Howard Graves Sr. of Unity Baptist Fellowship Church in May 2009. "Learning, believing, living, sharing, and teaching God's word is my passion and drive for life. However, being a positive influence on the life of someone else is my goal, but only through God's love, word, grace, and mercy shall I succeed."

Camille obtained a B.A. from Averett University in Business Administration and two Associate Degrees from Danville Community College. She is currently enrolled in the Master of Business Administration Graduate Professional Studies Program at Averett University. *A Mother's Prayer; Strong Towers* Copyright © 2015, Camille Stone Younger. Used by permission. All Rights Reserved.

My Mum the Major

General **Pauline Zawadi** is a married mother of four children and one grandchild. She serves as a public relations manager in her native Kenya. Deeply spiritual, Pauline lives her life in service to God and is in the process of helping others as a social entrepreneur who would like to create opportunities for those in need.

Due to her strong faith, she is thankful for her many blessings. *My Mum the Major General* Copyright © 2015 Pauline Zawadi. Used by permission. All Rights Reserved.

About the Creators and Designer

Sister Moma

Anita McGee Royston is a writer, publisher and education consultant specializing in engaging family and community involvement in the educational environment. She has worked for the Sacramento City Unified School District as a parent advisor.

She has also worked for UC Davis, where she was a 2001 Chancellors' Award winner for excellence in promoting racial diversity and Linking Education and Economic Development (LEED) and GEAR UP, as the family programs coordinator and director.

She is a former School board trustee, and Roberts Family Development Center family advocate and consultant. She is one third of Pryme Tyme, a Southern gospel trio out of Lexington, North Carolina. Currently, a radio personality who in addition to reporting the weather and playing music, she can be heard on WKBY 1080 AM Radio, Chatham, Virginia hosting THE VIEWPOINT, a Saturday morning talk show that provides a forum for the discussion of women's issues.

Ms. McGee Royston is a mother of five adult children, a grandmother, and a gifted connector of resources and needs for the academic and social equality of students one family at a time. *Sister Moma,* Copyright © 2015, Anita McGee Royston. Used by permission. All Rights Reserved.

My Mother the Advocate; Black Mamas; Something About Sydney; Testimony to the Spirit of Black Woman & The Book of Ruth

Joslyn Gaines Vanderpool is an entrepreneur, writer/editor and co-creator with Anita Mc Gee Royston of *The Brave, Bold & Beautiful* Book series.

She also is a proud mother and has been married for 28 years. Joslyn has worked in academia for more than 30 years and lectures on minority issues and conducts scholarship workshops and empowerment seminars to inspire individuals to live life passionately!

A graduate of the University of California at Berkeley, Joslyn has worked for the United States Congress, Howard University, and the University of New Mexico, as well as a writer and editor for *Youth Policy Magazine* and freelancer for *Washington Living Magazine*.

In addition, she has written about issues regarding youth, women, human rights, poverty, nuclear disarmament and a number of political issues for several publications and magazines. She has also served as the principle researcher on two educational documentaries, *Beyond the Dream I & II*.

Currently she is an outreach specialist at American River College in Sacramento, CA. ***My Mother the Advocate; Black Mamas; Something About Sydney; Testimony to the Spirit of Black Woman* and *The Book of Ruth*** Copyright © 2015, Joslyn Gaines Vanderpool. Used by permission. All Rights Reserved.

Book Designer
Fabiola Figueroa
fabiola3711@gmail.com

Resources

The organizations, agencies and resources listed are provided for informational purposes. At press time, we did our best to ensure the following was correct.

Please notify us at anitaroyston@gmail.com if the information is different so that we can make corrections for future editions.

Association for the Advancement of Retired Persons

http://www.aarp.org/

AARP advocates and provides information and resources for individuals who are age 50 and above, including articles and links for grandparents, and discount programs for members.

American Association of University Women

http://www.aauw.org/

For more than 100 years, the role of AAUW has been to improve the lives of women. The organization also offers scholarships to women seeking a higher education.

The Association of Black Psychologists

http://www.abpsi.org/

The Association of Black Psychologists was established to address the long-neglected needs of African-American professionals. The group's goal is to have a positive impact on the mental health of the African-American community by providing programs, services, training and advocacy.

Center for Disease Control Women's Health

http://www.cdc.gov/women/az/index.htm

The CDC website listed above has information about numerous health issues pertaining to women and guidelines for important examinations.

Center for Women Veterans

http://www.va.gov/womenvet/resources.asp

The Center for Women Veterans provides information on programs and services for women veterans.

Congressional Black Caucus Foundation

http://www.cbcfinc.org/

"CBCF works to advance the global black community by developing leaders, informing policy and educating the public. Each year, CBCF undertakes significant scholarship/internship, public health, and economic empowerment programs that benefit thousands of people both across the United States and throughout the global community." The Foundation has scholarships, internships and fellowships.

Housing and Urban Development

http://portal.hud.gov/hudportal/HUD?src=/topics

This HUD site has information on finding affordable housing which also includes programs for addressing homelessness.

Jack and Jill National Headquarters

http://jackandjillinc.org/test-page/national-headquarters/

Jack and Jill of America, Inc. is a membership organization of mothers with children ages 2-19. There are chapters across the country.

Mercy Housing

https://www.mercyhousing.org/FAQs

Mercy Housing has listings for low cost, affordable housing in various US Cities.

Mocha Moms

http://www.mochamoms.org/

Mocha Moms, is an advocacy group for women and is the "premier voice for mothers of color."

National Association for the Advancement of Colored People (NAACP)

http://www.naacp.org/

Established in 1909, the mission of the National Association for the Advancement of Colored People is to ensure the political, educational, social and economic equality of rights of all persons and to eliminate racial hatred and racial discrimination.

National Black Business Council, Inc.

http://www.nbbc.org/

The National Black Business Council is dedicated to creating and advancing African-American businesses through a national alliance of African-American companies and economic development organizations. The alliance was formed to encourage African-American business leaders to fully participate in the federal policy and legislative process.

National Coalition Against Domestic Violence

http://www.ncadv.org/

NCADV has zero tolerance for domestic violence, and is committed to helping those who are abused. The NADV website has information about shelters and resources in various states.

National Council of Negro Women, Inc. (NCNW)

http://ncnw.org/

The National Council of Negro Women is an assembly of national African-American women's organizations and community-based sections. Founded in 1935, the NCNW's mission is to lead, develop and advocate for women of African descent as they support their families and communities. NCNW fulfills this purpose through research, advocacy and national and community-based services and programs on issues of health, education and economic empowerment in the United States and Africa.

National Coalition of 100 Black Women (NCBW)

http://www.ncbw.org/

The mission of the National Coalition of 100 Black Women is to develop leaders who will help to rebuild their communities and redirect the energies of younger African-Americans in those communities. To meet the diverse needs of its members and to empower African American women in general, NCBW implements programs that provide an effective network among

African-American women, establish links between NCBW and the corporate and political sectors, enable African-American women to be a visible force in the socioeconomic arena and meet the career needs of these women and facilitate their access to mainstream America.

National Homeless Coalition

http://nationalhomeless.org/

The National Homeless Coalition provides information and resources for the homeless or those on the verge of homelessness. In addition, the NHC seeks remedies to eradicate homelessness.

National Partnership of Women and Families

http://www.nationalpartnership.org/issues/

The National Partnership of Women and Families "promotes fairness in the workplace, reproductive health and rights, access to quality, affordable health care, and policies that help women and men meet the dual demands of work and family."

National Urban League
http://nul.iamempowered.com/

The National Urban League is dedicated to economic empowerment of underserved communities and individuals. There are locations in various regions of the United States.

The National Urban League is a civil-rights organization focused on the economic empowerment of underserved urban communities. The National Urban League works through 100 local affiliates in 36 states and the District of Columbia to provide programming, public policy research and advocacy designed to improve the lives of more than 2 million people nationwide.

Quintessential Careers

http://www.quintcareers.com/mature_jobseekers.html

This website presents articles regarding tips for older job seekers.

Small Business Administration

https://www.sba.gov/

The SBA is an agency that helps burgeoning entrepreneurs find information about starting a business, developing a business plan and provides other useful resources.

Soroptimist International

http://www.soroptimistinternational.org/

Soroptimist International is a "global volunteer movement working together to transform the lives of women and girls. Our network of around 80,000 club members in 130 countries and territories works at a local, national and international level to educate, empower and enable opportunities for women and girls." There are soroptimist organizations around the United States that offer scholarships.

United Negro College Fund (UNCF)

http://www.uncf.org/

The United Negro College Fund is the nation's largest, oldest, most successful and most comprehensive minority higher-education assistance organization. The UNCF provides operating funds and technology enhancement services for 39 member historically African-American colleges and universities, scholarships and internships for students at approximately 900 institutions and faculty and administrative professional training.

Women's Independence Scholarship

http://www.wispinc.org/

WISP has a scholarship program that is "available nationally to women who have left an abusive domestic situation and who are pursuing an education designed to provide economic independence for themselves and their children."

Women Arts
http://www.womenarts.org/funding-resources/women-artist-directories/
Women Arts provides information about funding sources for artist (writers, poets, traditional artists, etc.) to create and the directory is a list of different women's art groups.

Women Traveling Together

http://www.women-traveling.com/

Women Traveling Together was established to provide resources and options for women who do not want to travel alone.

CPSIA information can be obtained at www.ICGtesting.com
Printed in the USA
BVOW05s2051200516

448849BV00005B/7/P